Stalking The Cyclops

A 25-Year Perspective

by

James Nathan Post

www.postpubco.com

ISBN: 978-14800-11762

Cover portrait of the author by Famin dBoy.

This book is dedicated to the late

Mark Steven Eisenberg,

editor of The Las Vegas Valley Explorer,
for publishing these viewpoints, and for helping to keep me focused
during times of frustration with the calling.

And to the Las Vegas Academy's

Dean Rosemary "Nurse Rachett" Murphy
and
Principal Robert "Reverend Hale" Guery,

whose exemplary performances in the roles of
the tight-lipped gray-souled tough-love petty tyrant
and the sympathetic but willingly impotent bureaucrat,
committed to protecting the institution they serve
at the expense of its student charges
motivated my first letter to The Valley Explorer,
which led to the publishing of this book.

"The Anti-Cyclops Papers"

The Cyclopes are sons of the Titans, who are weaponmakers to the Gods. Having only one eye, and thus singleness of vision, they lack all sense of perspective. They occupy the seats of power in our government, and wear the cassock of our major religions. Workers at the forge, and keepers of sheep, they dine on human flesh.

"I first encountered James Nathan Post while I was working on The Scribes Of Osiris project in Jerome, Arizona, in the late 1970's, and have always been impressed with the unusual sense of perspective he has toward the issues of the world. I can hardly imagine anyone agreeing with him all the time, but he will always make you take a second look, and think."

Alex St. Luc
Starship Academy

CONTENTS

You will find a complete table of contents, and a cross-index beginning on Page 271.

Note: Though many of them began as letters to editors and op-ed pieces in the late 1980's, the column essays as they appear in this book were written beginning in 1999. Many of them are old news, of course, and I may have changed my views since then, but these are for the most part published herein exactly as they first appeared, and in roughly the same order.

This volume includes all of those which were first published in three volumes titled,
> **"Good Nazis In Office, Good Niggers In Jail,"**
> **"Good Riddance To Rights, Thank God Now We're Safe!"**
> **"The Anti-Cyclops Papers."**

Crackpot Patriots

Are we really only crackpot idealists and intellectual Pollyannas who think the particulars of the Constitution are more than rhetorical statements used or denied at will by those who trade in power? Is belief in the truth of it like Santa Claus a pleasant myth we should acknowledge and grow past? At what point do I take in hand the trusting schoolboy I once was and admit that the world implied by the Bill Of Rights is not the real world at all. At what point do I concede that no Constitutional right exists to which agencies of the state are not granted enforceable exception by the courts? My copy of the Constitution weighs an ounce, in pamphlet form. Floors in the libraries are full of the arguments and rulings of various lawyers and judges proclaiming to "interpret" the precise meaning of its crudely unambiguous declarative statements. Those interpretations have largely supported granting the state exceptions to its Constitutional limits, and limiting the private citizen's Constitutional protections from state power. At what point do I concede there is no court in which the command structure – the state, the law, and the force – can be held accountable for exceeding Constitutional restraint?

There seems hardly any reason to encourage participation in the democratic process of election. The big-party faithful will toot their horns, cheer their slogans, and vote their party line. The internally-fuddled Reform Party will continue to get media coverage, because its lack of coherent ideology or definable agenda make it a scarecrow opponent. The freedomist's best kept secret, the Libertarian Party, will be denied exposure and ballot access because it does have coherent ideology and a definable agenda — precisely as represented by literal interpretation of the Bill Of Rights. Worse is recognition that no matter which party's champion gets into office, the offices will all be run exactly the same way, and the same laws will be enforced by the same agencies. It doesn't matter whether you choose Nikes or Adidas – you're gonna end up in a pair of rubber shoes, and you're gonna pay a hundred bucks for them. And you will learn to play ball, by the rules.

If we don't like it, what then, armed resistance? Even if armed like a fireteam of Marines, is it not beyond reality to imagine anyone might successfully resist enforcement of legislated rule? No matter what I think is meant by such phrases as, "....shall not be abridged," and "....shall make no law," there is in fact no power on earth to defend me from the full arsenal of armed enforcement of duly-enacted laws abridging each and every one of the rights in the Bill Of Rights. Where is the sense then in my whining that the Old Rules have been permanently broken by the lawmakers? At what point do I concede there nothing to be gained by it, and it might as well not be continued? When that point is reached, what do I write in hope of encouraging those who would like to live as responsible free citizens in a world of personal rights and opportunities? The vote is a sham, the courts are a big-bucks crap shoot (or a rubber-stamp fine mill), and the number and power of agencies conducting surveillance and imposing control are increasingly increasing. To permit the state to protect us from pornography and political subversion, we surrendered market and media to control by monitoring and censorship. To permit the state to protect us from temptation to indulge ourselves with the Devil's marijuana, we surrendered absolute power to search and seize any person or property at will, and we built a huge system of courts and prisons. And now, as the "tune in — turn on" generation grows gray, those powers are turned upon another group of Americans – a group most surprised to find themselves suddenly confronted with the machine they eagerly authorized. If we thought the War On Drugs was a draconian violation of all sense of truth, logic, or righteousness, a destroyer of rights, a destroyer of lives, and destroyer of communities – well, hang on, because the War On Guns could make that look like a peaceful afternoon in the exercise yard. For his surly and disrespectful attitude to a mall guard, Metro Police recently held down and beat up a slender 18-year-old Boy I know, smacking his face into the street while taunting him, "Does that hurt, bitch? It's supposed to." They arrested him for "obstructing an officer." DEA guys wear sneakers, carry pistols, beat up, and arrest dangerous degenerate dope dealers who immorally pollute themselves and tempt children. The ATF are loyal and pious, self-sacrificing extreme-stress specialists who wear battle armor, carry Federally-authorized assault rifles, and shoot to kill subversive gun-cult terrorists who refuse to be lawfully disarmed. Patriots, I want you to know it really sucks, to say, "I told you so."

Addicted To The Hype

To save us from addicting ourselves, the drug-warmongers have placed us all in protective incarceration. So why do Americans seem to have no power to resist addiction? Because we are indoctrinated from childhood to justify it. "Gotta get it!" cheers the self-indulgent Granny, clutching her cola cans. "Having a Big Max attack?" the jock-idol tempts the Madonna clone drooling on his biceps. "Gotta cop my Pops," cracks the New Order Boy Scout as he suckers little brother out of the last lip-smacking pop. The lesson is clear: "Your desire is justification for getting it now, by any means, and you ought to desire it, because it is so good." That attitude — rationalized compulsive consumption for sensual gratification — is a good definition of addiction. It is the driving force behind the American economy, and the hallmark of the American way of life. It is glorified in every form, and our heroes are those with the biggest appetites. "Does this commercial give you tension headache? Buy prescription-strength Feelgoodol over the counter now!" Pharmaceutical corporations — the drug makers — produce an array of non-curative drugs intended only to make the patient feel good. Called sedatives, relaxants, tranquilizers, or anti-depressants, they are sold to produce essentially the same mild euphoric effect as marijuana. The millions of Americans "self-prescribing" marijuana are not treating terminal glaucoma, but choosing the herb because they get exactly what the drug sellers promise with their pills —relaxation and mood enhancement. Since that threatens the drugmakers' market strangle-hold, they insist marijuana has no medicinal validity and self-indulgent users immorally abuse themselves. "Potheads get high on the devil's weed; patients receive therapeutic amelioration from miracle drugs." Frankly, if I were dying of cancer, I might like marijuana for attitude adjustment, but give me real homegrown opium for pain. Yes, it is addictive, but so what? So is the patentable opium-derivative artificial-molecule junk the insurance companies which own the drug companies will pay the doctors to permit the pharmacists to sell.

Those who make the rules concerning which addictive or medicinal products are forbidden each have vested interests in other commodities. The principal illegal drugs have one thing in common: they may be obtained and used by the consumer without the intervention of financier, manufacturer, packager, advertiser, wholesaler, retailer, or government inspector, not to mention the IRS. Those who market synthetic drugs have proclaimed themselves authorities on the value of the natural ones, and the last word on why they must be forbidden. It is a protectionist assault on free trade, usurping the power of law enforcement to prevent people from using naturally available substances in competition with their market for prescribed synthetic drugs. Our government's brutal persecution of "self-abuse dissidents" is not war on drugs, nor even war on addiction, but simply a world war on disobedience, and the crime is not using drugs, but buying drugs from anyone but the government's dealers.

If we would make war on addiction, then instead of basing our lives on sensual consumption, we should learn to value a lifestyle of frugality, healthful moderation, and prudent restraint. Curiously, this attitude of delight in simple life is most clearly observable in the self-sufficient philosophy of the marijuana-using hippie subculture of the 1960's. Mainstream America declared that fondness for humble but euphoric peasant life to be "loss of social motivation" and still takes it as evidence of marijuana's harm. It is considered weakness of character to lack prideful ambition in America. Where one's success is measured in consumption power, and national success is measured in volume of trade, addiction is a principal measure of patriotism.

Marijuana doesn't promote a lifestyle of status consumption, which fact is held against it. But there is one drug that makes us obsessive and competitive, and makes us want sensual indulgence, and more, more, more. Cocaine is most attractive to the conditioned middle class precisely because it enhances those qualities of aggression, consumption, and ego-centrism our success-images glorify. The way to beat cocaine is certainly not by prohibition. That makes it the blue-chip high-octane fuel of the hottest high-risk, high-thrill guns-lawyers-and-big-bucks game around, exponentially multiplying its power to be used for evil or destructive (even if well-wishing) ends. Cocaine — like every other vice — is defeated only by learning that *all* compulsive consumption for sensual gratification is ultimately self-destructive and must be *voluntarily* overcome to survive. Unfortunately, this is a heretical notion in America, even if one to which almost everyone will lend lip service.

Drugs are not the cause of our country's problems, just another symptom of our decay into one more of the world's great cults of pride, greed, and power, consuming the biosphere from cloud-top to bedrock in our rush to build a higher pyramid, to be raised upon it, exalted by reverent multitudes, and rewarded with endless stimulation.

Who Needs Freedom?

A War on Drugs? Pray, who might be the enemy? The unemployable untouchables, the city sludge, are junkies, because the narcotic makes their unbearable world go away. The minimum-wage class are potheads, because the affordable euphoric makes their shabby lives bearably mellow. The labor class are into booze and bennies, one because it numbs their pain without suppressing their aggressiveness, and the other because it keeps them on the job. The yuppies, the power-seekers and ambitious, and the serious criminals — are on cocaine, because it keeps them tense and hungry, and it's where the money is. The Doc sells downers so Dad can get some sleep. Mom takes uppers to lose weight. Junior dreams of steroids so girls will think he's cute. Sis wants abortion pills 'cause some other boy was cute. A War on Drugs? In the words of the great political philosopher Pogo Possum, "We have met the enemy, and he is us."

The most severe tyranny is not of simple lust for power, but of those who are convinced controlling others' lives is their responsibility. The War On Drugs is a war by us on us, and its price is our freedom. It is the stupidest of all possible wars, because nobody wins. If the enforcers win, we are imprisoned. If the kingpins win, we are intoxicated. Those who believe the Constitution grants too much freedom, and who prefer unlimited government power may gain through its prosecution, but that is hardly to say anybody wins. It was the most basic premise of my political education that the greatest crime against mankind is the imposition of authoritarian socialist power regimes like those of Hitler and Stalin, and the medicine which cures such social disease is the freedom of informed citizens to act among themselves according to the Bill Of Rights. Hitler would take a second mortgage on his soul for the powers granted to our Drug Czars.

It's my impression not many 21st Century Americans really desire or have any concept of day-to-day personal freedom. Most are happily locked into their worker/consumer slots enjoying the illusions which make up their perception of the world. It's hard to knock their lives. They are like the great ungulate herds that evolved to crop and fertilize the grasses of the plains, as they churn the beef, oil, and steel to grow fat and happy. Their existence certainly supports the case for socialism, and their willingness to join unions and sheep-cult religions shows they prefer things like that. P.T.Barnum said, "If He had not meant them to be shorn, God would not have made them sheep." These are good people, and they should have every right to be satisfied with their comfortable lives, notwithstanding they might look to some others like fat geldings locked to a treadmill in a padded stall with a virtual-reality hat over their heads. That's an important point: presuming one who would make of himself an activist for freedom is motivated by a desire to improve the general society, I'd say it's smart to avoid doing more damage to good people than what it is you're down on, like the Drug War does. And though the freedomist may champion freedoms that only the extremist will exercise, he must conduct himself in a manner which will protect the security of the working masses, no matter how numb from the neck up their keepers have them doped. It boils down to recognizing that to do something for "the people" of our country either as a system leader, or a revolutionary, our means and our ends must enable the best lives for the individuals which make up that illusory collective. Destroying a fat highly-ordered society in the name of granting to its members the freedom to behave otherwise than the order dictates is no better than destroying it to keep its members off marijuana. Given "freedom" to behave independently, what might cattle do? Wander from the herd? Stampede in all directions? Open a burger franchise? Or vote for a new bull and start butting heads picking a heifer to go make veal with? On the other hand, not all of us are beeves. The trick for those who would like to live by some other lifestyle, and must oppose the structure of the corral to do so, is to obtain the freedom to be different, without destroying the structure by which the ordered survive.

The means to obtain such voluntary cooperation of diverse individuals for a collective good is the full implementation of the Bill Of Rights, and the righteous protection of the citizen from violation of his rights by government or other citizens. To make such a society function, its people must be politically informed, respectfully tolerant of others as groups and individuals, and patriotically devoted to the government which protects their freedoms. Government should devote itself to defending and preserving the freedom of the people. Given such freedom, the people should devote themselves to the common good. That used to be called "The American Way."

Marijuana: Martyred In The Marketplace

Criminalization of hemp is an American tragedy with global and historic consequences. These facts are generally verifiable in the Encyclopedia Britannica, which was printed on Cannabis hemp paper for 150 years. Most high-quality books were hemp paper until the 1880's. It was legal to pay taxes with Cannabis hemp in America from 1631 until the early 1800's. George Washington and Thomas Jefferson grew it, and studied its many uses. Cannabis hemp is the longest, most durable, and longest-lasting natural fiber. From before Christ until the 1930's, 90% of all ships' sails were Cannabis hemp. The word 'canvas' is from Cannabis. 80% of all heavy textiles and rugs were hemp until the 1820's, when the industrial gin permitted cotton to be produced at lower cost. Even so, hemp was the second most widely used fiber until the 1930's, when it was renamed "marijuana" and outlawed as a "drug". Most of those fabrics have been replaced by synthetic fibers patented by DuPont and other petrochemical producers. Until 1937, most good paints were made with hemp seed oil, according to Sherwin Williams Paint Company speaking before Congress against the Hemp Tax Transfer Law. Over one hundred million pounds of hemp seed were consumed yearly for paint. After 1937, most paint used petrochemical oils made with DuPont patents. 90% of all paper was Cannabis hemp until 1883. The Gutenberg Bible in the 15th Century, Poor Richard's Almanac in the 18th, and Mark Twain in 19th were all printed on hemp linen paper. It is likely the Declaration of Independence is printed on hemp, though US Government Archives will not be more specific than "linen." Rembrandt and Van Gogh painted on hemp canvas. According to US Archives, hemp paper is most durable and long-lasting, the perfect archival medium.

In 1883, DuPont's patented woodpulp-sulfide process made it possible to produce cheap paper from evergreen trees and sulfuric acid, a petroleum bi-product. It decayed rapidly, but was useful for mass publication, like newspapers. In 1916, a process was patented to make inexpensive pulp hemp paper. Using modern technology, it could replace our present need for paper (except newsprint) with better paper, and it would eliminate the acid rain created by the sulfide process. Agriculture Department stated one acre of Cannabis hemp for paper pulp would replace four-and-one-half acres of evergreen trees. In the 1930's, technology to use the 1916 hemp patent became available. Hearst Paper Manufacturing Division stood to lose billions on its pulpwood timber reserves and its control of the paper market with woodpulp-sulfide paper. DuPont stood to lose billions on their acid-rain-producing, forest-stripping, woodpulp-sulfide patents. The third party in position to gain or lose was their banker, Andrew Mellon, Secretary of the Treasury. Whether by conspiracy or coincidence, these three united to become the major force to get marijuana prohibited by the government. In 1931, Mellon appointed his nephew Harry Anslinger Director of the new Federal Bureau of Narcotics (formerly his beer-busting G-Men) to crusade against "the demon weed." Before Congress, Anslinger's testimony was almost entirely Hearst newspaper releases read aloud in the emotionally-charged style of the exaggerated or contrived news called "yellow journalism." He declared marijuana the worst violence-inducing substance known, and implied its use (and not social injustice) was responsible for the well-known violent tendencies of the Negro and Latin. The culmination of the attack was the film "Reefer Madness," which time has revealed to be ludicrous. On the basis of that mentality, however, marijuana was outlawed. DuPont and Hearst in a single move wiped out their major competitor in paper, textiles, and paint. Treasury Secretary Andrew Mellon was no doubt pleased to deposit the fruits of their good fortune into their accounts at the Mellon Bank of Pittsburgh, which he happened to own.

Curiously, not only petroleum products increased in value by outlawing hemp. In Kentucky the useful crop was replaced by tobacco, which has no use except as a drug, no medicinal use, and has been admitted by the government to be a leading cause of death in America. For millennia, marijuana has been one of the most used herbs in traditional medicine, and from 1850 to 1937 it appeared in American pharmacopeia recommended for dozens of maladies. Testifying against the 1937 Marijuana Tax Act, representatives of the American Medical Association (AMA) declared, "...it is all a Hearst media scare intended to control Mexicans and Negroes, and once the active ingredients are isolated, it will likely be the miracle drug of the age." However, medical research on the possible benefits of marijuana were forbidden by the US Government until 1961, when Anslinger retired as Director of the Bureau of Narcotics.

In 1976, Eli Lilly and other drug manufacturers lobbied to outlaw all independent research into the medical potential of marijuana. In return, they promised to undertake development of synthetic THC they could patent, expecting the same benefits without the "abusable" high of the real thing. Lilly came out with Nabulone, a synthetic which did not produce the high, or any of the other effects of the natural product. It was never marketed, and after twenty-five years of research, drugmakers have not succeeded in creating a synthetic which works as well as the free-growing weed. Having the only research franchise the government is going to issue, they likely never will, no matter how long they keep trying. Until forced to admit they have exhausted every possibility, they need not resort to considering the merits of the natural substance, and they do not have to face loss of their "windfall" monopoly. Marijuana is an excellent mild analgesic, relaxant, and tranquilizer. It is the best for relief of intra-ocular eye pressure due to glaucoma. It is an excellent bronchial dilator. Unlike Valium, Librium, Thorazine, Prozac, and other such synthetic drugs, it has no toxic side effects, and it creates no physiological dependence. Unlike each of those manufactured attempts to create a safe mood lifter, its prolonged use produces no harmful withdrawal symptoms, other than irritability and loss of appetite for up to a week. Unlike each of those unnatural molecules, the purest THC can be grown free everywhere in America, and consumed raw in salads, smoked, or extracted as a drinkable tincture in any kitchen. If legal, it would replace a large part of the market for those profitable other substances, a market in the billions of dollars. Such were the findings of the US Costa Rican Studies, 1982, according to a copy of the original report sent to offices of NORML in 1983. The final report on the studies, the version accepted by NIH and the Reagan administration after rewriting it themselves, was a vague document offering only generalities and inconclusive summaries.

Hemp is not only valuable as medicine, and a fiber and oil source, but also is an excellent source of food. Hemp seed is second only to soybeans as a complete vegetable protein source. It is highest in certain enzymes and amino acids of any grain, and is less expensive to produce than soybeans. Using hemp seed as a byproduct of hemp fiber production, domestic animals and livestock could be fed for less than feeds now in common use. According to USDA, hemp is one of the best re-nitrogenizing rotation crops, and will grow in many regions where no other crop can profitably survive. Many Third World countries today could solve both their food problem and dependence on petroleum-based products by growing hemp. How does the US Government react to that news? By a systematic program of misinformation, suppression of positive evidence, and deliberate omission of the truth in presenting the subject to the American people, students, legislators, and the world. In the Third World, US foreign aid, loans, and military aid are directly tied to the willingness of leaders to impose restrictive drug control over their people. When American-imposed raids on their private lives cause those people to voice their objections, CIA and DEA are sent in to identify rebellious anti-government drug traffickers. The first time a dissenter points out that the ones who profit by the action are the American capitalists, he is declared a leftist, and the military advisors are called in. When somebody voices his objection loudly enough, he is called a terrorist, and America sends in the Security Fleet. Nations which submit themselves and their people to the anti-drug activity find their fields sprayed with paraquat, which the American government knows is poisonous, and their citizens rounded up and searched by armed troops.

The heirs of the Mellon, Hearst, and DuPont conspiracy don't want people to know about the beneficial aspects of marijuana, but they do want people to know about the law-enforcement problem, and its effect on the morality of their children. When powerful people in position to profit persuade legislators to make marijuana a felony, they may then assert that marijuana is making felons of our children, and nothing must be spared to protect them from that. Regardless what may be said about the desirability of marijuana as a recreational drug, it is clear that the benefits of the many products of hemp far outweigh whatever harmful effects have been documented in the many decades of study of this plant. Unfortunately, it is precisely because of the ability of hemp products to perform successfully against several powerful competing industries that it is kept illegal, and likely will be for the proximate future. Like cartoonist Al Capp's altruistic Schmoos, Cannabis provides too freely what others would prefer exclusive right to sell.

A Drug-War Questionnaire #1

Consider these options, which face young adults in our town today. Let's say they saved allowances and birthday presents, and now have a High School diploma and $1000. A: They can put the money into savings, and after one year, will have made about $50. B: They can put $800 into a used car, spend $200 on wardrobe, and get a minimum-wage job. After deductions and costs, they can take home about $100 a week. C: They can buy a pound of marijuana, sell ounces at $100 hanging out with friends, and double the money in a couple of months. (All they have to do is conceal their lives from parents, educators, pastors, and any officer of any agency of the government of The United States of America.)

QUESTION: If we are trying to create a drug-free family-oriented patriotic community, what could be stupider than making drug-dealing the easiest way for young people to get money, while thereby turning them into criminals who distrust anyone in public office? //

Our government made marijuana illegal declaring it too dangerous to let the citizen make up his own mind. Tobacco, cause of heart and lung disease, is the leading cause of death, killing more people than all other drugs, war and murder thrown in too. If we outlawed cigarettes today, would the result be fewer smokers, or more criminals? Would it prevent folks from growing it -- or would good citizens in North Carolina protect their families' secrets...for a piece of the action. If a pack of cigarettes cost fifty bucks -- about what the same amount of marijuana costs today -- a suitcase full would be worth about twenty-five grand. People become black-marketers, robbers, even murderers for that much loot.

QUESTION: Would it be fair to say tobacco caused those crimes? Are the tragedies, the crimes, and the punishments of the dope business the result of the smoke...or the heat? //

The decisions are made by our most senior policy makers -- from the President down. However, if a candidate for President, Congress, the Supreme Court, or DEA stands up and says, "I tried marijuana myself," that candidate is declared morally unfit for office. If a candidate for the Farm Bureau revealed he had never been a farmer; if a candidate for Secretary of Defense had never been a soldier or seen war; if a candidate for Trade Commissioner had never held a job, wouldn't we say they were incompetent? Yet when it comes to drugs, a primary requirement for making the decisions which affect the lives of not just drug users, but all of us, is a confession of total lack of first-hand knowledge. Our zero-tolerance policy has placed us all in the hands of the deliberately uninformed. What is worse, they consider themselves therefore morally superior.

QUESTION: If trust in authority, and personal ignorance of the subject are requisite for getting the drug-regulation jobs, how can we expect results other than dictatorial policy based on incompetent opinion? //

An ounce of marijuana at $100 is about the standard size purchase. It will make about fifty joints, and last from two weeks to a month. If you smoked it all at once, you would probably wake up with your mouth tasting like hippies camped there all night. A standard prescription purchase of Seconal, Qualuud, Placidyl, Nembutal, or Tuinal may run the same general price, intended to last about the same time. These drugs cure no illness, and are intended to provide the same thing the pothead seeks -- mood control, relaxation, freedom from anxiety, and sleep. But if you take all of a single purchase at once, any of those listed could kill you. The pot-peddler is locked up, stripped of liberty, voting franchise, security clearance, bondability, insurability, pilot's license, firearm ownership, and whatever property or vehicles he may own. The pill-pusher is a respected citizen with a secure income.

QUESTION: Why are the illegal drugs only those which can be grown and used without a manufacturer, inspector, packager, wholesaler, physician, pharmacist, and tax collector? Are marijuana, opium, and the like banned because they grow free -- and none of those guys get their protected piece of the action? //

America imprisons the highest percentage of its population. Dockets are backed up months, prisons jammed, and costs of more prisons go up and up. For disobedience to laws against self-abuse, relatively innocent lambs are forced to lie down with lions -- literally, sometimes. The naive young adult who goes into prison for selling dope to his friend is likely to come out a bitter sophisticated criminal. The cost to the taxpayer of that destructive incarceration is higher than the average national wage.

QUESTION: To relieve our courts and jails of a huge burden, and to stop turning small-time "self-abusers" into seasoned ex-cons, how about asking for a blanket Presidential pardon for all offenders now in jail for possession, distribution, and use of drugs? We could rent the vacated prison space to our friends in Singapore, whose zero-tolerance policies have recently included chewing gum.

A Drug-War Questionnaire #2

Same song, second verse; could get better, but more likely worse. Is the medicine worse than the disease? Prosecuting users has not stopped drug use, but instead has created a global criminal industry. Using drugs will not of itself make a person dangerous to society. Suffering years in prison for so-called self-abuse can make an angry, anti-social person of almost anyone. Prisons are universities for crime, and many who go in as petty drug offenders come out bitter sophisticated criminals. Because drug users are defined as criminals, millions of Americans see themselves as outside the law, and they view the US Government as an irrational and oppressive force to be feared and hated. What could drugs themselves possibly do to be worse for a nation than that?

QUESTION: Isn't using enforced prohibition to treat drug abuse like using a power sander to treat acne? It gets rid of the zits, all right, but...
//

Prohibition drives prices up, making drugs the most valuable crop in countries where they grow, and the peasants' only chance at rising above poverty, thereby disrupting their economies. It virtually guarantees that everyone who can grow it will do so. Having lured them into the drug market with our consumers' money, America then uses taxpayers' money to force them out of it by paying the local General to send troops to control them by force. The opportunity for the General to take over the drug market, and thus control the country, is obvious. If our foreign policy is supposed to be based on promoting democracy and free enterprise, how could we do worse than take actions which encourage corrupt military police regimes in the Third World?

QUESTION: Is America morally justified in arming foreign governments against their own people to prevent Americans from "self-abuse"? //

Would the death sentence for drug dealing stop the traffic? Put fifty thousand dollars and a briefcase of cocaine into the same secret room, and it draws predators like flies. Lots of folks will kill for that much loot, and for a major dealer to know the US government is officially adding itself to the list is merely an ironic footnote to the accepted risks of business. One certain result would be increased violence. Most dealers are not killer psychos, but ordinary folks, and if they get busted, they take their lumps and do their time. But if a bust meant a death sentence, they would have nothing to lose by trying to kill the arresting officer.

QUESTION: Would making drug-dealing a capital crime be an effective deterrent, or just a death sentence for the working cop? //

One killer put six bullets into a person for a forbidden sexual relation. A second killer put six bullets into a person for burning The Flag. Another killer put six bullets into a person over a drug deal. Was the first killer justified, because of morality — or was it lustful jealousy which led him to declare murder a fair wage for infidelity? Was the second killer justified, because of patriotism — or was it bigoted pride that led him to judge, sentence, and execute? As for the third killer, the motives most likely are simple greed, or payback for betrayal. Those motives are not caused by drugs. They are unavoidable elements of doing business in any highly-desired commodity forbidden by law. Making drugs legal will not stop people from killing for greed, nor for lust, pride, nor recreation. But it would stop people from killing each other for drugs.

QUESTION: Is there something special about drugs that makes it worse to commit a crime because of them, than to commit the same crime for some other reason? //

The natural drugs, opium, cocaine, and marijuana are not the only ones which can be abused. The most dangerous are manufactured as medicine. Though controlled by prescription, they are made in quantities far exceeding our prescription need. The extras are sold to other countries, then brought back into the US as black-market street drugs — Seconal, Tuinal, Qaaluud, Placidyl, and Amytal, to name a few which are lethal if overdosed.

QUESTION: To stop the deadly flow of black-market pharmaceuticals on the streets, why not attack them at the source by making it a crime for the "licensed kingpins" to make more than our prescription need calls for? //

The drug problem must be solved, but violent enforcement of prohibition has not and cannot solve the problem — it is in itself another problem, much more destructive than the drugs themselves. When a government institutes totalitarian measures, it becomes a tyranny, no matter how sincerely it was brought to that state. When permitted to bloom, tyranny can be brought down only by the horror and tragedy of internal violence. If we would halt the destruction of American civil freedom, and the plunge toward the tyranny of police-state bureaucracy, we must stop the War on Drugs now. "There was an old woman who swallowed a fly...." You remember what happened to her.

FAA: Just Another DEA Tool

Cannot someone establish a Maximum Authorized Altitude on the height of bureaucratic folly? Aircraft Owners and Pilots Association (AOPA), the largest general aviation organization, recently published figures provided by the Federal Aviation Administration (FAA) and the National Transportation Safety Board (NTSB) listing the major causes of aircraft accidents: poor pilot judgement, weather, structural or system failure, and so forth. Where are the figures which reveal the most critical cause of aircraft accidents is really drugs? Where are any data which conclusively show drugs to be a significant causal factor in any aircraft accident? If there are no such figures, then why was FAA pressured to be first in line with a Federal Aviation Regulation (FAR) calling for mandatory testing of pilots and other aviation professionals for illegal drugs in the name of increasing the safety of flying? Please spare me such leaps of reason as, "Cocaine was found in the pilot's corpse; the drug is illegal because it is dangerous; therefore drugs caused the accident." Please also spare me the conclusion, "An illegal drug caused the accident; the pilot was thus criminally negligent; therefore, the pilot's employer has to pay all the damages." Having taken those huge leaps, it becomes all too easy for employers to rationalize their all-too-reasonable fear of liability suit by further concluding, "Aviation safety is therefore best promoted by mandatory drug testing of everyone who flies for a living." Since employers would rather not take blame for demanding tests, and one can only blame so much on insurance companies, they would certainly prefer the order to come from some other desk. FAA was the expedient tool.

Pilots, however, are one of the worker groups least likely to be using the drugs which are the declared objects of the testing program. They are likely to be more safety-conscious, health-conscious, and self-disciplined than most others. Yet pilots (and their Air Traffic Controller counterparts) were the first group of workers singled out as without question having the job most severely mandating drug tests. If the generals of the "drug war" were looking for a group with a high likelihood of drug use while controlling public transportation vehicles which have an extremely high accident rate, the obvious top offender is automobiles — so why was there no clamor to make drug testing mandatory for cab drivers? Aviation's safety record is excellent, by any standard which could be applied to American industry across the board — and pilots operate in one of the more dangerous environments. Their standards are very high, despite all the media fear-mongering about incompetent pilots. The skeptical non-flier is invited to try putting the next two years into earning the Commercial-Instrument Pilot rating needed just to submit an application for airline training. To select pilots as the group most needing drug policing to ensure safety on the job is an insult to one of America's finest professional corps.

Then why was it done? If safety were truly the goal, the concern might more sensibly be with those drugs more likely to be used by pilots and more likely to cause interference with their ability. Those are their prescription sleeping aids, pain killers, and tranquilizers. However, those are not the subject of the tests. The tests are looking for marijuana, opiates, amphetamines, and cocaine, the big-bucks black market stuff. It is all too easy to infer this was never really an aviation safety matter, but a Drug Enforcement Agency program pursued for the sake of establishing an enforcement precedent. But why pilots? Because they are a group whose low level of use would probably produce a low level of protest, a group already accustomed to high levels of professional regulation. They are also a group associated with a high level of social paranoia. In spite of favorable statistics, lots of people still fear flying, and would vote to have pilots lobotomized and implanted with Mode-C Attitude Adjustors if they thought it would ease their discomfort at seeing another airplaneful of people spread across forty acres of newspaper headline.

If those who seek to increase government surveillance and control over Americans in the name of the Drug War had to take mandatory drug testing of anyone to the Supreme Court, the proposal would likely fail. By slipping it in as a Federal Aviation Regulation, which is not a law, they bypass all the legislative bodies. Making drug testing an FAR requirement was successful use of the FAA as the tool of another agency for a purpose of questionable legality. If anybody in a position of critical responsibility "needs" drug testing on the job, then let us begin with the Congress. They could be expected to claim immunity, proclaiming the Constitution of this free country protects them from such egregious invasion of their personal lives with a tool intended only to protect the citizen from degenerate criminals on drugs.

Who Wants Cancer Cured?

What if researchers discovered the cure for cancer is marijuana? Would the American Medical Association rejoice that lives could be spared and expensive procedures unnecessary if tobacco smokers all switched to hemp? Would the pharmaceutical industry rejoice to know the drugs they make to "treat" dying cancer patients at any cost might be replaced by a common herb grown free as cabbage anywhere in America? Would the Surgeon General proclaim the discovery and call for the right of Americans to grow and use the herb to protect their health? Would the Attorney General demand Congress stop the insanity of prosecuting the cure of a disease caused by the tobacco they cynically subsidize and greedily tax? Would Congress rise up cheering to give back to the people the Constitutional rights they have "needed" to take away so law enforcement might more efficiently bag marijuana users? Would the President stand up (as Libertarian candidate Harry Browne promised to do) and issue a blanket pardon for everyone now in prison on marijuana "self-abuse" charges? Might he even restore the voting rights of the millions disenfranchised as marijuana felons since Nixon invented the term "War On Drugs" trying to cop spin off Johnson's War On Poverty? Would the agents, administrators, and sub-contractors of the DEA, FBI, ATF, CIA, INS, and ETC of the FED, the Marshals, Sheriffs, Police, and schoolyard "safety" officers – not to mention the legions of prosecutors and dopewar defense lawyers – rejoice that they were no longer required to bear the burden of imposing marijuana prohibition by force on otherwise peaceful and productive citizens in America and all the other nations in which the "soldiers" of our War On Drugs are doing what soldiers do? Would they rejoice that large parts of their budgets, activities, and staff might not be necessary at all? Would they appreciate that their jobs might be harder without the otherwise-unconstitutional powers given to them in the name of protecting Americans from evil and destructive marijuana? Would stockholders and employees of the increasingly-privatized rapid-growth penal industry be pleased to see the cell blocks of their huge new state "correction and rehabilitation" facilities standing empty, and contracts for bigger ones canceled? Would the Marijuana Growers Association rejoice to see the price of their product fall from $100 for half an ounce to the same price as half an ounce of tobacco – that is, one pack of cigarettes? The market for recreational and medicinal marijuana and hemp products would thrive as competitive agriculture, but wouldn't the professional outlaw drop the product like PeeWee Herman, since there's not enough markup in legitimate trade, and farming is such damn hard work?

Or might all those folks find it reasonable and expedient to encourage the President to suppress the discovery, to place all research on marijuana into the hands of the drug companies, and to vigorously prosecute the War on Drugs? Come on, this is cancer we're talking about, number one killer of Americans. Surely no sane and responsible person could do such a thing, much less our trusted Presidents. Would you believe this has already happened? And not just once?

Raymond Cushing* reports researchers in Madrid have successfully destroyed brain cancer in rats with THC, the active ingredient in marijuana. They also tested to see if THC caused behavior problems, or any damage. They found no damage except to the cancer. No major US newspaper covered the story, which appeared once on the AP news wire, Feb. 29th. It is not the first time this has been discovered. In 1974, researchers at The Medical College of Virginia, funded by NIH to find evidence marijuana damages the immune system, found instead that THC slowed the growth of lung cancer and breast cancer. DEA shut down the Virginia study and in 1976, President Ford outlawed public marijuana research and granted exclusive research rights to certain pharmaceutical companies. Rather than confirm the herb's value, they set out to develop a synthetic (that is, patentable) THC to deliver the medical benefits without the "immoral" high which justifies keeping the free natural plant illegal. They are still asking for more time. In 1983, Reagan tried to force the universities to destroy all 1966-76 marijuana research data, including compendiums in libraries. Clinton fired his Surgeon General for suggesting renewed discussion of marijuana. Bush II supports a "meth-lab" bill to make it illegal to even link your computer to a website on which information about illegal drugs is published. It might be a crime to have read this. Legalize marijuana? Cure cancer? How could we even consider it – too many people have too much to lose.

"Annie, (we're here to) Get Your Gun!"

"You can take my gun when you pry my dead finger off the trigger. (PS: I won't save the last bullet for myself. I'll shoot one more fascist and die a free man.") These sentiments feel really great, especially for the veteran or immigrant who has seen the elephant up close. The same also feel genuine horror watching Americans disarmed physically and mentally by such anti-gun activism as the elimination of rifle training from High School ROTC, and the marketing of gun fear by media and political exploiters.

No government which feels it must arm itself against its citizens may rightly call itself a democracy, no matter what charades are played out on C-SPAN in the name of free elections. No zealous authoritarian bureaucracy in history has proved immune to the tragedy of statist power turned inward against its own people. In countries that have been our enemies, our allies, and our families' homelands, millions have been disarmed, rounded up, and exterminated as political, racial, religious, or behavioral undesirables. When our Founding Fathers wrote the Second Amendment, they did so openly declaring it was to protect the citizens' ability to defend themselves from tyrannous use of the power of government by those in office. Though it is horrifying to even consider having to take up arms against a US-Fed-Gone-Wrong, they believed from personal experience the best way to prevent that was to guarantee the right of every citizen to possess the means to do so. The Constitution uses the word "arms." Though there may be other types of guns, knives, and explosives, that word means specifically those things intended for lethal combat with other human beings. One does not "bear arms" against ducks and deer, even if hunting them with an assault rifle. The argument that registered sporting rifles fulfill our Constitutional right to possess armament is mental sleight-of-hand to divert attention from the Second Amendment's purpose.

Nonetheless, the issue of keeping arms for defense against the Fed is moot. The position is not defensible. To know a felony is in progress and not report it is a crime called misprision. Those who know their neighbors possess felonious weapons are obligated by law to report them. Using Zero Tolerance policies like the War On Drugs, any such report may be used to authorize no-knock invasion of any home by "peace officers" armed and mentally prepared to defend themselves from the weapon they have come to get. Likewise, any registered gun belongs to the State. The right authorities sign the right paper of permission, and an agent with a badge comes to take it. Refuse loudly, and you are called potential terrorist, and surrounded. Refuse strongly, and they send in the Waco vets and the B-52's – and that don't mean Fred Schneider's band. Therein lies the fallacy of the anti-tyranny argument for keeping personal military arms. Even if kept by patriotic local militia, rifles, even tanks could only be used in a futile gesture of self-sacrifice. That produces only increased Federal paranoia, and thus increased justification for oppressive measures used against the common citizen.

More important today is the right of the citizen to arm himself against aggression by other citizens. Unfortunately, that right is all too often abused by some Americans, and all too often needed by others. Attempts by the fearful bourgeois to make the abuse impossible through prohibition of personal self-defense only make the lawful citizen more vulnerable to predation, and more subject to authoritarian security measures. When personal defense weapons are banned, and the good sheep obey, then outlaws and police both become more heavily armed and confrontational. The lawful citizen has neither peace nor security, but armed antagonists on both sides, one imprisoning him to protect him from the other.

All rhetoric aside, the most pragmatic point of view seems clear. If the sane and free man knows he must go where his life is at risk, and he believes a pistol concealed in his jock will defend his life, it likely does not matter to him what opinion about his right to arm himself is held by the Sheriff, the Congress, Bill Clinton, Rosie O'Donnell, or the Pope. If he faces a gang of street predators, then anyone who tries by law to take away his pistol is simply another obstacle to his survival. To accede to the authority of their opinions, or submit to their threats of prosecution, and therefore give up the weapon could be seen as psychotic denial of the real threat he knows he faces, and therefore an irrational suicidal act. He might more sanely justify the juridical risks of carrying the forbidden weapon by saying, "I would rather be tried by twelve than carried by six."

A Government Bird-Safety Program

"Who governs least governs best." Certainly there is or ought to be some part of our lives in which government governs not at all. Offhand, I cannot think of one area of human experience about which the official position of the United States Federal, State, and Local Government is, "That is none of our business." To protect us from cheating each other, the government has outlawed free trade between citizens, making every transaction the subject of regulation and tax. To protect us from sinful self-abuse, the government has presumed mandatory stewardship over our bodies, regulating which drugs are forbidden, and which may not be refused, and enforcing their prescription with surveillance at the molecular level, and control at the lethal level. To protect us from robbing and killing each other, the government is taking away our right to defend ourselves from each other, and turning the peace officer corps into a military occupation force. There is little point in wailing about the fact that all of what were once called our Constitutional rights and freedoms are in practice long gone. All of our rights have been taken from us in the name of government responsibility to keep us protected from ourselves.

It is not possible to teach a bird to fly with safety guaranteed. If it were intended to be so, then God would have given birds parachutes. I wrote that like a joke, but I have some trepidation about it. I fear some cow-eyed bird-loving compulsive do-goodie will be moved to petition his senator to do something about the plight of our nation's eaglets, and she will decide the answer is a new branch of the Interior, responsible for retrofitting every eaglet with a parachute before it attempts the potentially-fatal act of flying. When it makes the TV news and starts selling tabloid woodpulp-and-ink and some airtime, the Senate starts the money flowing, the spin-doctors twirl their press agents, and the Federengi in the coke-filled back rooms play their master game of contacts, contracts, and gold-pressed latinum. Operation Safe Eagle is passed and funded to rousing cheers in the halls of Congress. The do-goodie gets to sleep in the Lincoln Bedroom. Everybody is happy. There is only one problem. It will take several fiscal years to award the contracts, do the research, develop programs, and to invent, test, approve, manufacture, and implement the fail-safe Federal feather-chutes. Meanwhile, the eaglets are risking their lives, and as the government has accepted responsibility for the safety of the

*<http://www.alternet.org/story.html?StoryID=9257>

birds, it feels obligated to take authoritative action to eliminate the risk. Someone quickly points out that the technology to protect the fledglings is already available. We have only to send out Federal Officers — such as the Forest Rangers — to put safety cages around all the nests to keep the birds from jumping out until their feather-chutes arrive. Think that's a joke too? There was a time when School Safety Programs were conducted by the School Nurse. Today that term describes the activities of armed law-enforcement officers employing both high-tech and hands-on investigative and control measures, and reporting to a staff of "disciplinary care-providers" in the Dean's office. They may do something to help safety, but they are enforcing obedience to a laundry-list of behavioral regulations, from totalitarian submission to drug policing to dress and language codes. Using procedures borrowed from the DA's office, they make top grades in categorizing each student's violations of other students' safety, filling out the forms, and administering the appropriate punishment, confident in the prime axiom of the bureaucracy, "If the paperwork is right, the act is right." The result is safety-cage schools, which for all the justifying rhetoric about the necessity, are nonetheless in practice run like penal institutions.

The function of government should most be to establish and protect the rights of each individual. Given such freedom, each individual should devote himself to the common good. Isn't that what we are taught America is about, voluntary cooperation of free people? People are only as free as their neighbors agree to respect their rights. If you cannot leave home without being mugged or burglarized, it does not matter what the laws say. If people do not respect each others rights, it does not matter if government grants them. If neighbors steal each others property, soon none of them have any. If they will not even respect each others lives, then even the best (or worst) police cannot save them by building protective birdcages around their lives.

It is not possible to teach a bird to fly in a cage. Those who will not be broken will destroy the cage if they must to get out, or they will destroy themselves against its bars, or against each other. Those who survive at best can only walk, and must be fed by agents of other government programs.

Educating Jailbirds

In the history of America, nothing has been more destructive to the nation than our own War On Drugs, which has caused more damage to citizens, to our legal rights, our business practices, our communities, our foreign policy, and to the trust between citizens and the state, many times more damage than all the drugs this persecution is intended to prohibit. Even so, perhaps the most destructive effects are yet to be seen, the results of anti-drug measures in the public school. Many government agencies have been made tools of DEA, since regulation and policy may be written at will, and need not fulfill the requirements of becoming duly-passed laws -- yet may be fully enforced. These agencies include the INS, IRS, FAA, FDA, ATF, FCC, CIA, DOL, DOT, ETC... all given roles and powers which exist only to enable greater surveillance and control of us all for drug interdiction, whatever the agency's nominal field of authority. Nothing more quickly arouses the willingness of the fearful sheep to surrender their power and rights to the sheepdogs than the cry to "protect the innocent children." Their media-stimulated fear of the dangers of the world (and their ecclesiastogenic revulsion for the "immoral") has enabled the drug fascists to impose practices in the schools which would be considered Stalinesque if declared as political policy, but which are accepted as anti-drug security measures. Our public schools are operated in the manner of penal institutions. School safety program designers are trained in police science. High school students are locked in, subject to restrictions enforced by uniformed armed guards. Though use of "obscene language" to an officer is a statutory crime, campus police exercise force to impose obedience. To ensure each suspicious student is free of drugs and weapons, they may sieze, arrest, and intimately search any dirty-mouth perp who speaks ill to authority. Though parent conference is mandatory, the system of campus discipline is not negotiable, but is a summary prosecution, to which the parent has only the principal to appeal. Administration finds it expedient for order's sake to look the other way, or to participate enthusiastically in running a safe, moral, and well-disciplined school.

Whether this policy is "right" or not, there are inescapable consequences of raising our children in a prison-like environment. If they are treated like prisoners – even for their own good – they will learn to think like prisoners, and to see themselves as prisoners. Since many are more sophisticated in real life than the schools' behavioral policies let them acknowledge on campus, they recognize the state is imposing restrictive illusions upon them. They might conclude the freedom of reality lies in escaping state oppression, and opposing those who support it. Raising kids in jail produces three kinds of adults: guards, inmates, and outlaws. Then we wonder why the ones that blow up the place are the smart ones from good homes... Public school is a mandatory term of incarceration in a state institution, under armed guard and physical duress. While being presented technical information and historical indoctrination, students are subject to behavioral regimentation to enforce the primary datum of the syllabus: belief in the rightness of and obedience to the authority of the state. Those who do not easily submit may be placed on mood-altering medication, and to refuse that is a crime. When practiced by other governments, placing the youth in mandatory behavior conditioning camps and using force, drugs, and propaganda to get them to obey The Leader is commonly called brainwashing.

Can the school system be fixed? No. Its problems are fundamental. The drugwar use of penal security in schools is only one of its fatal flaws. Another is federal requirements based on demographic academic statistics. Funding statistics have become the primary concern of administrators, which has led to breakdown of standards of academic excellence. Affirmative-action labor policies have further made the academic part of the education experience meaningless to the working-class student. Where authoritarian moralists predominate, schools obligate students to posture in obedience to puritanical dress, language, and behavior codes far different from their real lives, further alienating them. Is the system therefore going to collapse? If someday we just dispense with The Constitution altogether, and elevate some four-star Drug Czar to the White House with the authority to get the job done, the system evolving in public education today might be the salvation of those young enough to protect. And for those malcontents who just couldn't take the yoke? Well, school is after all an introduction to the penal system. "We've got just the place you're trained to be, Boy. Wh'say we start you off with three to five for that bag of dope?"

Student Chores: Child Abuse?

According to recent outcry in the news, the condition of school buildings in some areas of our country is so bad that it is deemed impossible for any student to be expected to learn anything at all therein. To solve such an inexcusable and opprobrious offense against our most valuable national resource of raw material, our children, the conventional wisdom must surely be to form a civic activist group to lobby the legislators to propose a study to float a bond to fund the school districts to employ a contractor to administer a program to hire an institutional sanitation engineering and physical plant maintenance specialist to write a multi-lingual manual of protocol and instruction to be used as a syllabus in a study group program to upgrade the skills of the administrators of the supervisors of the janitor whose job is to clean the place up. Such a program should surely be augmented by a new division of the State Zero-Tolerance Policy Administration (the most brilliant and indispensable addition to national education since Gutenberg's press) to assure that no student be permitted to commit such anti-education acts as dropping fast-food containers left from their healthful and delicious Nutrition-Department-approved cafeteria meals, without appropriate action taken by the Dean's Office to ensure that the prerequisite paperwork be impeccably completed to assign such appropriate punishment as suspension from classes, and that the responsible parent or guardian be mandatorily invited to meet with that Disciplinary Care Provider to lead his or her child in the correct rituals of obeisance before such duly-constituted authority.

In my albeit long-past training as a Marine and as an Army officer, I learned that the first step toward self-discipline is keeping oneself and one's surroundings clean. It seems to me that people can be distinguished as part of the problem or part of the solution by observing their behavior: some leave every situation they enter a little worse than they found it, something consumed, and something messy left behind, while others leave every room they enter a little cleaner than they found it, with something added, or something a little less disordered. In school our student are taught that the government's system is expected to provide everything ready for them to consume, and then to clean it all up while they are home watching meaningful Federally-regulated programs on TV. Worse, in our numerous public programs of social welfare and concern for the well-being of the disadvantaged, the prevailing opinion is that if persons belong to the correct demographic categories, they have a "right" to complain if it isn't done well enough to satisfy them, or to take what they deserve from anyone who appears to have it, or to express their understandable angst in righteous acts of civil violence. How could such attitudes instill in our children the desire to be among the cleaners and providers, instead of feeling most at home among the thoughtless consumers and the recreational vandals?

It seems to me there is one obvious solution to both the immediate problem of school building condition, and the long-range problem of instilling in our youth a sense of personal responsibility for the cleanliness of their surroundings. Dare I suggest that custodial skills and building maintenance be made a mandatory course of instruction in our schools, and each student obligated to a daily period of housekeeping duties? What if elementary students at recess were graded for bringing from the playground the odd bits of paper, bottle caps, cigarette butts, condom wrappers, and the like which comprise the common windblown detritus of the campuses of our cities? How soon in a child's development might it be possible to instruct him or her in the proper use of a push-broom, without abusing that child's rights, or violating the child-labor laws? Whether or not the school teaches its boys construction skills, or its girls household skills, at what point in a citizen's education might it be possible to safely teach the procedure to any boy or girl for replacing a fluorescent light-bulb, a blown electrical fuse, or a broken windowpane? Does one need a vocational-school curriculum to learn the complicated technique of operating a floor-buffer? Might a student who has demonstrated his expertise in the use of a spray-paint can to artistically tag a wall not be shown how to use the same street-wise talent to upgrade the condition of a scratched metal desk? Do we need to fund and build such magnet-school masterpieces as the Academy of Custodial Service Arts and International Neatness, or could just any good old country school actually be provided with the proper Federal and State wisdom and leadership to impart such skill and depth of character to our otherwise clueless progeny? And furthermore (not to frighten anyone with radical revolutionary concepts), what if (gasp!) the teachers even assigned homework?

They Can't Fix The Schools

Can the public school system be "fixed"? No. It's problems are fundamental, and more of the same will only make it worse. More money will only make it fail faster. Giving moralist authoritarian administrators more power will only make it more destructive to the children, and ultimately, to the nation. Gerrymandering curriculum and academic standards to produce politically-correct statistics for funding and propaganda lead to lower levels of student performance. Public school is a government-run industry to turn raw material – children – into input products needed by other industry: uniformly propagandized, unthinkingly obedient worker/consumers. Struggling to contain a sophisticated and aware generation, schools have become prep-schools for prison, statist propaganda mills masquerading as academic institutions by forcing students to maintain the illusion of pre-adolescent Sunday-school day camps.

The biggest offenders? Self-appointed moral police, drug warriors protecting the children from self-abuse, self-righteous zealots protecting them from knowledge of and opportunity to sin, and from the heresy of empiricism. Wet-eyed Pollyannas who believe enforcing ignorance in the name of defending innocence is better for youth than helping them gain access to all of the truth, and the wisdom to use their right to make their own decisions about it. Parents and other citizens willing to demand schools not only educate their children, but toilet train, and teach them basic social skills they do not or can not give them at home. To raise the children for them.

The unfortunate result of the government's willingness to do so is that the parent who objects to the system's judgements and procedures quickly finds he has no authority to place his own chosen teachings and values before those of the school in the upbringing of his child. The result of government presuming the responsibility and power of raising all the children denies the right of all parents to pass on their own ways, from the most deeply committed Pentecostal to the most libertine Libertarian. All of US.

The first fundamental change which would be necessary to "fix" the school system: public school must not be mandatory, but a voluntary opportunity. The parent or young person who prefers to choose some other path to destiny should be absolutely free to do so. The notion that the child must be industrially skilled and drilled in the history and doctrine of the state, even if by criminalizing the parent, is not a policy befitting any nation associating itself with the word <u>freedom</u>, but is cruel tyranny over the minds of its citizens, at the time when we are most trusting and vulnerable. Adding insult to cruelty is that as the student being indoctrinated in the proclaimed ideology of the state, The Constitution, grows in awareness, he sees (but is forced to behave as though he did not) that the practices of the government are anything but Constitutional. This awareness does not lead the believer in those principles to become loyal to the government. It follows then, that those most likely to be loyal to the system are either still living within the illusion they were taught, or they believe the Constitutional principles inferior to more authoritarian social structures such as the welfare police state. If the attendance in government-regulated school is mandatory upon punishment by incarceration, and imposing that "government benefit" enforced by the techniques of high security and correctionalism, then by any name, the school is a prison.

The next most important change is to eliminate the concept of age-determined or time-determined progress. The public education system should be open from its most elementary classes to anyone of any age or background for whom the level of the subject matter is relevant. An illiterate adult of thirty, or an immigrant seeking citizenship, should be able to take second-grade reading if that is his level of need; a twelve-year-old able to meaningfully address hieroglyphic should be admitted to any class of her intellectual peers. The key to progress must be mastery of the subject, at any level. That means not only do we dispense with forced age-grouping, we make progression totally dependent on ability to demonstrate 100% fluency with 100% of the syllabus. No sliding by with your age group with C's indicating you learned half of the subject. When you have all the answers, you pass, whether it takes you six weeks or six years. Nobody says you have to pass to get another birthday or a job, but until you get it all, you can't take the next course in the program. Though classes might have members of many ages and social backgrounds, they would have in common that they were all at the same level with respect to the subject. Some Americans would graduate at 16, and some at 61, but they would be the best.

NOT For The Children

Letting the public school system "fix" itself will not work, no matter how much money is poured into it, nor how much power over students and parents school administrators are given by politicians, moralist authoritarian board members, and sectarian activists. We need a supersonic multi-directional omni-targetable fleet, so letting them retool their battleship won't solve the fundamental problems. No solution can be made until we become honest about the purpose of public education. When attendance behind locked doors is mandatory to the minute, dress and behavior codes rigidly enforced to impose a uniform puritanical image, and safety concerns motivate penal-science methods of security and discipline, it becomes difficult to continue to accept the rhetoric that public education is a program operated at taxpayers expense for the benefit of the children and society. What is school really for? Every teacher, administrator, and security officer on every campus in the country will quickly affirm (with hand on heart and eyes glazed over) that the formal education, intellectual development, and personal growth of each individual student is the sole purpose of the entire system. Unfortunately, in spite of their desire or belief, it is simply not true. Concern for any individual student is easily observed to be the first factor sacrificed in the interest of any of various other motivations-in-fact. As with government restricting the rights of each person in the name of protecting the rights of the people, every student becomes a dehumanized unit in an implacably-run process claiming to serve "the individual student."

It is not indictment but observation to say the school system is strongly influenced by such other motivations as these: "Robotizing," that is, turning children into employable "worker units" trained to fill certain roles in other industry. Whether seen as socialist horror or as generation-transcending perpetuation of productive order, it is clear no industrial society can long perpetuate itself without instilling in the young the skill, discipline, and reward-motivation which enable them to be used in structured service by industry. This fact supports a certain logic that children are in some measure the property of the industrial state, "raw material" without which it cannot function. It is my personal libertarian opinion that educated free people engaged in professions they honor, proud members of guilds and unions, will not have to be forced to teach their children the ways of honest employment and hard work. Everywhere in history we look, we hate the state which claims to own the worker and his children like cattle or coal, and we call that worker's life "slavery."   Likewise, schools in fact perform a certain "Toilet training," that is, teaching basic rules of social behavior: punctuality, civility, respect, cleanliness, obedience, conformity, and taboo. Though some might argue these are matters which should be instilled in the home, it is clear our society does not consist only of families who know and practice these principles. If, however, in the name of these behavioral concerns, the schools in actual practice impose the same safety and security modalities used in correctional institutions, then the basic rules of social behavior the children actually learn will be those of the prison, and not of the voluntarily-cooperative democratic free country we keep telling those school children they are growing up in. Schools are responsible for keeping employable youth out of the labor market, yet off the streets, that is, for "Warehousing" them. Without such protective incarceration, adolescents would probably be a far more visible part of society as they work out the issues that naturally matter to them: self-discovery, pecking order, sexual stature, and the formation of protective alliances. Whether correctly or not, the school system rigidly inhibits all of these motivations. There is another consideration that has nothing to do with the children at all. That is the school system's role as an organ of "working welfare" in which a huge number of people are employed at public expense serving the children as a social-services "Client group". Like the prison system, the schools employ large numbers of people whose jobs and mortgaged lives depend on maintaining the status quo. Having identified school children as a client group, the government does not limit services to education, and the children become clients of other agencies also. Their well-being becomes motivation for further expansion of government power, more government jobs, and greater revenue flows. Among such programs are vaccinations, prescriptions, and other medical services (for refusing which, parents can lose children to other state agencies), and the ever-more-efficacious "drug interdiction services" by which "suspiciously-profiled" students come to the helpful attention of various counselors and other inquisitive persons acting for the good of the children in the name of The Senate and The People of Home.

The Lessons Learned

Years will pass before we reap fully the draconian horrors of Zero Tolerance policies in our schools, and in the workplace, and in our neighborhoods. We are all to be the victims of the tragic hypocrisy of using "safety" issues to justify the creation of a penal environment, in and out of school. With the liberals waving their crying towels and building the welfare state, and the conservatives wagging their fingers and building the police state, we have progressed into national socialism to the point where citizens who wave the Constitution are called radicals. Some of our national Zero Tolerance policies were originated by the highly-celebrated head of Las Vegas' school-safety program, a man who studied Police Science in order to play ball in college. If you take your problem to an architect, he will design a building. If you take it to a doctor, he will prescribe drugs. It should come as no surprise then that his solution is to run schools like prisons where students are taught to "play ball" within the system. As it is in prison, student discipline is a summary procedure administered through a labyrinth of official forms and authorizations. Schools are locked down at the bell, and the use of armed officers with metal detectors as campus guards is ubiquitous. A First Amendment exception forbids obscene speech to campus police, who are authorized to arrest offending students, and to submit them to body-cavity search for drugs, weapons, and other possible violations of the safety of the other students and the officers.

The Original Sin was a McGuffin – that is, it doesn't matter what the offense was, the sin was the willful disobedience. That is precisely the problem with Zero Tolerance, and with those who believe in it religiously. It soon no longer matters to ZT Enforcers whether the law is just or sensible. To have chosen to disobey at all is crime enough to deserve punishment. To guarantee that no student will risk anyone's safety by doing any forbidden thing, their solution is to make disobedience impossible. Disobedience to laws against self-abuse is detected in our schools and on our jobs by demanding the contents of our urinary bladders. Such Zero Tolerance for disobedience is totalitarianism at the molecular level.

What can the highly-credentialed, long-experienced (and no-doubt well-wishing) authors of our school policies possibly think students actually believe about the "fundamental American rights" they must acknowledge to pass government class? Do they think because the ZT policy forbidding nudity in films shown on campus bans "Schindler's List" from study in German class that the students had not seen it? Even a cursory objective examination of the literature they like (those violent bands and films you've been warned to fear) reveals readily that our youth are under no illusion about the fact that the practices of public school administration — and adult social regulation – are much like those of Himmler and Beria, the writings of Orwell and Kafka, or films like "Brasil" and "The Matrix".

It apparently eludes the entire power structure of our national school system that if you operate schools like prisons, it does not matter what is taught in the classroom. The lessons learned will be the lessons of life in the joint. Those are clearly observable. Two categories of people live and work there: agents of the State, and the population. To the population, the State is the oppressor, the enemy. To the statist, the population are immoral criminals who must be controlled for their own protection. If one is to have any privacy, it must be sneaked. To survive the coercion of the inmates, one must learn to say nothing, or lie. To survive the coercion of the administration, one must learn to snitch, that is, to tell on other inmates (which betrayal is a major motive for murder). To survive at all, one must belong to "an organized mutually-protective group" — which are almost always racial. Whether dealing with other cons or the keepers, the bottom line is violence — the fist, boot, club, knife, and gun. You sneak, snitch, lie, join a gang, hate authority, and submit or dominate through force – these are the lessons of survival under penal occupation. No one raised in such an environment can possibly be expected to become a successful part of a functioning democracy governing responsibly free citizens. Students "educated" in such an environment must ultimately make a choice between the only two options approved by the architects of the Penal State. Each must become one of the guards, or one of the cons – Good Nazis In Office, Good Niggers In Jail. Anyone who thinks that means goose-stepping Aryans or African-Americans has missed the point.

New Emperor; Same Old Clothes

One of my heroes has always been the little girl who pointed to the naked Emperor and said, "Look, he is wearing no clothes." In years of trying to emulate her, I have learned that the last chapter of the story has always been left off. Though it hasn't been so badly excised of its hard moral lesson as the Disney version of The Little Mermaid, the real story picks up where Little Lily is standing beside her parents watching The Emperor come parading down the street with all His Majesty's Ministers mincing magnanimously along behind. Being a simple child, and without guile, though possessed of at least average intelligence, she found it quite astonishing to see them all waving to the crowds of people, smiling and graciously accepting their applause. How much more astonishing to see her parents likewise smiling in adulation, and waving their patriotic placards proudly proclaiming, "I'd Vote For The Emp!"

"Look Little Lily," the little lady's lovely mother laughed, "here comes The Emperor! Isn't he impressive? Isn't he grand? Can't you tell how important he is? And look at his lovely clothes. Now tell me the truth, child, and don't you dare give me a foolish answer, aren't those the most beautiful clothes you have ever seen in your life?"

Little Lily looked and looked, and she could feel her parents looking very hard at her, and she could feel the hard glare from every Minister's eyes, and from her neighbors' hostile hooded eyes, and from the eyeless eyeglass gaze of the Emperor's Imperial Behavioral Conformance Assistance Officers. She was very much afraid that she might make a mistake, and she didn't want to do that, so she took a big brave breath, and said, "But Mother, look, he is wearing no clothes at all." Everyone gasped, smiles frozen on their faces, eyes wide as chickens waiting for the fox to pounce. "Oh come on," she plunged on precipitously, "look how fat he is, and what a funny little weenie he has."

Like lightning Little Lily's father slapped her smartly across the cheek. "Don't you ever say anything like that again!" he commanded. "Nobody is going to say a daughter of mine is a fool."

Little Lily's mother grabbed her girl away from her frothing father and put hands over her innocent eyes. "She must have some kind of disability," the pleading parent protested piteously. "She must be protected from believing she is seeing such things. Where is the Minister of Social Salvation?"

The Minister of Public Truth came huffing over, and hustling behind him came the Minister of Youth Elementary Enlightenment, and the Minister of Majestic Media. These monitors of the manufactured reality of the otherwise-mindless millions spoke as one, saying, "She speaks slanderous statements about His Majesty. To stabilize safety of society's state of mind, she must be silenced."

The Minister Most Martial marched over with his minions, manfully manifesting military might, and muttered through his megaphone, "She is causing a public disturbance with this subversive outburst, and must be arrested."

The Minister of Bishops, Blessed Babananda of the Baptized Blind Believers, walked across the goldfish pond and said, "Come now, confess. Don't you know it is a sin to call The Emperor a liar?"

"Wait!" cried The Minister of Wardrobe, knowing he was first in line for the hatchet-job attention of the Minister of Capital Relocation. "This only proves The Emperor's Royal Tailors are correct. Only a genuine fool would speak treason and blasphemy in the presence of His Majesty."

"Yes," agreed The Ministers of Mental Hygiene, Civility and Sanity, Humility and Humanity, "presumably her pre-pubescent preoccupation with His Primacy's prodigious pudenda is proof-patent probability of paternal hokey-pokey. How else could she have known what to say she was imagining she saw? If the father is not also a fool, he will submit her to appropriate therapy, and seek counseling."

The masses assembled began to mutter, to mumble, and to moo. Then a voice cried out, and then another, to bleat and bray, "Take her away! Take her away!" Little Lily's parents, pious, patriotic, and patiently pragmatic, presently agreed The Emperor and all his Ministers could not possibly be wrong, so they permitted them to lock up Little Lily for a lot of observation, to give her a good enema and a prescription for tranquilizers, and to send her back home. It is said she stayed in her room and never spoke another word, that is, until The Emperor announced the opening of his new school, a new hospital, and a new park, while she could see construction had begun only on the new Security Residence for Fools. But that is another story.

"Father Washington, Save Us From SEX!"

I have high regards for the good sheep of our communities, and for those who would be their good shepherds, but I know the nature of sheep is to be easily frightened, and to feel safe only in a secure fold guarded by a strong shepherd. Having been around the block a few times, however, I know also that not all the good guys are sheep, much as the shepherds would like to corral and shear us too. If the world of sheep is built of limitation and security, then the world of the goat is built of opportunity and risk. Given our Bill of Rights, America is a good place for both. However, if the taboos and fears of the sheep are imposed on all by force of law, it gets to be a pretty hard place to be a goat...or an eagle, or a unicorn, or anything else.

In the First Amendment to the Constitution, and in many of their other writings, the group of radical freedomists we call Our Founding Fathers made clear their intention that matters of religious doctrine and moral conscience should be made neither the subject of nor the justification for control by government. In blatant violation of that intention, the Christian Coalition has become a sectarian cabal within our government, in complete possession of the electoral power of one major party and the most publicized third party. Proclaiming themselves defenders of public morality, they are constructing a machine of statist power that would make Hitler, Stalin, and Mao drool with envy. They presume that certain things are so destructive to their religion's definitions of personal morality that all citizens must be denied the right to make up their own minds about them, and that the bodies and souls of the citizens are somehow the property of the state, to be protected from physical or moral self-abuse. From these fundamental presumptions depend all of the "blue laws" which have long justified media regulation, personal surveillance, and omnipresent combat-armed law enforcement to control all aspects of the citizens life — these are the prohibition of gambling, alcohol and drugs, suicide, and (the horror of horrors) sex, seeing sex, educating about sex, selling sex, having forbidden sex, showing pictures of sex, even writing words about sex.

Censorship for "protection" against obscenity is the basic foot-in-the-door law which slides those presumptions past the gullible good sheep. If people will believe that seeing pictures of genitals is morally damaging to the observer (or to the immaculate innocence and sanity of his children), they can be persuaded all too easily that government should protect all the people by controlling the communication media to make it impossible for such pictures to be seen. Censorship is the most basic state violation of First Amendment rights. If it is agreed they may take power over our communications to protect us from dangerous information, then they may control anything the sheep can be made to fear. Government would like laws to control the Internet, and their first level of justification is protection against "pornography," as being something dangerous to children and motivational to predatory perverts. There is a certain clear sense in the prohibition of yelling "Fire!" in a crowded theater, but it is a long leap of presumption to use the same logic to prohibit yelling "Fuck!" It is an easy step thereafter, however, to the prohibition of publishing, to the prohibition of private performance, and thus to building the state organs of surveillance and enforcement "necessary" to observe and prevent personal private practice of... well, of anything they decide it is their responsibility to prohibit.

Promoters of censorship justify banning sexual literature as dangerous to society, because it allegedly can motivate disturbed individuals to depraved acts against helpless victims. It may be true — and maybe other psychotics are motivated by old brown shoes, or Shirley Temple movies. If we take the possibility of inducing violence in the reader as justification for banning books, we enter upon very shaky ground. Of all the art and literature in the history of the world, surely none can compare in having motivated more readers to unreasoned violence, injustice, inquisition, hangings, burnings, genocides, and long-ongoing wars, to that trio of quarreling cousins, The Koran, The Torah, and The Bible. If looking at pictures of naked women makes some twisted individual want to kill one, he is certainly not typical of the readership. If we must take his peculiar reaction as just cause for banning all pictures of naked women, then how could we not take the homicidal reactions of those legions of crusaders and avenging angels as justification for banning all three of those contentious occult scriptures? To Hell with The Constitution, let's BAN THE BIBLE to SAVE AMERICA!

<u>Just say "NO!"... to Smut-Busters.</u>

Obscenity is in the eye of the beholder. Some people cannot tolerate even to think certain things, so they try to ban all which stimulates forbidden images in their minds. Unmoved that the acts they hate may be considered desirable by others, they can not acknowledge that each individual's reaction to any stimulus is his own. Blaming the publisher of words or pictures which distress them, they cry for law enforcement to protect them from their own feelings. A person who cannot confront his own reactions perhaps should be committed to some Institution for the Incompetent. Those who would impose public censorship to protect themselves from seeing things that uncontrollably upset them would make such an institution of the entire community, and would commit us all into it. What is worse, they would have those compelling reactions determine what should be forbidden to all of us inmates for our own good.

We solve no social problems by ordering police to force them out of sight. The very concept of "forbidden subjects of communication" is an invitation to social horror. That any abridging of Constitutional freedom should be granted to restrict publication because of "obscenity" is downright obscene. The obscenity censors' moralist position is strangely inverted. XX-rated stuff is mostly just about people having sex and enjoying it. However, in PG and R, sexual vulnerability and temptation enhance scenes of horror, pain, extortion, and murder. The women of prime-time TV-soaps wield sexual power like a chainsaw, and viewers cheer their cruelty with moral self-indulgence because the producers don't show them taking off their panties for the guest stars. By the curious standards of "obscenity" censorship, people who enjoy erotic subjects are lascivious perverts from whom the community must be protected, and those most disgusted by sex the most moral and sane. Furthermore, they believe their own self-righteous revulsion should be the standard to which the whole community is held.

Censorship abridges the right of the citizen to inform or amuse himself, restricts the right of parents to determine the moral upbringing of their children, usurps the power of the school board to select curriculum, and abrogates the power of the free market to determine which products are traded. Some attempt to justify censorship saying "community standards" demand it. It is never true. Given a free market, community behavior will reflect its actual standards, for better or for worse. If a community's standards-in-fact do not admit of some product, availability of a truckload of it would not lead the community to buy it. When some faction seeks to arm itself with the power of law enforcement to suppress a willing market, its cries of community standards are specious. Moreover, enforcing a show of officially-moral behavior creates the cruel hypocrisy of people stealing forbidden cookies with their left hands, while with their right hands they arrest their neighbors for the same. Suppression of a willing market produces a criminal underground -- which is taken as justification for further persecution, which is taken by the oppressed as grounds for active dissent. These are not socially beneficial results.

The central issue is whether adults can be trusted with the right to make their own decisions about what they see, hear, read, show, say, and print. Pro-censorship religious moralists say where sex is concerned, we cannot be trusted, and the power of law enforcement must impose correct standards -- that is, the proclaimed standards of their sect. The sanctimonious and self-righteous presumption that one has a moral obligation to take command of another's life if he will not conform to one's own taboos is bigotry enough in the individual. Given power to impose behavior by force of law, it quickly engenders the most intolerant tyranny, wherein dissent is evidence of moral weakness, and disobedience a fundamental sin. The typical obscenity ordinance serves principally to define what is obscene. Most define anything which is (even imagined to be) erotic to be obscene, and any sharing of offending words or pictures to be illicit traffic. Write a sexy love poem, take a snapshot of a naked friend (or God help you, your 8-year-old playing in the family pool), and let someone else see either -- and you could be convicted of "pandering obscenity" and fined and imprisoned. Given the freedom, I might like looking at pictures of naked people. I might even get naked with friends and take pictures. Shucks, we might even sell copies. If moralists whose pious concern for my soul leads them to judge any such behavior forbidden sin are able to make it prohibited by enforceable law, then I would be stuck with a choice: let officers of the Agency for Righteousness and Morality (ARM) inspect my home and my life, and cleanse those of whatever offends them, or draw my curtains and join yet another criminal self-abusers' underground.

Save us, Dub, from Bubba's sins.

Finally a pro-freedom move from Clinton: 130 pardons, but not fairly Presidential, merely personal pardons. Libertarian Harry Browne swore to pardon all drug-users, and cleanse corruption from office. Bubba Razorback pardoned his own family cokehead, his felonious business partners, and those in his camp who violated their offices for his gain, again proving himself the consummate swine. Promoting Ashcroft for AG, Bush II clearly intends from the start to promulgate the agenda of the Christian cabal which installed him. Today, more than ever before, we risk losing our rights, but not for being black, women, or gay. We all stand to lose. Most seem not even to see it coming, yelling "Hallelujah" while the doors close right before their eyes, because it is done in the name of morality, of protecting our daughters from lust, and our sons from iniquity. In free society, it is difficult to keep young Christians from seeing the world presents reasonable and successful social and spiritual alternatives to Christianity at every turn. To those who place their faith in some other name of God, or live by any other orientation, the effect of enforcement of Christian codes is as intrusive and oppressive as the Nazis, Rome under Caesars and Popes, or the ant-hill state of Maoist China.

"Lead us not into temptation," will be taken as political mandate by the regime of Jesus Christ, American, President by proxy, Lord and Fuhrer of the Righteous Rightist Revolution. Wherever the fundamentalist right gains political power, they use the law to see young Christians suffer not the temptation offered by Satan's alternative lifestyles. From tits on TV to Tsiolkovsky, from Charles Darwin to Gary Gygax, they scourge all they touch to save Christians from temptation to make a wrong choice. These are not weekend-Jesus-club Christians. They are consecrated activists, blind-faith fanatics, taught to respect a death of martyrdom, prepared to lay down their lives or take yours, and to vote as they are told is for Jesus sake, swayed by no reason, evidence, or emotion from their evangelical purpose. "Whatever peace man has on earth is won only through waging unending war against sin," they declare. "Only by persevering in that holy *war is peace* to be maintained." They call those who would be saved to submit themselves eternally, to "take the awl in the ear", a sign which identified a slave in Jesus' time. By their own declaration, Christian *freedom is slavery.* They call for the faithful to "know only Christ, and Him crucified", and declare secular knowledge to be Satan's lies, created to weaken their faith. To a believer in that doctrine, *ignorance is strength.* They call for each of God's servants to be his brother's keeper, and to watch his every move for signs of error. In Christian society, *every brother is watching you.* The exhortation to "love thy neighbor, and forgive thy brother,"is purged of liberal misinterpretation by the pious declaration, "A commie homo witch is not my neighbor, he is an evil invader. My brothers are the Jesus-saved Sons of God, not the Goddamned self-serving sons of Satan who won't sell everything to buy into the sacrifice of blood the Bible said Jesus said Moses said Abraham said God said is the One Way we get off the hook for whatever it was Satan talked Eve into talking Adam into doing."

Christianity is not a democratic social structure. It is fundamentally a monarchy, absolute dictatorship of a totalitarian God, by whose authority believers are obligated to live under and to enforce an inflexible law not subject to evidence or reason. Their government on earth will be a totalitarian government. If any group other than Christians (Scientologists or Sunni, for example) were making full use of the media and the courts to promote the wholesale dismantling of the democratic process by stacking the seats of power with their own fanatical agents, and overtly declaring their intentions to replace Constitutional American freedoms with their own oppressive moralistic doctrines, they would be declared treasonous, and the SWAT teams would be sent out to neutralize them. Those who wish for and take action to gain such power as to make the laws of the United States conform to the higher authority of the dogma of their cult, in so doing rendering the Constitution irrelevant, the Congress impotent, and law-enforcement a sectarian tool, are in fact conspiring to overthrow the government of the United States. A President who elevates to power a person whom he knows will interpret or change the Constitution so as to make it conform to the Bible or any other religious, occult, or philosophical creed is in violation of his oath to support and defend the Constitution, and is in fact an active member of that conspiracy. Is that not an impeachable offense?

Freedom Is Our Community Standard

We do not solve our social problems by ordering our police to keep them out of sight, but rather by open, honest, and tolerant examination of the truth in all our activities. The very concept of "forbidden communication of knowledge" seems to me an invitation to social horror. What a strange and backward attitude the erotic-censors' seems to me, their moralist position strangely inverted. The sexual violence they claim to be caused by "pornography" is not found in the X-rated stuff, which is pictures of people having sex and enjoying it. However, in the PG and R films, sexual vulnerability and temptation are used to enhance scenes of horror, pain, extortion, power, murder, and dismemberment. The women of prime-time TV soaps wield sexual power like a chainsaw, and viewers cheer their cruelty with moral self-indulgence because the producers refrain from showing the scenes where they take off their panties with the guest stars. It is not that pornography will engender sexual violence that moralists fear, but that forbidden acts might appear pleasant. By their standards, those who enjoy freedom of knowledge of erotic subjects are branded lascivious perverts, sickos from whom the community must be protected, while those whose reactions are disgust and loathing declare themselves most moral and sane. Insisting their self-righteous revulsion the standard by which the whole community is measured, promulgators of obscenity censorship demand the power of law enforcement to deny to all whatever offends their personal emotions and tastes.

If such a law is permitted in a community, what will prevent the overzealous from amending it to prohibit that which they find offensive for heresy, blasphemy, political subversiveness, ethnic sensitivity, or disrespect to sacred symbols and figures of authority in church and state? God save us from "public servants" who believe they must protect our children from their own visions of evil by using social shame, enforced ignorance, and criminal status to build stronger and higher walls around their minds...and ours. Some people cannot tolerate even to think certain things, so they try to ban anything which stimulates forbidden images in their minds. Unmoved that the acts they abhor may be harmless, voluntary, even considered desirable by others, they can not acknowledge that each individual's reaction to any stimulus is uniquely his own. Blaming the publisher of the words or pictures, they cry for the power of law enforcement to protect them from their own feelings. From one point of view, a person who cannot control his own reactions ought to be committed to institutional care for incompetence. Those who would impose public censorship to protect themselves from seeing things that upset them would make such an institution of the entire community, and would commit us all into it. What is worse, they would have themselves (that is, their uncontrollable reactions) be the judges of what should be forbidden to all of us inmates for our own good.

The obscenity ordinances some are trying to propose for our communities would specifically authorize the use of armed police to confiscate from our shops any literature deemed prurient, that is, pertaining to or showing anything sexual, and to take those books and tapes out and destroy them. Have we forgotten those piles of books burning in the streets of 1930's Berlin for the crime of pertaining to anything pro-Jewish? There is no easier way to create a sick and oppressive society than by declaring common human qualities to be evil and therefore illegal. The typical obscenity ordinance (usually based on Miller vs. California) serves principally to define in legal terms what is obscene. Specifically, it defines all that which is erotically explicit to be obscene. Further, it would impose the ban of censorship on all such material by forbidding the "promotion" of it by: "manufacture, issue, sell, rent, give, provide, advertise, lend, mail, deliver, transfer, transmit, publish, distribute, circulate, disseminate, present, display, exhibit, or to offer or agree to do the same." Should you write an erotic love poem, or take a snapshot of a naked friend, and offer to let someone else see either, you could by the letter of such an ordinance be convicted of "pandering obscenity", and fined and imprisoned. The central issue in censorship is whether or not adults in a free country can be trusted with the right to make their own decisions. Pro-censorship's position says where sex is concerned, we cannot be trusted, and the power of law enforcement must be applied to impose correct standards — that is, the prohibitionists' own. The reasoning: given choice, we make wrong moral judgements, proving ourselves too weak to exercise freedom. In compassion, they must therefore assume the burden of usurping our Constitutional right of individual citizen's power and exercising it on our behalf to control our unrighteous urges.

Given freedom, I might look at erotic pictures of naked people. I might get naked with friends and take pictures. Heck, we might even sell copies. Moralist authoritarians assert such acts are evil and obscene, and they take that as a mandate to impose control by civil force upon my untrustworthy abuse of my freedom. If they succeed in making that which is erotic illegal by calling it obscene, I will have a choice: let them cleanse my home of whatever offends them, or draw my curtains and become part of a brand new criminal underground. The sanctimonious and self-righteous idea that one has a moral obligation to take command of another's life if he will not conform to one's own taboos is bad enough in the individual. When it is given the power to impose behavior with the force of law, it quickly engenders the most intolerant tyranny, wherein dissent is evidence of moral weakness, and disobedience of the law is a fundamental sin. It is evil's most insidious trick that one who would defend freedom must appear to defend evil. For one group of people to forcibly usurp the freedom of choice of another group is evil, even if done with the best of faith in their own righteousness, and in compliance with the process of law.

I believe the Fathers of our Constitution were wise to guarantee that certain rights shall not be abridged, by law or in fact. Such freedom demands that standards of morality must be maintained by some means other than the power of civil law enforcement. It must come from the community, not as a cry for government to exercise more power by law, but as a collective act of establishing the community's standards in fact. Merely electing the rulers who command the police is a poor excuse for democracy.

We who oppose the so-called "anti-obscenity" laws do not seek to promote obscenity, though our detractors are quick to accuse us of just that. I should like to believe no citizen calling for such an ordinance wishes to destroy the basic rights which make our way of government the most just in history. I can acknowledge those socially-conscious citizens are attempting in good faith to define the "responsible" part of "responsible freedom", whereas we are attempting to defend the "freedom" part. The point of contention is the use of enforced prohibitionary law. If one group would ban obscenity, and the other would ban tyranny, then clearly the resolution must come from tolerance and respect of each other's rights and desires. We must all act upon the common goal of preserving both our communities' high moral standards and also our country's guarantees of freedom.

Some sects' morality exhorts abstention from certain acts which others might call normal sexual behavior. The penitent may voluntarily choose to accept such limitations as a sacrifice made in faith, and they violate the rights of no one. However, when moralists insist that to avoid temptation for such penitents to violate their vows, everyone else must be forced to behave as though we were also abstemious penitents, then they violate the rights of all, and invalidate the faith of the penitent.

Censorship would abridge the right of the citizen to inform or amuse himself, would restrict the right of parents to determine the moral upbringing of their children, would usurp the power of the school board to select the curriculum, and abrogate the power of the free market to determine which products are desired and which are spurned. By creating resentment, it would even undermine the power of the churches to create high moral standards through inspiration. And that is where our moral standards should come from, not from enforcement, but through inspiration, example, encouragement, and active participation of the citizen in the affairs of the community.

Some attempt to justify censorship with the declaration that community standards demand it. If that were true, availability of obscene material by the truckload would not lead the community to buy it. When one faction feels it must arm itself with the power of law enforcement to suppress a willing market among others, then cries of "community standards" are specious. Those who would impose some bizarre, paranoid, and oppressive obscenity ordinance are not reacting to community standards. They are attempting to dictate standards, and to impose them by force. I find that obscene.

Given a free market for ideas, community behavior will reflect the true standards of the community, for better or for worse. Enforcing an unwilling show of officially-moral behavior can only result in the cruel hypocrisy of a society in which people steal forbidden cookies with their left hands, while with their right hands they arrest their neighbors for the same. Suppression of a willing market among those who would be free produces a criminal underground, which is taken by the suppressors as justification for further persecution, which is taken by the suppressed as grounds for active social dissent, which justifies the riot squads... and history wonders why we were shooting at each other over pictures of naked people.

No Christmas in Town Hall?

I like Christmas, notwithstanding I do not subscribe to Christian theology or doctrine. I agree with the First Amendment that precludes making any law which would "respect" an establishment of religion. Adding my mote to the opinions of hundreds more learned, I interpret that to mean no law may be passed which grants official endorsement to any doctrine or dogma as being equivalent to empirical science, which grants favor before the law to any religious body, or which employs law enforcement to impose the taboos or sacraments of any particular sect. It would seem clear any reasonable interpretation would render thousands of laws now enforced in every state unquestionably unconstitutional. To begin with, consider laws which define what is and is not an establishment of religion. If any established congregation is, to use the new PC term, "faith-based," then it is the faith of the faithful which makes it a religious body, and not a decision made by any board of legislators. If government has no authority to define and so limit by law that which is an establishment of religion, so as to deny unqualified establishments, there is not even reason to keep an official government registry of them. Though any group of faithful are certainly free to call themselves a congregation and conduct their rituals in public or in secret, it is only by registry and licensing by government that such a group becomes an "establishment" of any kind. Why should any religious organization wish to permit (or even encourage) the government to make any unconstitutional laws respecting them? Even a cursory look at the most common laws respecting religious establishments as different from other establishments makes the answer all too tragically simple: power and money. The most obvious is of course the exemption from paying taxes that other establishments must submit to. Others include "blue laws" imposing restrictions on property owners and businesses respecting their proximity to religious establishments or schedule of ritual. Since the first Vestry with the most members in office agreed to permit Legislature the power to define and license religious establishments in return for that fiduciary respect, the Church has been whoring its constituency to the State for public money and law enforcement. This relationship is proclaimed illicit by both Constitution and Scripture, for reasons clear to anyone who appreciates Constitutional freedom from government, or who celebrates personal communion of the individual soul with the eternal spirit without an idolatrous authoritarian chain of communication and command.

Unfortunately, the most vocal of the opponents of this meretriciousness have taken the stand that the government must therefore purge itself of all that might be seen as supporting one or another religion...any religion. Wrong! Read the Amendment: "Congress shall make no law respecting an establishment of religion, or prohibiting the free exercise thereof...." We seem to have forgotten that second part. We have a majority of one religion in America, and that one is openly seeking to use its plurality to obtain high office and thereby impose its notions of morality and truth by enforced law. Others call for the power of government to be exercised to remove from any "public" place any display of the symbols or celebrations of that particularly predatory sect, and all others as well. Both seek greater government license to pass laws respecting that establishment of religion, one for it, the other against. Both have missed the point. The point of religious freedom without respect for any establishment is that all religious activity may flourish without any sect seizing secular power, and without anyone being prevented by government forces from openly celebrating his faith, especially on public property. Though I decry and rebuke the sectarian cabal which so proudly and publically wears its robes in the halls of Congress, I must still object to prohibition of their colors. No Christmas in Town Hall? Didn't that line up there say, "no law....prohibiting the free exercise thereof"? Run the carolers off the Court House steps with riot control troopers? Tear down the World War I memorial in Idaho because it is cross-shaped? Valgame Dios! God forbid that should come to pass in America. Which means, of course, that we must be as willing to accommodate other public celebrants who are well enough established to put on a good show. The Mary and Joseph thing is a joy to watch, no matter how seriously you take their offspring's reputation. I'll take all that kind of stuff I can get, whether it's about Winnie the Witch, Mahmoud the Muslim, Deirdre the Druid, Hassan the Sufi, Buddha-Belly Baba, Benji the Buddhist (and Benji the Bahai), Norman the Mormon, Jersey Jerzy Jew, Ziggy Zen, Harry Krishna, Ozzie Osiris, Thuper Thor, or Hey-Zeus. The God I know is big enough for all of them. Merry Christmas!

Is Halloween Satanic?

Once upon a time there was a beautiful religion based on respect for nature, on creating safe and loving communities, maintaining health by knowing nature's ways and remedies, and worshiping the eternal spirit through ritual celebrations of fertility and the holy cycle of life. They call their religion Wicca, from which we get the words "wise" and "witch". Wiccans did not believe mankind was evil, or born in debt to God, or had to shed anybody's blood to please God and keep from Hell. Therefore, they did not wish to join the cult of guilt, fear, and sacrifice which swept their land with armed priests, and flaming stakes. They refused to bow down to the idol that cult had made of a martyred Jewish prophet. For refusing their divinely-ordained yoke, those militant self-proclaimed agents of God declared Wiccans were worshipers of Satan and deserved the torch, though Wiccans knew Satan is only a mythological character. Wiccans still have a celebration about the same time as Halloween, called Samhain. It is devoted not to Satan, but to the Goddess, for the goodness of plentiful earth. The idea God might be female is heresy by Christian dogma, and those who believed it were hunted down, tried by pious male judges, divested of their estates, and killed. After persecution drove Wiccans into hiding, Christians created a day of "giving the Devil his due," the shtick being to dress up in images of death and evil: corpses, devils, and witches. It is a mockery by which the young are taught that witches are sadistic evil old hunchback women who cook bat soup, consort with the Devil, and presumably eat Christian children. Halloween identifies other such "occult" symbols with Satan as pointed hats and those mysterious evil wraiths called ghosts. (Is St. Jude a ghost? What does necromancy mean?) The truth, of course, is that the only evil in black cats, bats, skeletons, pentagrams, astrological symbols, Hebrew letters, or out-thrust tongues, is the evil the judgmental insist on putting there. Then they self-righteously accuse anyone associated with those images of their own sinister judgements. Christian paranoia and bigotry created the absurd spectacle of Halloween to teach children that certain non-Christians are evil. The symbols used are as far from the truth about witchcraft as the rabbit with the technicolor eggs is from the truth about Christ. The fact that young people stretching the limitations of their elders' conventions choose number 666 or the inverted star as symbols of independence hardly means they become minions of The

Infinitely Evil Satan (minor chord; drum roll). If Happy Meals for a pair of Cub Scouts costs $6.66, that does not mean Ronald McDonald or one of the Cubs is the Anti-Christ. Putting a star on his hat would not make your kid a Communist; a star on his shoulder would not make him a General; and even carving one on his forehead would not of itself make him a Satanist.

But no, Christians who fear Satan's insidious influence are not really paranoid. Satan is everywhere, ready to poison their minds. Consider that even our days of the week (taught in public schools from kindergarten) are named for Pagan gods. Sun-day, and Mon(moon)day are straight from Astrology, a superstitious doctrine practiced by Satanists, promiscuous LSD-heads, and weekly-tabloid false prophets. Saturday (Saturn's day) is not only Astrological, it is even named for a false god worshiped by Pontius Pilate's deicidal Roman stormtroopers. Wednesday is Wotan's day, after the deity of bloodthirsty Vikings, as is Thursday (Thor's day), named for his (not His) son. Friday is Frigga's day, taken blatantly from the mythology of Druids and evil witches. Tuesday is Tiu's day, for the Teutonic god of war, a false deity from the same myths Adolf Hitler believed in when he said Germans were the master race, diabolically giving "White ethnic pride" a very bad name. Satan would like us to keep the names of ancient false gods alive, along with other diabolical notions like evolution, reincarnation, geophysics, herbal medicine, and water-witching. If Evil is not to triumph in America, surely we must stop using our social institutions to promote the opponents of God by at least eliminating the horde of Satan's demigods whose names we are forced to honor weekly. Why can't we name our days in character with our role as a nation under God, a nation so tolerant as to legally harbor every doctrine no matter how false good Christian reasoning reveals it to be. For Monday, let us have Lukes (which will be good for Spanish speakers used to Lunes). For Tuesday, Markes, which mirrors the Spanish Martes. For Wednesday, Matthes, and for Thursday, Johnnes. For Friday, not Thor's mother, but Maryday. Following the Spanish again, Saturday is simply Sabbaday, and Sunday is obviously Sonday. The old days' characters, Thor, Roman, and Hippie Astrologer, will become fearfully-evil Halloween masks.

There Is No Millennium.

The power of the millennium is attributed to being 1000 years after the birth of Jesus. So what was the "date" then? There is no record of it in writings from the time, all dated according to some other calendar. Each calendar traced its origin to some event – the "date" of which is meaningful only if traced from some other event .So "when" did any of it happen, and what makes one time more important than another? Timekeeping through history has been done by observing celestial bodies, a science called astronomy. The notion that any arrangement of planets, or date, has psychological or divine significance is called astrology. Using computers, we can determine the position of planets at any time in history. In the year we call 7 BC, a conjunction — "a sign in the stars"— occurred which would be interpreted by astrologers east of Bethlehem as heralding the birth of a new king in the west. If that astrological interpretation of that astronomical event might be taken as correct dating of the birth of Jesus, then anything intended to happen 2000 years after that happened in 1993. Did we miss the end of the world? Or worse, has it already ended, and is this the hell to which we have been damned?

Extrapolating present trends creates a picture of a hellish world to come. It seems negativistic to point out terrible consequences of steps we are blithely taking, when our lives today are so abundant. In the buffets of Las Vegas, the variety, quantity, and quality of food is unmatched in the world, and in history. In all of human existence, no one has ever eaten better than we do. That is a sobering thought. Even so, a few things seem clear. Though the War On Drugs has been the most destructive influence on Constitutional freedom, civil security, and trust in government in this century, it continues to escalate. It will pale in comparison to the War On Guns. Whereas the first is justified by the presumption that your body is the State's to protect, and its destruction of your life done to protect you from yourself, the War On Guns is presumed to be protecting others from you, so anything goes. Domestic terrorists, after all, have no rights at all. When freedom-loving Americans resist drug laws by smoking dope, nobody gets hurt. But when "2nd Amendment gun-nuts" stand up for their rights by shooting back at storm-troopers who come to get their Vietnam War trophies, the do-do will hit the fan. Even one such incident will initiate an entry-on-demand / no-knock-if-we-want policy, and people will be killed believing they have the right to defend their homes. It will also justify domestic use of all high-tech surveillance and intervention equipment available to the military.

However, the War On Guns is only Act II. Perhaps the year 2000 will be significant after all as the year the War On Sin began. The presumption that your body is property of the State, to be protected with laws against self-abuse is piddling compared to the presumption that your soul is property of the Church, to be protected from the eternal consequences of your sin — by law enforcement. This is not new – all "blue laws" are enforced statutes which forbid acts only because they are moral taboo to the prevailing religion. The fact the Constitution forbids union of Church and State does not deter them. The fact that Scripture refers to a religious body which beds down with civil authority and embraces the deadly sword of law enforcement as a "whore fornicating with the kings of the Earth" does not deter them. This is to be their year of victory, and they are filled with rejoicing in themselves, in God's name. In Cabal, the high-priests of the Coalition speak of "Dominion" as their filial divine responsibility and right, and insofar as they worship a totalitarian idol of God, they will not be satisfied until they command a totalitarian regime in His name. A Christian Ayatollah in the White House will use the power of American might to smite the sinful of the earth — starting at home. What can be done about it? Nothing. Most will vote for it in the year 2000, and still be surprised when they find reason to come for you.

Here are some predictions for the coming year: The End of the World will not happen. California will not fall into the sea. The aliens will not return to Area 51 with Jesus after a thirty-year trip at light-speed. No one will rise up into the sky to the strains of a brass sextet with wings. The computers are not going to crash — The Borg will survive just fine. Cher will marry again, to me.

Keep It Private, Citizen.

An important freedom is the right to privacy, as intended by the term "private citizen". It is not specifically mentioned in the Constitution, though many of the stipulated rights obviously depend upon it. Though any social activity requires giving up a degree of one's privacy, and most prefer not to be hermits, it should be possible in a free state to live without any official body demanding to know one's location, sex, race, age, extent of personal holdings including home, pockets, or bladder, income including money, trade, or service, or the names of those with whom one does business, has sex, or discusses politics. The demand that automobiles be registered and display the number is a good example of government invasion of privacy disguised as public service. Registration is touted as protecting the citizen from theft. This is illusion, as license plates do not prevent theft, nor much improve the chance of recovery. Even if service were the true objective, it should be voluntary. Even mandatory, it need be done only once, not annually. Clearly, the primary benefit is to enable government to establish identity and observe the movement of the owner. Licensing provides no service to the citizen, but grants higher levels of surveillance and control over him — and he must pay for it! It is argued that fees provide revenue needed to operate the public service system. That is like being interrogated by electroshock to obtain information the State would use to control you, then being charged for the electricity. When it comes to pressing the citizen for details of his life, the Motor Vehicle Department is small time. If, God forbid, it should become a matter of State interest to know where all the Jews live, how many places have records stipulating religious or ethnic denomination? How about that new pan-demographic Census? What about that IRS? Sometime, just for fun, try to convert $20,000 of your resources into $100 bills, carry them to another state by airline, spend the money on firearms and gold, and get the stuff home...without leaving your name on anything.

Here is a little parable to illustrate the problem. "Back In The USSR?"

Two men huddled in a bleak corner of the drab concrete city. Clothes threadbare, they were gaunt men, but they felt lucky to have a small brazier to warm their hands. One drew reflectively on a pipe, though he had nothing to put into it. "Tell me, friend," he said, "why you sit here in the cold with me, who has nothing, when I know you own a fine vehicle. Here there is no food, while crops lie heavy in the rural fields. Surely if you went out and brought back produce, you could become rich. Do not the principles of Capitalism say real power lies in private ownership of the means of production?"

The other chuckled wryly. "Yes, free enterprise is the rule. There are just a few minor technicalities. First I must register my vehicle (and pay a fee), get a license to drive, for which I must take an exam on the regulations (instructor's fee), then a driving test in a vehicle that meets regulations — mandatory inspection (mechanic's fee), safety equipment (retailer's fee), and insurance (agent's fee) — after which I may pay the fee to get a business licence. To carry and sell produce, I must have a Health Code inspection (fee), and an environmental impact assessment (fee). To conduct commercial transport, I must pay for a drug-test program on my only employee, myself. To conduct interstate trade, I must pay a bonding fee. Since I have no money, I must borrow on my vehicle to buy produce, and pay interest. When I buy, I pay sales tax. When I sell, I pay receipts tax. Since I have an employee (myself), I pay Social Security and worker's government insurance fees. I pay self-employment tax on everything after expenses, and when I keep what remains, I pay personal income tax on that. What I must pay for government permission, mandatory expenses which increase neither productivity nor value, mandatory insurance, and taxes outweigh what profit might be made in the produce I could carry — that is, without gouging the consumer. And the consumer can only pay so much before he cannot afford to buy at all, whereupon my produce and my capital investment both rot in the vehicle, while the hungry curse me for my greed. For failure to pay them back, my creditors will sieze my vehicle, and for failure to pay their taxes and fees, the government will take whatever else I have. If I tried to obey all the laws, it would ruin me. If I got caught breaking one, they would destroy me. Perhaps someday we will have free enterprise, and success will lie in ownership of the means of production, the entrepreneurial spirit, and the willingness to work. Until then, success depends on paying for government permission, regulation, and protection. Since those belong exclusively to the federal-contract mega-businessmen who own the government, my vehicle might as well be a rock." And nothing ever happened to them, forever and ever after.

You Bet, You Can Bet!

You bet, betting should be permitted on College sports. The players are doing nothing more or less wicked no matter who bets on their game, skims tickets, or sleeps with the coach. Heck, why not bet on the Little League? The temptation to tempt the babes to cheat? Are those who write the do-do-no-no's into law just reacting to their own paranoid image of demonic game-fixers lurking the Middle Schools like happy-pill-peddling pedophiles looking to tempt their innocent lambs with the rewards of learning the subtle skills of point-shaving?

How true is the notion that a free citizen has the right to spend, give away, throw away, or otherwise dispose of whatever property he owns? Do we have ANY property the government may not control if it chooses to? I think not. It would make criminals of those who risk our personal property on the outcome of a ballgame, or the roll of dice. Everyone who enters a game knows not everybody wins, and nobody wins all the time (except maybe those who haven't heard cigarettes hurt them (or school kids used to races where everyone gets a ribbon, so nobody goes home a loser)). That is why casinos call it a game, instead of something sneaky like "mandatory insurance" ...also a bet, on the outcome of your accident. If betting is legal activity the citizen is free to do, why should the subject of the bet matter? On what grounds might government insist one may spend money on tobacco, but may not bet it on a duck race? If not for the understandable racket called "licensing" (that is, government granting to one citizen a right it denies to others, upon payment of money to the right agency's bagma...I mean, citizen-service revenue-receiving associate) why should not any free citizens agree among themselves upon the terms of any bet? "Hey, buddy, 'betcha two t'one my kid scores before yerz. A hunnert bucks." "Yer on, chumpo."

Where do they come from, all these so-called "blue laws" regulating such personal practices as drinking, drug use, gambling, and prostitution? The generalist term most often used is "moral values." Sometimes given weight as "traditional values," these laws are well-intentioned as protecting the weak-willed from self-destruction. Since ancient cultures in holy books also discouraged certain activities, many presume these prohibitions are "God's laws." Be that as it may, it does not make them law of the land.

Making any sectarian taboo a generally enforced law would seem a violation of the Constitution's prohibition of using law enforcement to grant respect to any religion as above all. Each of these laws prohibiting something "moralists" think nobody should make their own choices about depends on certain presumptions. First, that anyone other than the free citizen should use power to make his moral decisions for him, and second, that government should let those decisions be made by legislators to follow any doctrine of religion.

For a well-intentioned busybody to believe he serves his fellow man by law-enforced punishment for disobedience to those closer to God than themselves, is some presumption. To believe he serves God by making his brother a better soul than God made him, is the height of self-righteousness. To believe himself morally superior, favored by his God because he is willing in the name of "protecting his brothers' souls from their sins of vice" to declare them criminals, to persecute, imprison, disenfranchise, impoverish by statutory asset-robbery, to beat, interrogate, "medicate," coerce into dangerous "informant" roles, even to kill them...is, well, if it were being done by anyone other than state-employed followers of the predominant religious sect, it would be called psychopathic by the shrinks and lawyers, and Satanic by you-know-who. Such a person, well-intentioned as he may be, presumes that the bodies, and even the souls of those brothers somehow belong to him, that he as God's steward should take upon himself to protect them from the moral errors of those to whom God so unwisely gave them.

No self-styled moralist has any right to prohibit gambling by others. That fact doesn't change the law or the reality. If it were no longer prohibited, free citizens might decide to bet on all kinds of things. The "powers that be" would organize and collect the vig, but they would for sure open the games up, not put some tight-shoe schoolmarm squeeze on us for our own good. Could be a lot of fun. Why, fer example, should we not bet on politics? Offer a spread on electoral votes: Bush -34, flat; Browne +42, Gore... who cares. Who's got a line on Libertarian Carla Howell vs. Ted Kennedy? 125 to 1? I saw the Rams at that last year, didn't I?

Only Crooks Use Cash.

Only criminals use lots of cash, right? To stop the drugs, guns, and bet runners, follow the cash. Would there be no crime if we outlawed cash, and switched to universal card accounts, which like your VISA know what you purchased, where, and when? If using a card means identifying yourself and your location, then no one wanted for anything could use it. Far from eliminating all the criminals, this would force people into the underground who were leading productive even if furtive lives. This is not unlike government giving welfare to unwed mothers if they name the "deadbeat dad" failing to provide, making him unemployable, of necessity a criminal. To say total accounting of everyone's transactions may fairly be called "free enterprise" is like saying there is freedom in prison to obey the rules. It "levels the field" by prostrating all. If government can rule what you may possess, which of your assets you may trade, the price, and how much you must pay for the privilege of trading (as it does today), then the only free enterprise is underground. Only there can two citizens agree upon the worth of their assets and exchange them freely, without a government agent in the middle dictating the terms of the deal, for a forced fee. The Drugwar is promulgated in spite of clear evidence it causes more damage than drugs do, because (among other reasons) it entitles government surveillance and control over our personal transactions, and global transactions. It is war on privacy of person, privacy of possession, and privacy of transaction. The Devil's Dope is just the football, but the game is control of your life and money. If any agency had power to know, permit or deny every transaction, then everything would belong to it in practice, to do with as its policy dictated. Elimination of private exchange in favor of a "crime-proof" FEDCARD Agency would make its officers the rulers of the world, and create a huge, hostile, and resourceful underground.

The FEDBANK Empire opens with the key that says TAX. If the card is used to collect tax, then government may control how it treats its account holders. If taxation continues to be item-specific, and region-specific, then every product and service will require an identifier, a location code, tax rate, and official fair market value. The resulting World Blue Book would be a global price-fixing tool. It would have thousands of authorized terminals constantly updating some category or other, the consequences of new legislation, or recalculation of some index. The ability to access the database for marketing would be more valuable than blood, and black-market FEDCARD data might become a medium of illicit exchange at a certain level of society. The power to control the master program is to drink from the Holy Grail while wearing the Ring of the Niebelung, wrapped in Superman's cape. The opportunity to trade an important oil evaluation fix for a crop of cocaine to distribute for the swing vote of a demographic group might make a kingpin of Colombia's elected and trusted delegate to the Board of Trustees, and not leave a track for the bean-counter robots to follow. The door slams shut with the lock that says LAW. Once in place for taxation, its potential takes totalitarianism to draconian new levels. Gum is illegal in Singapore, raw eggs in California. The gun you bought at Sears last year is illegal now and must be surrendered. That book has been declared obscene by City Ordinance 264-A1, and cash registers in this town won't sell it. Everything has a legal category, and every person's category would be checked with every purchase. Felon? Can't buy a gun. DWI? Can't buy beer. Driver's license expired? Can't buy gasoline. Business license expired? The Master Control Program will not permit deposits to your account. People do not stop eating when their bank account is closed by aparatchiks or subroutine 264-D. The "unaccountables" find some way to survive. Barter media are spontaneously created, and like the regulated counterpart the stock market, are faddish in valuation. Lots of things become media for illegal or other cashless trade, as hippies used beadwork, hash-pipes, and the like to take the place of dollars which demanded somebody get straight jobs. Was a time when cocaine dealers used Indian jewelry to avoid carrying cash. You might expect something like baseball cards, CD records maybe, but with rare ones known to be more valuable. "A '92 Madonna? Give ya fifty... tell ya what, sixty gallons, FED-clean, no record, my brother."

Cross-breed the cell phone, global locator, driver's license, and your bank card, and you've got the USACARD. When you hold it (or implant it), its built-in skin-resistivity meter (that's a lie detector) tells the USA how you feel about the questions it asks, and you don't even have to answer. Hey, that'll stop crime for sure, and then we can enjoy a little peace and freedom around here.

The Green Police

Citizen activists of Elko NV's Jarbridge Rebellion are drawing national attention attempting to prevent The Mighty Fed from closing a popular road to protect endangered trout. The hard fact is, of course, that keeping all human beings out of any area is the only way to keep it wilderness. To permit people to visit is to destroy it, like it or not. Is the only answer to this dilemma to permit government to decide which places the citizen may visit, and which are forbidden zones? Liberal authoritarians are quick to abridge the rights of all to protect the interest of a helpless few. Conservative authoritarians as quickly abridge the rights of all to protect a powerful few. Libertarians proclaim the government should remain hands-off, permitting private owners of land to protect it or develop it as they wish. In practice, government has demonstrated it might choose to force the private conservationist to permit an easement for a public road, or might just as likely forbid the private developer to move one stone if doing so appears to destroy some form of habitat it may happen to identify on his property. Unfortunately, none of these government policies is able to guarantee the survival of any species, nor to guarantee future generations the right to visit the primordial wilderness their grandparents knew.

Here is a bit of speculative "future history" to illustrate my take on the problem.

"Once upon a time, at the insistence of mobilized popular concern for the survival of endangered species and the preservation of the natural environment, well-wishing public servants in government instituted The Green Police. These armed agents of the Department of The Interior were given the responsibility and power to make sure nobody broke any of the laws, statutes, regulations, policies, rulings, or restraining orders protecting the forest and its natural inhabitants. Since motor vehicles, structures, campsites, fires, fuels and toxic substances, firearms, hunting or trapping devices, chainsaws and axes, mining, digging, or dredging equipment, refuse dumping, construction, damming, drainage, et cetera, and etc. were potentially harmful to the forest, or to the natural habitat of some indigenous species, all were made illegal within the EPZ's – that is, the Environmental Protection Zones.

"Being confident they had thus done their part to save the planet and sooth the hearts of their concerned constituents, the legislators retired to the baths with their favorite lobbyists. They were soon disturbed by new outcry from those same environmental activists whose demands they had just fulfilled. Those passionate saviors of nature were calling for something to be done about the sudden increase in the number of criminals who were desecrating the newly-hallowed ground of the EPZ. Not to be gainsaid by insubordinate, lawless, and socially irresponsible commoners, the Officers of State dutifully met the demand by substantially increasing the number of Green Police, and providing them with every modern technological advantage so as to accomplish their sworn duty to the People and the Land. Naturally, costs were very high for their competitive salaries and extensive training, their fine new equipment, and the many new employees needed for their administrative support -- not to mention the costs of involving other law-enforcement agencies to protect them from hostile hordes of squatters, poachers, Sunday-coachers, fence-jumpers, scum-dumpers, and other trespassing environmental terrorists. To fund such expensive public service, the Department Of Interior was granted the power to award government contracts to manage certain resources of the EPZ – that is, to conduct the business of limited logging, trapping, mineral development, and (for those with very special permission) tourism. To save the forest, armies of The Green Police patrolled the limits of the legally-habitable areas, while government-sanctioned environmental defense contractors cut down the trees."

Want To Go To Space? Learn Russian.

Best recent news is that entrepreneurs plan to turn Mir Space Station into a resort, and Russia is eager to let anyone with the money play. Growing up at White Sands, I was thrilled to see my Dad and his friends shoot the last of Hitler's V-2's, and embarrassed to see Sputnik and Gagarin reach orbit first. The greatest tragedy of Challenger was not the loss of seven pioneers, but that the Shuttle did not fly for so long thereafter. The notion we could not continue to accept known risks while lawyers, politicians, and journalists held up development of space whining for guaranteed safety, liability litigation, or politically-motivated investigations is an insult to American pioneering courage. Though test crews since the beginning of flight have lost lives in pursuit of progress, lawyers took advantage of the celebrity of Challenger to press for huge settlements, driving up the cost of insuring everything in the program. Money for space goes not to research, but to insurance companies, to protect the engineers from the lawyers. Our safety record is high, not because lawyers are concerned for the feelings of heirs of the brave, but because our engineers are damn good. The only thing stupider than letting preachers dictate science to school boards is letting lawyers dictate science to engineers. Any one-eyed moron not brainwashed by catechism can tell the religion is fantasy, but since lawyers spend years in school memorizing books of arcane rulings, they can pose as educated, and it is harder to tell they have no clue what reality is.

Whence the notion it is atrocity to permit any American the right to risk life for progress, or amusement? Until Chuck Yeager started hanging it out on his meager Captain's pay, most aeronautical envelope-stretching was done by civilians like Howard Hughes, Wiley Post, and Amelia Earhart, whose only motivation was to go faster, farther, or to do it first. How about a vote of confidence from Americans? Give us a chance to prove our faith in the Shuttle, and we'll pay our way doing it. How about a raffle, a big ballyhoo wherein we may buy a chance at a seat equivalent to Christa McAuliffe's on the next STS? At $25, it wouldn't take many to pay for the payload. Millions every year pay more to watch a ballgame. It could be NASA's most profitable cargo! No matter how practical the money and public interest generated may seem, it is not likely. NASA would instantly be bound in gambling litigation, and insurance would exceed the cost of the payload. Congress would take the money to be accounted, appropriated, and re-disbursed (minus handling charges). Security paranoids would label any assertion the people have a right to use the Shuttle "suspiciously leftist".

Perhaps no issue has greater long-term significance than commercial development of Space. Low Earth Orbit, Geosynchronous Orbit, the LaGrange points, and the Moon comprise the high ground of the 21st Century. Whoever controls those places will inevitably dominate the world, and control will fall to those most able to establish permanent presence and profitable use. In our country's first century, mastery of the sea meant world control. When asked to fund America's first Army airplanes, Calvin Coolidge inquired, "Why not buy one and let the pilots take turns?" General Billy Mitchell was cashiered for declaring his superiors irresponsible for the same short-sightedness. When war compelled the bureaucrats to step aside for the engineers, American air power won World War II, and has been the controlling factor in all things military and commercial since. Letting Russia or Japan or anyone else have controlling presence in space is like being able to build the best ships in the world, but refusing to go to sea.

Most space experts are cool-tempered people with no use for hype or hokum, but Americans in general seem most moved by sports, soap-opera politics, give-away shows, and fantasy epic adventures. NASA's best public advocate was probably Gene Roddenberry, whether or not they knew it. American space development can succeed only if supported enthusiastically by the public, and they will support it only in terms of their own interests. Kennedy hit it on the head: "Hey, let's have a race to the moon!" We will be moved only by seeing Americans working and playing in space, and making money doing it. As long as the argument is whether DOD/CIA has exclusive use of space, or a few big corporations can go too, we will not be moved. When the price of a raffle ticket will buy a chance to be "The First American Nobody-Special In Space," we will get involved at the grassroots again, the money will flow, and the rockets will fly. Until then, it looks like Sergei Korolev's old John-Deere-style hardware will once again put Russia first in space.

Public Health or Animal Rights?

Being a desert community, our town has its share of problems with civil animal control. A recent proposal called for an ordinance limiting private dog ownership to four animals. More would mandate licensing as a commercial kennel. Concern about numbers of animals may draw attention to the problems of animal control, but it does not provide a solution. It seems to me the issue is whether keeping of animals constitutes a violation of rights of any individual, or of animals themselves. The correct concerns are whether the animals are a public nuisance, a health hazard, a safety hazard, or are themselves abused. Ten clean, quiet, well-cared-for, well-behaved dogs are no violation of neighbors' rights, even on a half-acre lot. One dirty, fertile, fence-jumping, garbage-slinging, cat-eating, kid-chomping howler is too many for a whole county, even if his owner has put a plum in every pocket in the County Court House, and has his license sewn into the seat of his pants. Proponents justified their actions saying, "Nobody needs more than four pets." Maybe it is true nobody needs more than four pampered baby surrogates poochie-pooping around the trailer park, but a blanket law based on such thinking does not address the needs or rights of those who live on four sections and use dogs in their ranching operations, nor of the users of canine security, nor of the responsible citizens who enjoy the profitable hobby of breeding the family dog.

The local Kennel Association defended the right of private animal-owners to compete with their own business because they savor the relationship between owner and dog, and train both in socially-responsible behavior. It is likely none who operate as professional businesses would object to a license fee as such. The problem lies not in paying the fee, but in determining who has *permission* to do so. It is a matter of how one may get — or block someone else from getting — the special use permits, environmental clearances, neighbors' release statements, noise abatement studies, etc., etc., which a responsible board of bureaucrats might eventually come to require. In pursuit of such civil power, animal control ordinances are often created as an attempt to gain broad-brush authority so that the ability of landowners to freely use their own property, to own and raise animals, and to conduct legitimate trade would be subject to the decrees of a small appointed board. Many are passed regardless of whether or not any actual violation of any person's rights was shown to have occurred. By focusing upon such limitations as numbers, breeding rights, and the like applied to all in hope of limiting the violating few, these ordinances do not address the real violations of rights at all: noise, health, safety, care, and the citizen's privacy of ownership from bureaucratic authority. It neatly avoids all of them!

Licensing does not address the problem of uncontrolled strays or wandering pets. The solution depends on first establishing a clear definition of the problem: by Animal Control, are we talking about human public health, or about animals' rights? If granting "humanitarian" rights to certain species is the objective of the publically-funded activity, then perhaps the adoptable residents of the Animal Shelter should be imposed by law upon every human family as a civic duty, like jury duty, a kind of animal affirmative action? If on the other hand, the problem is defined as control of vermin population of domestic species, nothing beats a bounty. Voluntary registration and lip-tattoo would protect owners. A dead "lipped" animal would bring a fine, not a bounty, giving bounty hunters cause for respect. A live one would bring a ransom. Folks who value their animals would protect them, and strays would be very rare.

Whether unwanted animals are eliminated by bounty hunters or by paid employees of the State, communities face expensive problems of feeding resident populations in the Animal Shelter, and disposing of thousands of euthanized animals. Except for sentimental attachment to the species, why can we not find some profitable way to recycle the tons of meat they represent, as we could if they were sheep, horses, or goats? That is abhorrent to many people, no matter how practical it may be, but it points out one significant difficulty in facing the problem. Are we solving the technical problems of animal control, or merely pandering to public emotion? We have all heard someone cluck that Hindus will starve while there are mountains of beef strolling uneaten all around them. We have hungry people in our country also, yet we still spend public money to dispose of hundreds of tons of usable food because we have a cultural taboo against eating dog and cat... even as livestock feed, or animal-shelter rations. How much of the issue of civil animal control stems from squeamish citizens' wishing certain emotion-provoking matters kept from their view? Is not "humane euthanasia" employed more to ease the shock of the observer than that of the animal?

Regardless of the means of disposal of the unwanted, the correct solution to the problem is not to restrict the rights of property owners, but instead to create laws which protect the rights of citizens from violation by their neighbors' practices or pets. These would include clear definitions of noise nuisance standards, health hazard standards, and animal care standards, and the uncontested right to trap, shoot, or otherwise dispose of any unwanted animal upon one's own property, and to use effective force in protecting one's person, family, pets, or property from attack by any animal on public property. Clearly, neither the approach of the pragmatic exterminator nor of the dewy-eyed puppy messiah can serve the needs of the entire community, but hopefully, by keeping rights of the individual citizen foremost, and tempering that reasoning with compassion for both innocent animals and sensitive people, it is possible to create a workable system which balances human social well-being, animal rights, and costs.

I like cats and dogs, but who needs a billion of them? But for that matter, who needs a billion of us? Even so, I'm still a chauvinist when it comes to my species. An attack dog with a badge on his collar is not a police officer, and don't even start about how Peaches should be able to vote, since she already eats at the table. And I won't call you Harvey Woolbanger just cause you say you're really fond of sheep.

"I just don't feel like a real man
if I can't take a whiz outdoors now and then."

An Open Letter To Pro-Life

I resent pro-life advocates putting words in my mouth: when I say pro-choice, that is exactly what I mean, and not pro-abortion. I believe abortion should be opposed without using criminal law, and instead with inspiration and offering positive options to the mother. It would be equally unjust of me to insist when you say pro-life, you mean pro-tyranny, for wanting to impose your choice at gunpoint by law enforcement. Reduced to simplistic form, the logic of the pro-life argument is clean and compelling: abortion is murder, and should be prohibited by enforcable law. This taken as morally fundamental, the only uncompromising resolution is total prohibition of abortion of pregnancy...for any reason whatsoever. Though protection of the unborn is the declared moral mandate of the pro-life movement, I believe very few would agree with total prohibition. More believe that certain exceptions should be made, that some pre-natal homicide is justified by their moral evaluations. These exceptions include pregnancy by rape or incest, and risk to the life of the mother. The moralist logic supporting these exclusions reveals the existence of a "hidden agenda" in the pro-life movement: not so much to protect the lives of the unborn, but to promulgate the position that sexual indulgence not intended for procreation is immoral and culpable. Abbey Lawrence of Libertarians For Life reveals the underlying moral theme: "....abortion [is] a vile act of aggression and an abdication of responsibility for the consequences of a freely chosen act...." This obligation being a matter of moral opinion, it is unjust to impose it by force of law upon others.

What about the rape exclusion? Because a woman raped did not willingly permit the sexual act which caused the pregnancy, she is not morally bound to bear the burden of parental obligation, says the rationale. The circumstances of the conception do not change the fact that any abortion is homicide. The significant factor is thus revealed to be not the life of the unborn, but the mother's moral posture at conception. Under the rape exception, the unborn must be saved if she submitted to sex for erotic pleasure, but may be aborted if she resisted sex on moral grounds. Why so, if not for her personal convenience, or the moralist posturing of her society?

What about the incest exclusion? As there is no actual harm in it, incest (that is, voluntary inter-familial copulation and breeding) is an offense only by taboo, but it is a strong and deeply felt taboo. What besides such revulsion to the moral circumstances of the conception could justify aborting the innocent unborn of such union? "What about how incest creates genetic defects?" you ask. If you would justify abortion of the unborn of an incestuous union because it *might* have genetic defects, then would you also admit abortion of an unborn shown to actually have a defect? If not, you reveal the issue is not the defects, but again the moral posture of the parents. If you would admit abortion of genetic defects, then why not terminate the defective upon identification at birth, instead of creating special care programs for them? If you would make that distinction on the basis of parturition, then you defeat your own case for pre-natal vs. post-natal rights. Further, if incest is an exclusion, would you grant legal abortion to any woman willing to testify that her father is also the child's? Would you grant freedom of choice in the death of the unborn to the willfully incestuous, where you would deny it to others? Or might you insist that the unborn may be aborted only so long as the parents are punished for sex crime? The issue is again revealed to be not foetal rights, but moral posture.

What about abortion to save the mother's life? On what grounds do you place the mother's life above that of the unborn? The unborn is innocent of its mother's suffering, and historically women died in childbirth to save the child. If unwanted pregnancy is imposed upon the woman by law as a moral obligation to accept the consequences of her voluntary copulation, then what makes her unwanted death different? If you concede death is punishment too severe for her sin of lust, so as to justify killing the innocent unborn instead, then you presume even to judge one person's suffering against another's life, and to back up your judgement with the power and might of law enforcement.

If you may create exceptions to your own rule to justify homicide by your moral evaluations, then why should not others have the right to create their own exceptions, in accordance with their moral evaluations? *What makes you so special?* **You say** the mother has a moral obligation because of her complicity in the conception. **You say** any unborn has a right to your protection by armed law enforcement from its mother's intention. **You say** your willful assumption of power over the mother's life is not only justified, it identifies you as the mother's moral superior. These contentions are all matters of opinion, no matter how serious you feel about them, or upon whose authority you choose to take them. If any exclusions are permitted, based on moral evaluation of the circumstances of conception or inconvenience to the mother, we are no longer discussing the issue of whether or not to permit legal abortion. We are only arguing over the moral grounds on which it may be justified. That is to say, if you are to base your cause upon a moral mandate to protect the lives of the unborn, then you must support total prohibition or concede you have no right at all to impose your personal judgement upon the moral decisions of others. If you would presume your moral convictions give you the right to take forcible control of the lives of others to protect their children, would you also admit the right of others to take control of your children by force of law to protect them from your choice of work, medicine, school, religion, or family structure just because they were in their own opinion morally justified? If not, your will to assume power over others for their children's sake is *self-righteous hypocrisy.*

What about total prohibition? If you would support total prohibition, subject to the full extent of law enforcement, as the War On Abortion, then the issue becomes no longer one of abstract moral or ethical questions, but of mundane practicality. To what quality of motherhood do you consign the children you would save? If you use power to take away a woman's right to control her life and body because you judge her morally unfit (as a fornicator and would-be murderer), and thus force an unwanted child upon her, should not that obligate you to fulfill the responsibility to the child that you have presumed to delegate? How can you justify leaving that child in the hands of a parent you have already judged to be morally unfit to make her own decisions? Short of raising the child yourself, the only way you could be sure you have fulfilled your duty is to insure the mother's care by official observation, regulation, and enforcement of legislated standards of parenthood. Who will set those standards? You? And how will you enforce them? Will you impose money fines upon women for being poor, ignorant, and unemployable school-dropout mothers? Will you put them in prison for trading in street crime, drugs, fencing, and whoring to feed the babies you saved? Who will care for the children then? You? Why do we not hear pro-lifers offering to take away the burdens of the unwilling mother, to bear her expenses, to feed the child, and see to its upbringing? Apart from demanding its unwelcome birth, pro-life's actions do nothing for the child, but are all directed against the mother.

If abortion is murder, how would you enforce it? If punishment is a fine, then you are only quibbling about the price of abortion, and to whom that price is paid. If you would promote imprisonment, then how long do we incarcerate a woman for seeking, attempting, or having an abortion? Would her sentence begin before or after the birth of the surviving unborn? Might a long prison sentence be grounds for granting an abortion by the staff physician? If not, do we expand our prisons into State OB wards and nurseries? If you make murder of the unborn a capital crime, who would you indict as accomplices — her doctor, parents, husband, or the manufacturer of the surgical equipment used? If abortion were crime, having a miscarriage would place a woman under suspicion of murder. If a woman miscarried as the result of an accident suffered through her voluntary exposure to risk, skiing, for example, she could be tried for manslaughter. An underground network would quickly be established among social workers and physicians to help make medically-competent secret abortion available to those who seek it in spite of the law. A second underground would also be created among the truly criminal to prey upon the same seekers. So pervasive are the requirements for monitoring and controlling such activity that only a Federal agency could have the necessary oversight and authority. Of that necessity would be born the APU, the Agency for the Protection of the Unborn.

To begin with, physicians would be obligated to report all positive pregnancy tests to the APU. Each positive test would be assigned a Social Security number, and a caseworker would monitor its progress until it was awarded a birth certificate or a legitimate obituary. Failure of any woman to obtain a test during the first trimester would constitute a misdemeanor. Since pregnancy once detected must be carried to term, employers could stand to lose valuable woman-hours as a result of their employees' moral shortcomings. Pregnancy without notice could be grounds for dismissal. Companies failing to demand periodic and random pregnancy tests of women employees could be held accountable for criminal negligence to the unborn if one of them was discovered to have had an abortion. (Just as airlines failing to demand drug tests can be held accountable if the pilot in an accident took an illegal drug). If a woman were injured or killed in an abortion attempt, her accident and life insurance would be invalid because she was committing a felony. No hospital would touch her, lest they be charged as accessary after the fact.

"Make abortion illegal and there will be no more dead babies. Women will become chaste and fathers responsible. Everything will be peachy." It is a nice dream, but an escapist fantasy. To use the law to save the lives of the unborn is a beautiful hope, but the real-life result would not be beautiful at all. Your laws would create a turbulent, crime-ridden hell in which women, their unwelcome children, and many others would be the victims. Your hope is laudable, but your desire to use power to enforce your hope is self-delusion by pride in your moral choices. We are exhorted somewhere in Scripture to accomplish God's work not by power and might, but by the Spirit. I call upon you to abandon the shortsighted expedient of force by civil law, and instead find positive ways to persuade the women you encounter to accept your reasoning and be moved in spirit to voluntarily forswear abortion and to lovingly raise their children. When you have changed their hearts, then you have done the work of God. If you are only forcing goats to behave as sheep in order to make yourself appear a better shepherd, you may be disillusioned to discover God is neither deceived nor impressed, and you shall have nothing but discord in the fold you would thus create.

Do We Have Bodily Rights?

The State presumes the citizen is his body, and as the citizen's protector, it has a duty to prevent his self-abuse of it. The Church declares he is a body with a soul to lose, and as God's anointed protector of souls, it has a sacred duty to control him to prevent his eternal damnation. Truth is, of course, every person is an eternal sovereign soul in God's universe, possessing an ephemeral body in the world. Neither is property of Church or State. Neither meretricious Church nor her incestuously-miscegenate brother State has any right to presume power in the name of protecting our bodies or souls from our own God-granted freedom of choice. That fact has not stopped them from getting into bed together, embracing the deadly sword of civil law, and establishing lifetime control over every activity any citizen might pursue. There should be no law against suicide, or assisting another, nor against self-abuse. If a joe wants to dope himself to death, let him. We have global over-population. People here have a right to stay, and to keep on breeding, but there is no purpose enforcing laws against things just because people get killed doing them. Abortion? On demand, at cost, and next-day pills at any drugstore. Yes, abortion terminates life, and masturbation is potential genocide. The self-righteous may cluck back to their chairs. No woman's body is property of Church or State such that she might be forced to commit that most personal resource against her will. Disapprove loudly as you wish, but it is between her and God, and nobody's rinkydink bizzniss. Sterilization? Likewise, on demand (or give a $50 bonus).

Is a dead body anybody's property? If people want to process bodies some particular way, they should have the right. Grandpa's mummy in the parlor, why not? Recycled body parts, unclaimed bodies, and donated ones are a resource, a wealth of transplant parts, non-specific protein byproduct, a skeleton in every biology classroom. If any service should be public, it is disposal of bodies, and health-care recycling. What's the dumbest? People die waiting for costly organs while others go in debt to pickle and bury a million bodies a year.

If our bodies are not property of the State, then the State has no right to prohibit self-abuse. Recognizing that truth demands abolishment of DEA, release of all in jail for drug crimes, and the end of all activity by any agency to detect or apprehend anyone for use or production of unpatented or natural drugs. Likewise, acknowledging our right and responsibility for our bodies' wellbeing lies with ourselves and not the government calls for abolishment of the Bureau of Alcohol, Tobacco, and Firearms. Alcohol can be made by anyone with the recipe, and should not be regulated. If it is OK for one joe to sell beer, any joe should be free to sell beer, out of his basement like Amway soap. For all its known harmfulness, tobacco should not be the subject of government regulation — along with marijuana, opium, coca, peyote, psilocybin, comfrey, or vitamin Z. If our souls are not Church property, and the Constitution forbids imposing its doctrine through law, then right demands revocation of all "blue laws". If it is OK to sell beer on Saturday, it is OK to sell it Sunday. If it is OK down the street, it is OK next to the church, or the gun store. Firearms? The Constitution forbids restricting our right to arm ourselves. All laws limiting our right to own weapons should be revoked. The right to use force defending your body or other property should be absolute. However, punishment for initiating force against an innocent should be severe. Kill somebody in a robbery, lets weed the gene pool of you, now. Use deadly force to compel submission, you're in the cage with the boogeyman, bozo, and we put the videos on late-night TV. Capital trials should be a public event. In the rainforest, cannibalism by the community is used as capital punishment. Man, that is pure! You've got some joe up for capital crime. Come jury time, you strap him into the chair center stage. Each juror votes by pushing a Yes or No button. If there are enough Yes votes to convict, the perp is fried on the spot. If not, he walks out a free man. Would that be sane and just? Not likely, which might actually make a better deterrent. Nobody wants to star on "Judgement Day," and people are lining up to be jurors.

Suicide, Slavery, and Sin

Saw a bumper sticker: "Kevorkian for President". We might better make him the President's health aide... Government policy toward suicide again reveals the presumption that our bodies are property of the state, to be protected (or as with the draft, expended) even if in opposition to our personal will, as it suits the Suits in DC. How is it not clear to everyone that every human being has the right to terminate his life? It is after all, his body, her body, your body... not their body. It has been made Constitutional law that no person in America may own another person. Opposition to slavery is one thing people of all races here agree with. But if the government is just a group of individuals who have gained a position to wield collective power, why should they have the right to own persons? How is it that in so many ways, they presume to own our bodies, and to treat us all as incarcerated slaves? They proclaim it is for our own good, and therefore for the good of the collective that they should use the power of the gun – law enforcement – to take from us the right to behave as free citizens with respect to our own bodies. Is the slavemonger who forces his slaves to exercise his notions of good health and fitness (so they will be good collective workers) any less a slavemonger, or does his generosity to his slaves justify his ownership? Even if government kept us all fat and safe from risk, would that justify its taking away our right to choose to be something else, even if to our own destruction? Unfortunately, many seem happy being fat and stimulated, put to work and taxed to create the Massa' State that feeds and medicates them and makes all their hard choices for them. The policies of the present government are totally committed to the proposition that your body, soul, and property are the responsibility of the government to be observed, documented, regulated, and manipulated, at the point of a gun when it is expedient for the controllers. Both Republican and Democrat politicians will continue this policy if people continue to vote them into office.

The roots of authoritarian opposition to suicide are politically influenced by the large money flows associated with insurance and probate, and as always, supported by those who believe suicide to be sin, and who feel they must therefore do whatever necessary to others in order to protect their souls. Taking their sect's edition of God's Laws in one hand, and the might of civil enforcement in the other, they proclaim themselves by virtue of their moral superiority their brothers' keepers. Here's the straight word on that subject: God's laws cannot be broken. Not "may not" but <u>cannot</u>. That which we can do, does not violate God's law. All those rules about whether or not we <u>may</u> do that which we have "free will" to do are just that – rules somebody decided to proclaim and enforce. Good ideas, lots of them, but not God's laws. If you can be persuaded to believe you are guilty of violating God's law by your act, you can be controlled, and led to make payments of propitiation in both substance and deed. Gravity is a good example of God's law. We did not get to the moon by violating that divine law, but by obeying it perfectly. Orbital physics is a manifestation of God's law, "What goes around comes around." This law is clearly observable in the Vedic notion of karma, and in the cyclicity of the I Ching, even if obscured by the Biblical paradigm of commandment, disobedience, and punishment vs. divine gratuitousness toward the awled-eared obedient slave. If as the moralist authoritarians say, God is down on suicide, then it is surely between that soul and God, and not the business of self-appointed Divine Judges in the world.

Personally, I think anybody who needs to call a doctor to help him kill himself is short a couple of organs to begin with, not to mention imagination and a sense of adventure. But even giving them that, why should there be a question of whether a doctor may do it? Why not anyone? The government's right to grant the doctor's sacred exclusive privilege to practice medicine is based upon the presumption that the government is protecting the collective patient from quacks. In the case of assisted suicide, a practitioner could only be rightly called a quack if the patient survived. If we have the right to own our own bodies, and to dispose of them, we should have the right not only to the assistance of a doctor, but of anyone we might wish to choose to be with us in such a profound moment.

"We'll Protect You, Body and Soul."

When a gambler and his kid go to the casino, the kid is forbidden to operate the gambling machines, and graciously provided with non-gambling entertainment. The gambler sits in front of a video, feeds quarters into a slot, and is entertained with games of skill and luck. The kid sits in front of a video, feeds quarters into a slot, and is likewise entertained. According to the "moralist" viewpoint, the gambler's play is vice, an immoral thing to which only a responsible adult should have even limited access, and the other an appropriate activity for the chiiildren whom they would presume to protect from temptation. The only difference between the games is that the gambler's machine gives him a chance to use skill and luck to win, whereas the kid's machine takes every quarter every time.

Whether or not things like sex, drugs, and gambling are immoral should certainly be a matter of personal opinion. They should not be the subject of any enforced government opinion. If individuals or the members of any sect, party, or other group believe a particular activity is immoral, they are guaranteed the right by the Constitution to say so openly. If they choose to eschew those activities in their lives, they are free to do that without infringing upon anyone's right to their moral opinions, and without involving the power and might of law enforcement. But beyond that, the presumption that everyone must be forced to eschew them likewise is most unrighteous.

Purveyors of forgiveness must persuade their market to believe they are guilty. The priesthood may not be the oldest profession, but it is certainly the oldest racket. If you believe you are damned by somebody else's "original" sin, you can be sold anything to get you off the hook. Anything we might enjoy – but lowing praise to an authoritarian idol – is at least suspected of having roots in sin, and therefore any desire for pleasure should motivate the penitent to conviction. If one can be made to believe his most precious God-given natural pleasures are evil, and his desire evidence condemning him to eternal whatever-you-fear-the-most, he can be made to subject himself, and sacrifice his estate. It is spiritual blackmail.

Here is a clear index by which the use of State power can be seen to be unrighteous: your body and your soul are not the property of the State. The State has no righteous authority to protect your body as though it were government property, by taking over your life by force. All of the laws against "self-abuse" – the penal occupation of America through the Drug War – presume the right to forcibly take control of your body to protect it from you. Likewise the laws against prostitution, pornography, and personal non-standard sex deny the right of the individual citizen to willingly grant to another citizen any level of access to his or her body, for whatever reason or reward is mutually agreeable. Whose body is it? Do you believe your body is Federal Property?

Why does the State presume to meddle forcibly in these areas of our lives? Because of an even more insidious presumption. They have a "moral obligation" to the community, and therefore not only a right, but a mandate. To begin with, there is no such thing as a community – there are only us individuals. To say the community may be protected from abuse by taking the rights from its individuals is hardly different from saying the forest may be protected from fire by cutting down all the trees. Though protecting your body from abuse with drugs is a practical objective, morality is not so derived. Most precisely, morality has to do with one's perceived state of grace before God. When a well-intentioned but self-righteous (or sect-righteous) zealot presumes himself to be the spiritual guardian of his fellow man, he is seeking to prevent spiritual self-abuse, seeking to protect your soul, as though it were his to protect. "The Soul is God's," I hear someone bleat. Yes, which fact does not make it the property of any religious institution, no matter how deeply they believe their bigotry to be equivalent to faith. Therefore when a religious body takes upon itself to bed down with the kings of the earth, to seize the deadly sword of civil law, and to impose its doctrine and taboo upon all by force, its acting in the name of protecting our souls is presumptuously blasphemous.

If our government in its self-proclaimed desire to improve our lives were as honest and generous to the citizen as the casino industry is to its customers, and respected our personal rights to our lives, our private pleasures, and our property like the casinos do, our candidates for office would not need to sell their loyalty to buy ad time on TV to get out the vote.

Memorial In Vain

I write this on Memorial Day. Yes, I know, yesterday's holiday is old news, and therefore no news. We take our Federally-mandated free day's pay, put away the Flag, and go back to the "Veterans' issues...ho-hum" attitude we maintain the other 364. I'm a veteran, with the Distinguished Flying Cross, among other honorable decorations. Though I hold my service in high regard, and belong to several veterans' organizations, I am not able to comfortably attend meetings of most. I am too often gently rebuked for being "political" instead of maintaining the posture toward God and Flag expected of the soldier. To my thinking, a soldier who does not know or agree to the politics of those who command him is an amoral mercenary, no matter how pious and honorable he may be, or how glorious the government which hires or conscripts him. A soldier who willingly fights unto death, confident he knows his leaders' righteous principles, is spiritually fulfilled and a champion in the world, you can take that from me. It is a fine feeling to fight for a righteous cause, even if in retrospect the cause you trusted seems less noble than at the time.

The professional soldier and the veteran I believe should be more "political" than others, since they are the ones who must go (or send their sons) to kill other people because of their politics. If a soldier is pious, and truly concerned for his soul, it would seem important his homicide be done for righteous reasons. If having pledged to obey The Flag, he sees his leaders' actions are immoral, or hypocrisy, he must make a critical decision – whether patriotism means defending the rights and principles which define the country, or defending the regime holding the authoritarian offices, regardless of their violation of those principles. If the leaders' attitude is, "Victory is worth suspending the rights and principles for which we fight," then any moralist justification is merely expedient propaganda. Defensive war is morally moot – if they come, you fight. They sink your navy, you sink their island, budda-boom. However, attacking a country in the name of defending a principle is not defensive war, right or wrong. It is police action, authoritarian political aggression. When we justify sending fighters to kill people to defend their rights from their bad political regimes, then deny them and our own citizens those same rights that define us as a nation, we make murderous hypocrites of ourselves. By any standard I know of, that is immoral. If our Bill Of Rights is what justifies us, we damn sure better be getting those rights at home, and seeing to it all the people we "save" get those rights too.

I am no longer able to recite the Pledge of Allegiance. We are taught as children to drone, "I plejaleejus tuda flag..." without knowing what it means. The Flag is a symbol of authority, and to pledge allegiance means to promise to subject oneself and obey. That's a fine idea, but our judges at Nuremberg all agreed the individual German was not absolved of personal moral failing by having faithfully given allegiance to his Flag. "...and to the Republic for which it stands," is still all right with me, if I take that to mean as the Constitution defines it, and not the corrupt and oppressive structure of greed, pride, and power festering in Washington DC. I do NOT pledge allegiance to the Flag. I pledge allegiance to the Constitutional principles which a certain group of British subjects made traitors, outlaws, and terrorists of themselves to grant to their heirs and to history. I'm with them. They got it right, POLITICALLY. When our government -- "The Flag" we are to owe allegiance -- rapes us of those rights for which the Veterans died, and imposes upon us the socialist police policies of the regimes they died to defeat, then all those honored dead have died in vain.

Lots of flame going around about the New World Order, a conspiracy to impose some global regime. As an American patriot, I am pretty wary of seeing the USA swallowed up as one more Free Peoples' State in the United Sodality of Terra. My trepidation comes from observing that seems to be occurring, perhaps inevitably, but it is not a Bill Of Rights world they are forming. The present US government is clearly directed toward such globalism, and also clearly directed toward a highly-policed socialism as its format. If I saw my government standing up in the world demanding that every country unite to grant every citizen every right in the Bill Of Rights, repealing every law in every country starting with THIS country which abridge or violate those rights... well, fellows, this old rotorhead burnout would RE-UP!

Our Flags: Burn the Ban.

The movement to amend the Constitution to ban burning the Stars and Stripes as a political statement is well-intentioned, but a terrible mistake. Our flag is a symbol of a special relationship between citizen and state: the voluntary loyalty of free private individuals. I was taught in Army officer training that obedience can be compelled, but respect must be earned. If a citizen may be prosecuted for disrespect toward a symbol of freedom, then his right to any dissent is eroded, and the flag is thus truly tarnished. How sad when the right to make public statements against the government is being newly granted in Russia to see that right attacked in America. When a politician wraps himself in the flag, then calls for a law against flag-burning, what is he really trying to protect? Would a flag-burning amendment also prohibit shredding the flag as a statement against covert government? How about throwing acid on the flag to protest toxic pollution, or staining the flag pink as a statement against pro-socialist sentiment in Congress? How about such disrespectful acts as burning the President in effigy, or peeing on The Wall we Vietnam veterans hold sacred? Surely these are deplorable acts, but where the rights protecting such declarations of political opinion are absent in the world, it is there we declare oppressive government exists, and where we feel most justified in sending our soldiers as "defenders of freedom." If in the name of defending the flag we abandon those rights, we have lost the battle for freedom without facing an enemy.

The enslaved may be compelled to obey — the free must be inspired. So let the dogs bark at the flag, and if they tear it down, raise high another. Let us stand firm as champions of personal liberty throughout the world to defend others' right to yell insults and cast dung at any icon of power, and when those who see this are moved to revulsion for those who desecrate symbols, and respect for those who defend rights, then our purpose will have truly prevailed.

As a combat veteran, I proudly fly the Stars and Stripes, but I certainly did not, nor would I ever fight for "The Flag". I fought, and would fight again against any enemy, to preserve those principles of responsible freedom for which I was taught the flag stands. As a libertarian refinement of a democratic Constitution, the Bill Of Rights is a pinnacle of achievement in applied social philosophy. It is unique in that it is intended not to impose limitations on the citizen, but instead to guarantee that statist limitations shall not be imposed. Those who promote the No-Burn Amendment wish to add to the Constitution not another guarantee of liberty, but a punitive restriction of political expression. They would make of the flag a symbol not of civil freedom, but of enforced display of civil obedience. The movement is an attempt to rally the unthinking around the flag as a symbol of patriotic obedience, where they lack commitment to an issue that might mobilize an informed citizenry — a practice sometimes called jingoism. As such, the Jingo Amendment is the antithesis of those principles for which the flag stands.

Equally offensive is the recent movement to ban the display of the flag of the Confederacy, as a "symbol of racism". The Civil War was not fought over slavery — which was an issue, but hardly THE issue. As any knowledgeable southerner will point out, that terrible holocaust was fought by the Confederacy in defense of the Constitutionally-defined rights of the sovereign states to regulate their own internal affairs without forced intervention by the Federal government. Those who fly the Stars and Bars do so in respect for those long-abridged states' rights. No American today would stand up for the practice of racist slavery – so should we therefore ban Federal Reserve Notes because they bear portraits of American Presidents whose administrations permitted slavery?

The First Amendment guarantees the right of an American to display or desecrate ANY symbol as a statement of his or her personal opinion. If that freedom is sacrificed to prevent destruction of any such symbol as a statement of political dissent, then is the American flag truly desecrated. If the libertarian spirit of the Bill of Rights is not kept alive in the United States of America, then that great document becomes only the hemp linen shroud in which the greatest political experiment in the history of mankind is mummified for the historians — and perhaps the hopeful idealists — of another day. This is our day. Let us not lose it. Defend what each of those gallant banners have once stood for: our Constitutional guarantees of personal freedom, states' rights, and voluntary loyalty to a righteous representative government.

Affirmative Action in the White House?

Equality of opportunity is neither a fact nor the law in America. There is individual prejudice among people of all racial groups against others, and the result of such prejudice is cruel and unjust in every case. Though well-intentioned, perhaps even pragmatically correct at one point in our history, the laws collectively known as "affirmative action" give discriminatory precedence to some people by race, in the name of eliminating the practice of giving precedence to some people by race. Though the severe inequity suffered by blacks and others in our past (and in spite of enormous progress, still suffered today) deserves righting, AA was not in practice a move toward racial justice, but instead is a sacrifice of the rights of certain white people, done to mollify minorities' desire for revenge against their ancestors. In the name of justice (but for the purpose of organizing minority groups into manipulable voting masses), the rich whites in power gave away neither their rights nor privileges, but the rights and jobs of lower class whites. The AA laws stripped working-class whites of a precious American heritage, that same heritage which was cruelly denied to non-whites once, but which white social activists the last forty years have gone to such trouble to guarantee to others: the right to compete fairly for the advantages of success in America with equal opportunity, without discrimination against them for race or color.

Open competition may not always produce racially-equal results. Does anyone suppose Evander Holyfield and Venus Williams are where they are today because of some affirmative action law obligating white athletes to take a dive if up against a minority competitor? Or should white athletes demand such a law to give them "a fighting chance at equality" against the (naturally superior?) black champions? Since the concept has been expanded to include other forms of "disadvantage" besides just race - such as gender, age, handicap, etc - there is only one group of Americans who do not have some kind of demographic category around which they can rally politically to seek laws specifically "protecting the equal rights" of themselves as opposed to those of other demographics. In each case of "protection" it is assumed that the "minority" needs its rights defended, while the "non-minority" is presumed to need no defense. More and more, the view is taken that our rights inhere not in our being individual citizens, but in the demographic group to which we belong. Every protection program excludes the same group, the SWABWAM ...the straight, white, able-bodied, working-age male... who is presumed to be an arrogant, exploitive elitist, a sexist, racist villain... and rich.

In city, state, or any other government-regulated job, these laws mean when a swabwam applies, any applicant of the correct minority is given "cuts" ahead of him. Where taxpayer-funded "internships" will pay half a job's wage if the employer will hire an otherwise-unqualified applicant from some particular minority group, employers will go looking for one, and agree to teach her the job before they will pay the full wage to hire a non-minority regardless of his qualifications, or how hard he studied and worked to acquire them. (Consider how highschool students might feel about this fact.) To fulfill mandatory "quotas," the AA lawmakers have criminalized fair employee-qualifying process in labor law. Even if an employer is truly non-discriminatory, the law takes away his right to select his employees in his own business to suit his own choices, and imposes its racially-specific decisions upon him.

If affirmative action is as the Congress and the Justices have said, the fair, just, and lawful thing to do down at the working-class level, then let's see how they like it. In the name of racial justice and equality, let us dispense with the Presidential Election. Why should it be different in the White House? Let us not forget that so far 100% of the holders of that job have been white, and a quota of even 1% would at this point obligate the Electoral College to select the "best qualified ethnic-minority candidate." We could just save the American people all those tax-paid campaign millions, and free the TV sets of politics the whole year in favor of the ball games we find so much more important anyway, by invoking the laws of affirmative action, and just giving the job to the first candidate of the most-politically-correct minority group who shows up. Forget Al Gore, Son Of Bush, and Harry Browne – in the name of affirmative action for racial equality at all class levels, lets just give the job to Jesse Jackson... or Dennis Rodman, or Whoopi Goldberg. Heck, I'd VOTE for Whoopi!

Really Cut Government Spending?

<u>Art</u>: Eliminate the NEA, and all government activity which judges or regulates the artistic, moral, political, or other merits of literature or art, other than needed for the architecture of government facilities.

<u>Social Security</u>: Offer voluntary freedom from FICA tax by waiving rights to benefits. Base receipt of non-taxed benefits on need, to provide subsistence to the elderly, not guaranteed gravy for the able.

<u>Defense Industry</u>: Give necessary defense industry something else to do. Improve by redirecting money for parallel civilian purposes. Examples: pursue space for commercial success. Get security and liability concerns out of the way of anyone who can make money in space — feature films, tourism, industrial colonies in orbit or on the moon; develop military-usable water, waste treatment, and alternative-energy systems for homes, companies, and small communities; maintain a large Corps of Engineers manpower pool for disaster and environmental projects, including civil construction, toxic waste dumps, highway cleanup, etc; create an Army "Alien Corps", in which refugees can work under discipline, learn English, American culture and basic laws, to be granted citizenship upon completion of a tour of duty; expand military hospitals and medical schools, make them available to all veterans, dependents, identified disaster victims, etc, and price their services at cost, in direct competition with the physician/insurance monster.

<u>Contracts</u>: Mandate in the budget of any contractor accepting Federal funds that no individual's salary may exceed that of the President of the United States. No CEO, hot-shot engineer, genius ad-flack, nor celebrity endorsing the product on TV should be more highly paid on any government-contract job.

<u>Drugs</u>: Eliminate all funds to subsidize tobacco. Eliminate funding for drugs prescribed not to cure illness, but only to give the patient an artificial sense of wellness, including tranquilizers, anti-depressants, and sedatives. Decriminalize marijuana. Don't tax it, regulate it, prescribe it, or otherwise mandate control of its natural market. Drop all marijuana cases, grant

presidential pardon to all marijuana offenders, and release them. Terminate funding for surveillance, apprehension, and prosecution of marijuana traffic. Economic advantages: empty half our prisons; end billions flowing out of our country to buy a crop we can profitably grow; end billions more given to governments of pot-growing nations to oppress their people with paramilitary narc forces; open the market to the benefits of hemp, including non-acid paper, livestock feed, and environmentally-beneficial replacements for petro-chemical fibers. Grant prescribed access to heroin. We permit such medical addiction now to tranquilizers, sleeping pills, and sedatives sold on a perpetual basis to millions. This will bring the opium market under competitive pressure, breaking the power structure of organized crime now supplying the demand. The greatest benefit would be eliminating small-time criminals who now prey upon the common citizen to supply themselves. This benefit is a decrease in the expense of law enforcement and insurance claims. If any drug should be outlawed, it is cocaine. Unfortunately, making it a black-market commodity multiplies its power to do evil many times. As a democracy of concerned individuals and responsible government, we must find a way to treat cocaine as a personal behavior problem, and not as a criminal disobedience problem.

Churches: In accordance with the Constitutional requirement that government shall not respect institutions of religion, terminate their tax-exempt status. Churches should pay full taxes on all revenues made through the sale of religious tracts, sacrificial items, or religious practitioner services. Why should this not extend to our foreign policy? Provide no "foreign aid" to any institution of world religion, even if it may have gained the trappings of statehood, including the Vatican, Israel, all Islamic governments, or any such nation in which civil power is vested in a religious sect.

Public School: Education should be available to all eligible children at government expense. It should be neither mandatory nor "guaranteed", but a voluntary privilege. Curricula should be strictly secular and empirical. Children who fail to conform to standards of behavior or performance could be denied attendance. It should be very easy to license private schools, and to operate them as businesses in competition with other educators. The choice of private curricula should be agreed upon between the schools and parents, and not made to conform to any standards established by government. No public money should be paid for the attendance of any student in a private school, whether parochial or secular.

Though Americans call for reduced government spending, very few mean it. The most common position is probably, "Cut off that freeloader over there — and fund my deserving program."

(You can see this was done a while ago.)

Prison, Punishment, and Public Good

Why put people into prison? To punish them, to make them better citizens, to deter others, and to protect others from them. Punishment for its own sake is pointless moral exercise. It makes sense only as corrective improvement of the individual, or as a deterrent, a step toward improvement in the public. The usual punishments are fines, denial of rights, imprisonment, and death. Fines are good punishment, particularly for crimes of acquisition. The problem is temptation for individuals or agencies in power to make arrests to seize assets for themselves. Fines and punitive property seizure cause the crime of robbery by prosecution, corruption which can exist only within the system of law enforcement, causing net destruction to the public good. Denial of rights, such as disenfranchisement, inability to get bonding, insurance, security clearance, etc, makes it more difficult for the punished to rejoin the public. Denied access to legitimate enterprise, they are more likely to seek anti-social activities, making them more dangerous than before punishment. The policy is net destructive to the public good. The forced isolation of incarceration is also good punishment, but with destructive potential. The difference lies in creation of unpleasant conditions in prison as punishment – that is, torture. Forcing prisoners together in fear and hate under the oppression of violent guards is definitely punishment, but the effect on the subjects is destructive. The effect of teaching "jailhouse mentality" to large numbers of citizens (particularly the young) is net destructive to the public good. The problem with punishment as a deterrent to future crime is the inherent injustice of "making an example" by punishing the individual for the imagined future crimes of others. The presumed deterrent is the would-be offender's fear, and though the public may accept it, it is nonetheless injustice to the individual. Punishment done to inspire fear of the law is statist terrorism, exactly the practice identified as villainy in Darth Vader (chief of Imperial security, enforcing law without tolerance). Where that is acknowledged, soon grows the seed of resentment and distrust of government – which breakdown of confidence is net destructive to the public good.

As protection of the public from the subject, execution is absolute. As punishment, death is either best or worst. If the most severe punishment is a lifetime of torture, death might be a merciful option. Merciful also, yet punishing indeed might be isolation without media, mail, phone, visitors, or any other contact. However, if the objective of temporary incarceration is truly "corrective" as advertised, then the effect upon the subject should clearly be improvement in attitude toward himself, the public, and the law. If the effect is instead clearly destructive to the subjects' social potential, then for what reason perpetuate the practices? If the objective is to accrue something to the public good by the tax expenditure, surrender of public rights, and damage to the lives of the imprisoned, then those practices which have a net destructive effect might best be stopped, and practices which best accomplish advantage to the public good be kept or initiated. Short of executing dangerous offenders, protecting the public is best done by imprisonment, the longer sentence the better. The public is protected as long as the subject is isolated, whether tortured or living in luxury. Since the socially-destructive effects of jail result from harsh conditions created as punishment, perhaps the most beneficial practice might be to reverse that. Prison life costs taxpayers $40,000 per year. How many of us have that to live on? Jail could be cheaper using less security, and more luxury. When the point is reached where jail is better than life outside, there is a curious incentive to stay. If indefinite sentence in a soft cell is cheaper than a carousel of crime, arrest, prosecution, and high-security lockup, if the public is protected, and the prisoner has a better life than ever, where is the objection? Why not turn old apartment neighborhoods into high-surveillance cell blocks where prisoners have TV, recreation, and a Vegas buffet, if it meant greater public security at lower public cost? Add work, beer, choice of Valium or marijuana, and overnight visitation, and some folks might forget they were in prison. Some might even call it a workable social format. Everybody has a debt to the State, as public servant or public offender. Everybody has a cell, job assignment, check-in schedule, and mess-hall pass. All that's need is for everybody either to be guilty of some crime, or to have taken State employment maintaining the comfortable residence blocks, and controlling the lives of those who live there. Add slot machines and a sports book and, hey, maybe The Millennium has arrived after all.

Freedom Schmeedom. It's Over.

I'll say it again: the golden age of liberty in America is over, and nobody misses it. The Constitution is only middle-school mumbo-jumbo to most Americans, a few questions to be answered on a Social Studies test and then forgotten. Few could state the freedoms from government granted by the Bill of Rights, beyond "freedom of speech, separation of church and state, and the right to bear arms," all of which are flagrantly violated by the Cult of Power in Washington in numerous ways, all supported by the courts and enforced with lethal power. Worse, all of the violations are accepted as justified exceptions by the overwhelming majority of Americans. The minorities crying most loudly for freedom still vote for state-created jobs and increased entitlements and benefits from Massa Washington. The gun-rights nuts swear they will kill or die for the Second Amendment, but they vote for martially-armed law enforcement for prohibition of personal rights proclaimed immoral by the politically-predominant church. The abusive use of guns by citizens and by uniformed agents of the State is escalating, and the desire of government and large masses of socialized citizens is to take the guns away from those the masses fear, and leave only the occupying military power of law enforcement armed to protect us all. The result can only be a three-way fight between the heavily-armed genuine criminal out to prey on the citizen, the citizen who arms himself unlawfully in self-defense, and the armies of Darth Metro's Ubiquitous Security, for each of whom the other two are deadly enemies. Another group which whines impotently about the genuine abuses of our rights and freedoms is the Drug War protesters. Since the generation that first protested drug persecution also protested against the Vietnam War, the WWII generation concluded drug protesting is unpatriotic. Since those young freedomists also led in the sex revolution, their elders in power concluded drug use leads to immorality. Having lived in the drug underground for some time in my life, I know personally all the common shit and the lifestyles of the users of each. I wouldn't claim any of it is any good, but the government's draconian War has caused a hundred times more damage to our country than the combined effects of all of it. I recommend we all get off the stuff, from America's number-one killer, tobacco, the insidious ego-inflater cocaine, mind-numbing heroin, even the relatively harmless mild euphoric marijuana, and particularly all of the tranquilizers, sedatives, mood-enhancers, anti-depressants, uppers and downers, and such synthetic garbage your benevolent legal pill-pusher Dr. Feelgood will happily prescribe for you. Making it all legal might end the damage of the Drug War, but only we ourselves can end the damage drugs cause, legal or not, so clean up your act.

The Holy War On Drugs has been the single most destructive influence on the knowledge and practice of Constitutional freedom in America's history. As with Hitler's Jews, the enemy in that cruel war is the private citizen, and the purpose of his persecution is the creation of the security state. If the urine sample we are forced to surrender on demand to employer, Dean of Students, or police were tested for DNA instead of devil weed, our racial groups could be immediately identified, so that nobody could lie about his race to get on welfare... or any other reason the government might like to impose. The last Presidential Election was settled by a few hundred votes. Since even the simple possession of the most common and least harmful of the forbidden substances is by law a felonious disobedience, the Drug War has disenfranchised millions of Americans as felons. Marijuana is used as a litmus test for those who might make up their own minds about how reasonable any particular law might be, and who might decide not to do something just because some board of puffed-up professional power-freaks with law degrees write a rule saying they must. A dope felon never votes again, even if too young to vote when convicted. The potential dissident, the free thinker, is identified, and systematically disenfranchised, leaving to vote only those who have proved they will take the law as fundamentalists, and obey it. Would two million re-enfranchised free-thinking marijuana felons have made a significant difference in the last election? No, whether they all voted for Harry Browne or not. No, because both of The Major Parties will conduct the business of Government the same way. Both the Left and the Right will perpetuate the Drug War, Social Security, the IRS, ATF, ETC, and the general growth of the authoritarian wealth-distribution and behavior-control mechanism of the welfare police state in America. The system is two-fisted, one hand cupped supporting the citizen, the other cupped over it confining him. The difference between the Republicans and the Democrats? Turn the hands over. You're in good hands now, Schmuckos.

I Resign

I once thought myself some kind of prophet crying out warning in the wilderness, but it seems I have only been pissing into the wind. Congress has made laws respecting establishments of religion, from oppressive blue laws, prayer healing on Medicare, drug use made legal for a particular race's church, even granting certain religions recognized political states supported by our taxes. Some are opposed by calling them cults, or supported by calling them faith-based organizations, and some respected by making their mythology equivalent to science in school, while prohibiting them to celebrate on public grounds. Freedom of speech is abridged by making certain words illegal if addressed to uniformed agents of State, calling other words hate-crime if applied to persons darker than the speaker, or calling words legally spoken conspiracy if someone is present to hear them. People may assemble peaceably, unless to petition for redress of grievances, or are young members of ethnic groups declared to be gangs of criminals. Leaders of well-regulated militia are persecuted, and strident efforts to disarm the people fill newspapers every day. Dogs are being trained to locate guns, and even where right to possess a gun is still respected, it is illegal to fire it. The right to be secure against unreasonable search has long passed, as any search is considered reasonable if the word "drugs" is uttered by an agent of State or his dog, while government gluts itself upon seizure of property any suspect of drug crime may own, failure to convict notwithstanding. Just compensation for property taken is just whatever government decides to pay. Public trial is what the jury gets to see after the lawyers have decided what part of the evidence presented to them is admissible, and perversion of the process of jury selection prevents the impartial from being seated. Powers not delegated to government are presumed its privilege upon recognition, and there is no area of human activity which any agent of government will declare definitively to belong to the people, and to no agency of State. Such abstract concepts as reason, righteousness, and reality have no bearing, if they conflict with process, precedent, admissibility, celebrity, or money. Such concepts are likewise dismissed in the system of discipline used in schools, so upcoming generations are accustomed to the summary judgement of deans and boards, and do not expect more as adults from the wardens and nannies of the State. It is in our schools that destruction of all Constitutional protection of the people from the State is seen most clearly. The presumption that children must be protected by government authority has been taken in such fundamental sense that the *a priori* presumption they are property of State is not even examined. Parents too are now subject to punitive commands of school bureaucrats, without recourse. Disciplinary process is entirely prosecutorial, and there exists in the school system no person whose office is to defend the rights of student or parent against its machinations, no matter how those may conflict the letter or intention of Constitutional rights. It is hardly fair, however, to blame the schools, churches, or officers of government for these grievances. It is clear almost all Americans are content with the way things have developed, and are prepared to vote and behave in support of the welfare police State. We have long cried warning of the walls closing in as the authoritarian left reduced individual rights in the name of collective well-being, and the authoritarian right reduced rights in the name of collective morality. As indicated by the recent election, the walls have met in the middle, and less than two percent voted for the only party calling for defense of Constitutional freedom. We all drink our favorite of two brands of cola, wear our favorite of two brands of rubber shoes, and vote for our favorite of the two brands of Massa Washington's socialism. The Chief Justice of the Supreme Court recently stated the most important issue facing him is the need to increase the salary of federal judges. We have all become good Nazis in office or good niggers in jail, proud public servants, fat dumb cattle, or criminals locked down and shut up for correctional therapy. The greatest experiment in political freedom in the history of mankind is over. Welcome to your Animal Farm, friends, I'm retiring the pen.

The Ego Rallies, But For What?

Publisher Mark says I am a tired old crybaby feeling sorry for myself because I figure I am wasting my breath casting parlance before the fattened masses of brain-dead US Federal livestock who don't give a pickled poot about the passing of our Constitutional freedoms. Knowing he is right chafes the ego enough I am compelled to take another shot at it, so I press this upon his indulgence and attempt a comeback. Questions that come to mind are, "Whom should I try to rally, against whom or what should we rally, what should we do to reclaim our freedoms, and what should we do when we've got them back?" Perhaps a more important question is, "Do we really need them?" If our Founders established the Bill of Rights so Americans might live long and prosper, it is hard to object to today's America. In the history of mankind, nobody has ever had more of anything than we have. Perhaps my concern is more for the future, observing when you stand at the top of the pyramid, every step you take can lead to a fall.

To whom do I cry my Cassandra's warning? We are all divided into demographic voting blocs, each told some "right" (socialist entitlement) can be obtained for our own group by agreeing to some thus-justifiable limitation of the "privileges" (Constitutional rights) of all. The results have been predictable, though largely unspeakable. The racial group most loudly (and justly) crying for freedom the last forty years are blacks. Led by various demagogues and agitators to demand greater and greater benefits at the Federal trough, they have produced two generations of welfare-addicted, illegitimate, illiterate, irresponsible, crime-ridden, and violent people turning once-affluent communities from which they were previously barred into barren slums wherein they prey most cruelly upon each other, a terrible waste of a very fine bloodline of human beings. To use Paul McCartney's line, Brothers, you got your lucky break, and you broke it. For all the good those who like myself hate racism in any form might wish for you, nobody can fix it but yourselves. Don't waste your time whining to Massa Washington, who will only feed you crumbs with one hand for being good niggers, and whup you with the other when you get bad. Likewise for Hispanics, Indians, women, old folks, and the like whose leaders are trying to get you organized to vote for them by tempting you with chile, low-fat sugar, or Viagra on your cornbread for getting in line with the blacks. Only one group of Americans may not join together to whine about some alleged disadvantage, so as to obtain legislation to win a place closer to the Federal trough. Those are straight, white, able-bodied, working-aged males (like myself), whose attempt to do that would earn instant censure as homophobic, racist, uncaring, exploitive, sexist villains – precisely the image necessary for any of the other whiners to obtain their objectives. So we have nothing to gain by bitching either.

If the "enemies" of freedom are as they seem, the self-serving pork-fed career politicians chumming the masses with subsistence welfare to protect the privileged corporate barons who own them, self-righteous dominionist preachers promulgating the idolatry of their authoritarian cults of guilt and sacrifice, correctional-institution-minded school administrators brainwashing the young with statist propaganda and behavioral conditioning, less-than-zero-tolerant hanging judges and the eager and arrogant guard dogs of their law enforcement armies, racist agitators elevating themselves on the shoulders of masses gathered around banners of their own skin color in hatred of all others, and hordes of amoral lawyers, lobbyists, and legislators willing to defend or attack any person or position regardless of righteousness or reality for the right fee... if these are the enemies of freedom, then what might be done by the letter of any law to defeat them? Since they own the law, the schools, the money, and the power, looks to me like: nothing. What might be done by working "within the system" of electoral process, which clearly has been usurped by the media-perfected techniques of marketing celebrity? As evidenced by the pathetic dribble of votes for the Bill-Of-Rights-based Libertarian Party: nothing. What might be accomplished by the assassination of any or all of the above? As evidenced by the tragic folly of bombing — or even resisting — Federal forces: nothing. If we have all become like ants milking the honey from our aphids on the high green branches of a burning bush, then what can we do to save ourselves, our children, or the political principles which brought us to our present state of affluence? Nothing? So you tell me, friends, am I just pissing into the wind, and likely to have it thrown back into my face by all of those above mentioned, or can you say I am doing anyone any good? And while you're thinking about that, what are you doing about it?

Talkin' 'Bout My Revolution

It's my impression few Americans desire or have any concept of day-to-day personal freedom. Most are happily locked into worker/consumer slots enjoying the illusions that make up their world. It's hard to knock. They are like great ungulate herds that evolved to crop and fertilize the plains, churning the beef, oil, and steel to grow fat and happy. They support the case for socialism, as their willingness to join unions and sheep-cult religions demonstrates. These are good people, with every right to be satisfied, even if they might look to some others like fat geldings locked to a treadmill in a padded stall with a virtual reality hat over their heads.

Any successful revolution must protect the working masses, no matter how numb from the neck up they are doped. I'd say it's smart to avoid doing more damage to good people than what you're down on, like the Drug War does, for example. Armed revolution to impose a new force-won command state to replace the old force-run command state has proved outdated, the obvious folly of replacing a military monster with a new military monster. All you're doing is putting the peaked hats on new pinheads, and the workers' concern is going to be for the rations and the hours. As long as labor is fat, dumb, and happy, it is pretty hard to justify a revolution on their behalf. The rising-of-the-oppressed-masses type of revolution not only is impossible, it is inappropriate. Though freedomists might deplore limitations imposed by financial, religious, marital, sexual, literary, contractual, physical, and psychological profiling, regulation, and propaganda, only an idiot would start a revolution to put labor out of work to set them free of the regulations that come with the Federal contracts that keep them employed. That would be dumb, like putting teenagers in jail, disenfranchising them for life, denying them education, security clearance, bondability, and teaching them the hard values of prison life, in order to protect them from destroying their lives by smoking marijuana instead of tobacco like Mommy does.

The question is, "Who needs a revolution?" The politicians, patricians, and police (the pigs and dogs, in Orwell's vision) are happy with the status quo, and the cattle and sheep agree. So who else is here, and what is our problem with the things that the pigs and dogs will do in order to maintain the structure and order of their working class. The answer would seem to me to be to identify and pursue activities that might tend to make it easier to live in a country with the technical capacity to run a totalitarian regime of unprecedented intimacy, and still remain in practice free of the limitations which the pigs and dogs impose to protect their power over the sheep. The lifetime-job, lifetime-mortgage lifestyle of the worker-consumer accommodates a detailed IRS report. I am a patriot, and willing to carry my share of a fair tax to run good government, and a reasonably honest person, and willing to voluntarily declare my income and pay the money. Willingly. But I deeply resent having to not only pay the money, but also to document and display the details of my life, my property, my family relationships, my business relationships, and my every transaction. It's bad enough the Sixteenth Amendment created the income tax, but where does it grant the right to force me to make my life an open set of books?

If they make private free trade a crime to keep the sheep paying taxes, they can then insist the only folks who are objecting to their limitations are criminals. That makes it tough to stand up for your right to conduct personal trade freely with anybody you want, for whatever you own. "Why do you need freedom," we freedomists are often asked, "unless you are trying to commit crimes?" Seems to me that is the kind of question that if you have to ask it, there is no way I can explain the answer to you. "Why do you refuse to be searched, since you have nothing to fear as long as you have nothing to hide?" the Good Sheep ask us, voting away their rights and mine and yours in fear of whatever they suspect you are hiding, and happily trusting that the pigs will never tell the dogs to start looking for the beans in their jeans. These people will never be won over to a revolution to keep Constitutional freedoms safe and exercise them fully. These masses, by far the majority, will be the ones processing the paperwork, stamping the death certificates, keeping the trains running, and stuffing their neighbors' children into the drug camps and crematoria. They are the ones we must learn to live among, since there are no longer any wild animals. The freedom of the wilderness is no longer available to beast or man. The planet has been paved, and whatever freedom is to mean in the future, we must start there, no matter how tough that makes it to be a coyote, or an eagle.

Revolution In What Direction

Want to be a revolutionary, do you? It is satisfying to proclaim that the self-righteous swine in power, by virtue of their greedy and prideful exploitation of us lesser beings, deserve to be proclaimed evil, and to oppose them unto death in glorious sacrifice as a heroic defender of freedom. It's a damn good feeling, one taught to us in school. First great social legend we "sons of World War II" got handed in school was the glory of The Minutemen, and the band of hunted men with guns, led by a renegade officer they called General at their hidden militia training camp at Valley Forge. We were taught to say "we Americans" gathered in the forest of winter there for freedom's sake. "We" took up arms against the Divinely Ordained government's law enforcement troopers for our freedom, and for other people's freedom. To stand against tyranny for the common man was the first cause glorified in that primal myth I so took to heart. Close upon it was the myth of the small kid pushed too far who makes the bully cry, the skinny guy who buffs up to get revenge on the goon who kicked sand on him, and who eventually must take on the gang to save his sister... even if the gang is led by his father, the sinister Director of Imperial Law Enforcement, Darth Drugwar. It is good to be a freedom fighter, and to stand against the Bully State.

The pitfall here, of course, is insofar as I take that heroic Dick-and-Jane's-world image of the musket-fife-and-drum revolutionary to heart, I'm likely to seek reasons to see government as tyrannical to justify feeling good about going underground against it, that is, to create a revolution to jerk myself off. The world has a way of presenting evidence to support anything we desire to believe. I have not forgotten how proud I felt wearing my hard-won wings into harms way believing I was flying as a champion freedom fighter against The Big Bad Red Thing in Vietnam. Nor have I forgotten how I was shaken to recognize in retrospect I had been flying an anti-personnel land-skimmer enforcing the will of The Empire, as far as the local folks involved were concerned. It has a lot to do with the viewpoint.

The United States of America is a kind of illusion, a collection of images many people take as real, and so behave as though they were real, and so give them a reality. There is no such real thing as a "border". When we imagine a border, and put up a gate with a machine gun, and collect toll, and examine body cavities, we create a real thing we must live with. That does not change the fact that the border, even if dramatized with a wall and an army, is fundamentally an illusion. The problem with trying to guarantee freedom is how to be free of other people's illusions, when they are backing them up with a gun. Which brings me back to revolution. It's about perspective. Making sense of how to be a revolutionary calls for a focal point. If we are to rally the free of mind to pursue a freedomist revolution in 21st Century America, what freedom are we talking about? The best format for creating a good balance of liberty and responsibility I know of is our own American Bill of Rights. "We" fought two world wars to destroy governments who did not honor those rights. The history of the last century has made abundantly clear, however, that the US government has not felt obligated to honor the protections from government proscribed by the Bill Of Rights, but has given itself license to abridge all of them. Ideologically, that makes the government a tyrannous usurper of our Constitutional rights, therefore deserving to be opposed, brought down. Ideologically.

Perhaps more pragmatically, we might put people who promote authoritarian government of the non-Bill-Of-Rights variety on a list of Enemies Of The People, and before focusing our revolution on overthrowing the neo-Fascist Fed, see who else might belong on that list. First off, there are racist activists groups. They are a bummer to everybody, no matter whom they are puffing or putting down. Racism of any color is low-grade thinking, but it seems an absolute among humans and all other life forms. Suppressing it is inflammatory, and abetting it is incendiary. Religious sects seeking political power to impose their malarkey at the point of a peace officer's gun work to create new classes of persecuted criminals. Perhaps the hardest enemies of freedom to combat are attitudes and ideas held by the people, toxic thought – mistrust of lawyers, doctors, judges, insurance companies, banks, the CIA, Jesuits, and the other J-word. There is another significant category of enemy. Though for many of us, the government is not an ally, but a penal-system guard, we share as an enemy the true criminals, the cannibals, muggers, rapists, robbers, vandals, and burglars, the murderers, the usurers and scam-artists. Enemies of the people are on all sides. Who does that leave to be us?

"In real life, your rights depend totally on how your neighbors treat you, not what the law says."

Superman Or Batman?

Who are the enemies of the people? And what do we do about them? We are taught in public school that our great wars were fought to free people from the greatest enemy of all, the totalitarian welfare-police-security state, like the socialist and communist regimes of Nazi Germany, the Soviet Union, and Red China. Everyone I have ever met who has lived under such government power has agreed. Defeating such regimes once they are established has traditionally taken extreme violence from without and from within. Defeating them while they are developing can only be accomplished by aware people in the society taking steps to prevent the practices, attitudes, and laws which enable and define them. Sounds easy, except that such practices and attitudes are precisely those which government finds best suited to its ends, and will naturally find justification for taking. If it is done well, the people will be cheering. It's tough to point out such behavior in one's own government without appearing to be unpatriotic, especially when your government is still the most egalitarian and libertarian around, hopefully the world's champion of freedom. So here's an idea you ought to get used to: government will naturally keep giving itself more power and taking over more of your life if it can, not because it is evil, or staffed by sinister fanatics, but because it believes you need it. If you do not at some point stand against it, you will eventually be consumed by it. The best place to stand against it is at the first sign of its transgression, the fact you might be regarded as a radical or a loony notwithstanding. Look at it this way: if cats eat you, then you best kill kittens. Here's another one to get used to: if you are going to be defending our rights as human beings on God's world, or at least our rights as defined by the Bill Of Rights, you will be defending the rights of other people to do things that might absolutely revolt you personally, puke or not. Worse, lots of good people are going to be against you for it. If you desire that you and those around you should have freedom, then you better pray for tolerance, cause you're going to need lots of it.

Here is another group of enemies of the people: the real criminals. No, I don't mean the potheads, hookers, bet-runners, and sodomists, I mean people who prey on their neighbors, the cannibals, muggers, rapists, robbers, vandals, and thieves. The government will tell you to leave that problem to them, which they will solve with laws, and law enforcement. Problem with that is, it is in the interest of law enforcement to have the highest levels of surveillance, regulation, and control of our private lives as possible, if it is to fulfill the responsibility of protecting us from our neighbors. Eventually, we all become incarcerated, in protective custody, or in uniform. Back to the USSR. If we would have rights then, it is ultimately not the government which grants them to us, but our neighbors. If you want rights, you must grant rights, which means you don't take your neighbor's goods, and you don't step on his face. It also means this: if you do not want to live in the police state it would take to protect us from each other, then at some point, you have got to do your own policing, because there will be predators. It follows pretty strongly then if you are not absolutely ready to trust government law enforcement to protect your personal life from the predators around you, then you might be well advised to learn the techniques of predator extermination, and defend your right to own and use the weapons you will need to defend your life. Once you have exercised your right to arm yourself, here's another thought for you.

A favorite fantasy of mine, a guaranteed endorphin rush to thrill the mind, would be to wear a face not quite my own, to stalk alone the alleys of the night, to track down, set up, sight in, and then with the burning cold precision of the family torpedo, the jarhead ninja, to squeeze off the silenced magic bullet, to splat some well-deserving scumbag's brain, to do the world a favor, and then to softly slip back home again to wipe the sweat and calm the trembling, to smile and say, "Hi, kids, I'm home," as though I'd spent the hour with a lover. Is there no point at which it is right to take up my deadly tool of social surgery, to go forth into the alleys of the night to defend myself and my neighbors from those who have chosen to make predatory vermin of themselves? And if there is such a point where I may rightly go out sniping cannibals, is there something wrong with enjoying it? This is no job for Superman, or some Roboputz who'll shoot up the neighborhood then give them to the courts and counselors again. Is this not a job for Batman? How nasty would it have to get for you to put on the cape?

Surrender To Me, Osama

To Osama bin Laden, from Angelo and James: The world is hunting you, and you will eventually be found. We would like to offer you an option. Born a Montenegrin Muslim, Angelo is an American citizen working in Las Vegas, and James is an ex-Christian libertine libertarian writer. As the American Montenegro Freedom Initiative, we are producing a novel about life in Montenegro to bring about creation of a hospital for children there. We are not uncommon Americans, and have neither celebrity nor position to do anything on your behalf, except under one condition. That is if you would volunteer to surrender yourself to us, personally. Consider these points:
    1. The people suffering most from your actions are Muslims. We do not argue that America is right in bombing Afghanistan for harboring you, but without your provocation, there would be no bombing. The Americans hurt most are not Christians in government nor Jews with Israeli connections (both are making hay), but common citizens who happen to be Muslim or Arab. We neither defend nor apologize for America's desire to defend and promote itself, nor Israel's desire to maintain its identity and influence. In your desire to harm them, however, you cause greatest pain to Muslims. Your devotion to God's will for good is no doubt sincere, but you have deceived yourself, and your actions are most painful to Muslims and to Islam.   2. You have tarnished Islam before the world. The image of Muslims is fragile enough, and your confirmation of the belief all are fanatical mad bombers is reflected in the suspicion and hatred with which Muslims and Arabs are now treated by many Americans, and in the presumption of criminality by the US and other governments. We do not defend racial or religious stereotyping, or the cruel prejudice which grows of them, but the injustice Muslims and Arabs suffer in America today is in reaction to what you have said and done.   3. Your family disagreements and your dissatisfaction with the business affairs of Saudi Arabia do not justify your rallying Muslims to make war upon the rest of the world. God is not impressed with your self-absorbed piety, no matter how loudly you quote Koran, nor how pridefully you claim the name of Allah.   4. You know there is only one Hashemite King in Islam who can trace his line to Mohammed, and he is the King of Jordan. If you hope to receive the justice of Islam in whose name you claim to act, then you must make your peace with him before God, and before the eyes of the world.   5. There

is a bounty of $25,000,000 dollars placed upon your head, and the odds of someone eventually claiming it are 100%. Most likely it will go to someone who betrays you, or to one of the generals or politicians. Most likely either will spend it in stupid self-indulgence, or in promoting things you stand against.

We do not expect you to denounce your choice to harm those you see as God's enemies. We only call upon you to let us perform an act of charity in your name toward those whom you claim to serve. Therefore, Osama bin Laden, we call upon you to make contact with the world media, and to surrender to us, and only to us. As the recipients of the bounty, we would have access to the world media, and we would be able to speak with world powers on your behalf without having to represent any particular political body. It would be our objective to see that you should be placed in protective custody in the hands of the King of Jordan. We cannot speak for him, of course, but we should expect he would favorably entertain our proposal to make him the executor of your fate before the courts of the world, and before God. We should expect America's agreement to permit that would be seen with great favor and respect by the many nations and peoples of the Muslim world. For our part, we shall dedicate the ransom to the creation of a hospital for children in Afghanistan. This will be pursued in concert with our ongoing efforts to bring about such a hospital in Montenegro, another place where Christians and Muslims find reasons to place each other's children in harms way in the name of the one God all claim to believe in. Because we believe in that One God, we dedicate ourselves to the children of all religions. The laws of God may be absolute, but the living Spirit of God is very flexible, and compassionate. In the name of God, Osama, repent of your prideful desire to personally rid God's world of those you believe are God's enemies. God is capable of much more love and tolerance than you believe, and God's justice is complete without your interference. Therefore place your fate into the hands of God, surrender yourself to us, and let us commence this good act in your name. We await your response, Sincerely yours, Bajram Angelo Koljenovic and James Nathan Post. (Please forward to addressee.)

The Big Bad Bush-Bin Laden Bash

We are too quick to identify The United States Government as Osama bin Laden's principal opponent. We want to see him mano a mano with "Texas Dub" Bush, our champion of freedom and righteousness, hell, he ought to be a pastor, give it up, ladies and gentlemen, for The President Of The United States of America. Rally round the Flag, boys, and no price too high to back up Our Leader. It is not surprising the political body and its symbiotic façade-maker the media should take such advantage of the emotion of the WTC attack to rally the American people around their own seats of power. Though it is true Osama is motivated by a blood feud involving the president's father, his hatred of us has many more targets. We should not be distracted by media's making this a High Noon showdown on NEWS-TV between, in this corner, America's favorite celebrity son, and his challenger from Bunghol, Al-Nowhere, Dirty Sam bin Laden, who has just kicked the President right in the balls, and nobody saw him move.

Though news politely avoids the matter so as to not offend one of America's valued minorities, nor to offend one of our valued allies, it is true Osama is more anti-Semitic than Hitler, and his hatred for Israel is boundless. Israel is a curious entity, able to represent itself as a race, a religion, or nation. In Osama's world, Israel is his enemy on all three counts. To a very large extent, this attack on Americans is not about America, much less G.W. Bush. It is about Israel. Whether it is true or not, he perceives America – not just the rich Christians in office and the Jews in finance who own them, but all America – to be the tool of Israel, the big dumb goon who enables the offensive little prick with the six-point badge on his sleeve to push his people around. His hatred is particularly directed at the common American he sees as a fat, arrogant swine, self-righteously commanding the proud dogs of war, mindlessly addicted to the gluttony of the virtual world of TV shows, obscenely jerking off with the daughters of his whore, that perversion of the Jews' usurpation of Abraham's eldest son's estate called Christianity. From his point of view, such swine are fit only for slaughter, and as he doesn't eat swine, would like nothing better than to see them eaten by their own guard dogs. He would like nothing better than to see Americans living under the brutal police-state oppression common in his part of the world. He knows there is no way that he and his followers could conquer America, invade us, and impose such a government upon us. Yet that is exactly what we are in danger of at this moment. He does not care which government oppresses us, as long as we become oppressed. Think. Which government would it most delight him to see oppress us?

The US government thinks of itself as being the United States of America, and of us citizens as its wards, or human resources. Before 1776, serfdom meant people on land were like the cattle and deer, property of the authorized estate. If by using our freedoms to attack the US government, Osama can get them seeing each of us as a potential enemy of the state, and taking from us those freedoms he abused, then he has succeeded in making us oppressed by government. Those who resist government's trying to protect itself from "domestic terrorists" by limiting all our freedoms will be accused of abetting terrorists. "Patriots" will be those who support the aggressive policies of the US government, foreign or domestic, Constitutional or institutional. Though the important distinction between police and soldiers has been badly blurred in recent years, it is clear that an armed force conducting pre-emptive acts of violence against citizens to eliminate opposition to the government is indistinguishable from an occupying army. Those who believe themselves to be patriots for defending the principles of freedom will quickly suffer at the hands of government, and also at the hands of the flag-wavers who insist the fight for others' freedom begins with giving up yours.

If Osama bin Laden can get the US government to try to lock Americans into a security state, then he has won. He will have imprisoned the American people, by tricking the US government into doing it to us as protective custody. If he can provoke Americans to be either one of those resisting government security by fighting for American freedom, or one of those in uniform imposing American law, then he will have us killing each other over the government's right to inspect and control us in order to protect us from everything it can imagine a terrorist might do. Watch out, Sports Fans, this guy's gung fu is better than Ho Chi's, even if he does look like nothing more than a Koran-whacking raghead walking out of the desert with a twisted messiah complex and a machine gun.

Is Pro-Muslim Anti-Israeli?

Is it anti-Semitic, racist, or bigoted to be opposed to the policies of the government of Israel? Likewise is it anti-Arab, or anti-Muslim to be opposed to the policies of the several Islamic governed nations who are the declared enemies of Israel? If the policies of any government violate the human rights I respect as enumerated in the Bill Of Rights, should I not speak out against that government? American apologists for Israel's behavior point out that it is "democratic." That is, which of a small circle of persons of the prevailing religion holds the highest offices is determined by elections among those who may run, by those who may vote. As for how they behave in office, I know I suffer from the limitations and biases of any media-programmed American, but I am too often reminded of their former antagonists, the Nazis, and of a growing trend in the same attitudes and practices within my government. When people who are legitimately elected perform unrighteous acts in office, are those acts not still unrighteous, no matter how they got their jobs?

Do people in America at heart largely agree with the precepts of Hitler's form of government, while demonizing The Leader only for his use of those ruthless state powers against Jews? Does America somehow render those practices virtuous, when they are used in support of the Jewish nation/race/religion? Is every American Jew expected to support such policies when practiced by Israel, even if they are against Constitutional law in America? Is every American Jew expected to agree that unconstitutional practices should be permitted in America, if it is in the interest of Israel? Has an American Jew who opposes the policies of Israel betrayed his race, his religion, or his country? Does America support Israel because as the conspiracy nuts proclaim, Jews control the only banks big enough to handle the business in oil, drugs, and war which empowers those winning the elections in America? Do the Israelis' Semitic race or Judaic religion really have nothing to do with America's true motivations?

Having a background in theater and science, I like the Jews I've known. Is the Jew stereotyped? Well, yes and no. Jewish culture is a whole collection of stereotypes, which makes for great drama on stage and off, and their "stereotype" intelligence and tenacity should be an inspiration to the rest of the world. As with the Cosa Nostra, however, the "Jewish thing" is undefined and amorphous, but highly esoteric, at some level becoming each individual's primary self-identification. This esoteric nature is evident in Israeli law respecting only Ashkenazi, the bloodline to which it is not possible to convert. The few Muslims I have known, Arab, Jordanian, and Bosnian, have been delightfully passionate about life, and in matters of honor intractable, which characterization seems to conform to the image I have from the media, that is, the most generous of friends and the most ruthless of enemies. I would not want to make an enemy of either of the sides aligned over the fate of Jerusalem, or to lose their friendship.

As for supporting either side, we have Constitutional grounds for non-intervention. If our Constitution forbids laws respecting an establishment of religion within our borders, why should we then make laws respecting a foreign establishment of religion, even going so far as to grant to it the rights and privileges of political statehood? Is not the fundamental error being fought over in Jerusalem that two factions of an ancient religious cult have each been given the mechanisms of power of the secular political state? Could we Americans do worse than to give the reins of power in Washington to proclaimed devotees of a third contesting faction of that same ancient cult?

How am I as an American Libertarian, dedicated to the righteousness of the fundamental principles of human freedom and dignity as expressed in the Bill Of Rights, to relate to the fact that in the Middle East conflict, no nation grants its citizens any of those precious freedoms and protections? Where are freedom of religion, freedom of speech, equal (or any) rights for women, freedom of personal sexual practice, artistic freedom, freedom of enterprise, equality of the right of ownership of property, equality of opportunity for education, and for holding office? We still have these rights, for the most part, though significant freedoms and protections have been badly eroded by legislation against fiscal privacy and victimless dissent. If a government attempted to impose Arab style Islamic law upon the citizens of the United States, every single one of us would have reason to object. Surely none would object louder or sooner than the Christians, except perhaps liberated women, deviant eroticists, and the like, and the cage-rattling gadfly blowhard opinion mongers like myself, who would be exterminated in the first wave.

Our Buzzards

Everybody admits Americans are propagandized, but we don't believe it. We learn on TV what is real, and what is good, and why people we don't like do things we don't like. We are taught to believe the parent, the pedagogue, the preacher, the policeman, and the president. We're even taught to believe the psychiatrist and the politician. Because our media are declared free, we presume what we see on TV is the truth, all the truth. We know better, but we continue to presume our Red, White, and Blue righteousness justifies any less-than-true expedients to which we have been forced by the evil nature of the world.

Here are some unfortunate truths about our present situation. The enemies we face are all creatures of our own actions. Osama bin Laden is a former ally and agent of US secret foreign policy. We built his Al Qaida network, using his money and also weapons and money from proprietary assets of the CIA and our other covert foreign policy agencies. Why? We were still fighting the Cold War, using our nation's credit card to bankrupt Russia with an arms race. The Soviets were trying to take Afghanistan. The word 'jihad' does not mean 'war for Islam' as we are encouraged to believe in the media, but the struggle to be righteous in an evil world. When a small group of Muslim extremists declared themselves mujahidin, taking the last resort of violence against the Soviets in the name of Allah, our Special Ops folks decided it would be a smart idea to start a Muslim uprising against our Cold War enemy. So we set up a wealthy young Saudi radical with the means to create an organization clearly a monster by the standards of any religion. But as it was our monster, we thought it was OK.

It was not our first monster in the region. In 1953, the leader of the popularly elected representative democratic government in Iran decided to nationalize the oil business. America's President Eisenhower, unwilling to permit the oil-barons of the military-industrial complex who owned him to lose their concessions, declared Iran's leader too far left for America's brand of democracy, and our covert operations specialists disrupted the government and backed the dictatorship of the monarch Shah. Installed to protect the interests of the richest Americans, the Shah typically learned to enjoy American indulgences, and to protect himself from the objections of his less generously indulged citizens, using as police the "defensive" military machine created by American foreign aid to protect "his" oil fields. This led to the Islamic revolution in which members of the Muslim clergy took over the country and threw out the puppet king of the America they had learned to hate. Iran became our enemy, and we blamed it on Islam.

We solved the problem the same way we got into it. We created another monster. Again using such covert channels as the CIA and White House special project teams, we elevated to power an ambitious young Iraqi officer named Saddam Hussein, and we encouraged him to wage war against our former ally and new enemy, Iran. Thinking himself blessed with our backing in all his ventures, he moved against another of his neighbors, Kuwait. Like Saudi Arabia and others in the region, Kuwait came to be a country through the collaboration of a few influential local families, the oil industry, and the United States government. Hussein's bold grab of Kuwait reached into the pockets of very powerful Americans, who used their positions as the leaders of the American government to launch yet another war against another former ally. So we camped our army on holy ground in Arabia to defeat our new enemy, Iraq. Because we have not left his holy land Arabia, we oppose the Taliban in Afghanistan and Pakistan, and we support the Muslim-oppressing Israelis, our former CIA asset Osama bin Laden has become our enemy too.

When the Islamic Party won a fair election in Algeria, we supported a military crackdown to keep the party out of power, claiming Islamic fundamentalists would put an end to democracy. In a situation now developing in Macedonia, Orthodox Macedonians and Serbs stand ready to launch an ethnic cleansing bloodbath against the Muslim Albanian minority. Our unwillingness or inability to defend them will be seen as abandonment by America of all Muslims, and confirmation that it is Christian America, and not the Muslim Taliban, which seeks to promote a Holy War.

Like a cuckoo, our Eagle of Democracy laid the eggs of peaked-hat-pinhead dictatorships in others' nests all over the world, and what hatched have preyed upon their people and glutted themselves upon our leavings of their countries' resources like predators and eaters of carrion. From Afghanistan, the Shah's Iran, Saddam's Iraq, Batista's Cuba, Samoza's Nicaragua, Pinochet's Chile, Thieu's Vietnam, Savang's Laos, Noriega's Panama, and a dozen other places, our buzzards are coming home to roost.

You Are A Terrorist

"Greetings: You have been identified as a terrorist suspect, a potential terrorist, or a witness to terrorist activity. Please report immediately to the nearest Federal...." What will you do when you find you are a terrorist, that is, by the government's definition? What if you think you are an American patriot, maybe even served in the military, but something you hold to be a true and dear American thing is forbidden because of commies, drugs, or terrorists? As a patriot, do you fight for it, or do you surrender it to the Peace Trooper with the body armor, machinegun, VR hat, and badge? Do you decide you can get along fine without it, and you prefer to march in the ranks for the Red, White, and Blue no matter what, than be named an outlaw by the country you love, for standing on the Constitution against those who are acting outside it, but wearing the badges, and carrying the flag?

If "we" are those who would call ourselves patriots because of our country's founding principles, whether we were born here or not, and who would oppose any power group trying to pervert the United States government away from those principles, foreign or domestic, then we face an obvious decision now. Every one of the guarantees of liberty and protections from government intrusion proclaimed as the Law Of The Land have been utterly abrogated in practice by the power cult in Washington, and the New Order capos have made it clear that no right, no protection, no Amendment, no interpretation is held so sacred that it is immune to exception if the Reverend Darth Ashcroft says it interferes with the objectives of His President's Holy War to bring freedom from fear to the world.

Is there really something sacred about the guarantees of the Bill Of Rights? Or has defending the Bill Of Rights become reactionary clinging to the obsolete? When I was taught in public school that we were the good guys in the wars against fascism and communism because those bad governments denied those rights to their people, was that just bullshit propaganda for brainwashed good scouts after all? Do those rights really mean nothing, when it comes to the character of a nation, and the lives of its people?

If our moral right was based in the righteousness of those founding principles, and we have abandoned them, then on what grounds do we proclaim our use of power to be more righteous now? We have so confounded ourselves that we are being propagandized to believe we hold the moral high ground because our leaders subscribe to the righteousness of a mystical and fanatical cult movement among American Christians. Even such a blatant semantic gimmick as using the term "faith-based" to permit themselves to fund their church at the public trough where "establishments of religion" are forbidden to feed slides right by the public mind, the flocks of good sheep bleating praises to the Man Of God in the White House, the "Burning Bush" whose voice thunders in the otherwise Godless hell of Afghanistan.

It is apparent the group of weapon makers, oil dealers, drug and anti-drug Czars, and extremist Christian cult devotees now rampant in Washington are intent upon establishing a vast empire, a defacto world hegemony. It is also apparent that they do not intend that their New World Order be based upon the principles of the Constitution of the United States of America, neither here nor anywhere else in the world. Their American World Empire will not honor the Bill Of Rights (though like today's administration, they may profess to). Does that not make them anti-American in some fundamental way? And if it does, so what? Is an empire without it necessarily an Evil Empire? Might an American empire be a good empire, even without the Bill Of Rights? Or is merely taking and exercising the historically corrupting absolute power of Imperial Law what is meant by "turning to the dark side"?

Is there something fundamentally wrong with Americans trying to establish a world empire, then? Does not some kind of unified world political pact seem inevitable? Lots of nationalist patriotic Americans object to the One World idea as selling out US sovereignty to a world socialism. They are not unlike the states-rights folks objecting to the Fed usurping their state powers. Do we really need state-level government at all these days in the One Nation Indivisible? If there is to be a World Empire, shouldn't we prefer it be American? But then, if that American Empire acts like any fascist or communist authoritarian zero-tolerance media-propagandized child-brainwashed speech-behavior-and-thought-controlling police state, then why should we prefer it to any other? I would be much happier to break out the colors I once so proudly held high, and re-up to champion the United States of Earth if I saw the guys carrying the flag proclaiming they will make the Bill Of Rights the Law Of All The Lands.

We'll Defend You. Trust Us.

The American people, for all our insensitivity to the extreme virtual violence of our media, are easily frightened by reality. Once Americans took pride in being "shoot your own dog" folks, who were able to deal with their own problems and keep their own houses in order. Now we not only have huge agencies taking care of such problems, we are even forbidden to do it for ourselves. You must call the government to exercise their responsibility to have that nuisance stray dog captured by a uniformed officer, confined in a government facility for observation, then compassionately euthanized in a non-traumatic environment by a licensed veterinarian using a controlled substance, while soft music and gentle bow-wows play. If instead you shoot that garbage-slinging, kid-chomping, fence-jumping, free-breeding flea-bag mongrel, you are guilty of crimes against its rights, and you will be captured by a uniformed officer, confined in a facility for observation, and, if the right paperwork can be obtained from the right agencies of government, euthanized. The same seems to be true of the feral humans who might wander like stray dogs into others' neighborhoods to scavenge in the garbage or prey upon the young and weak. I am glad my country offers 911 service, and having a cell phone has pulled me through some tough times. Even so, when the time factor is less than the response time of a SWAT team in the next room, I will take 9mm to 911 every time. If we were armed and clearly entitled to use lethal force to defend ourselves and our homes and neighborhoods from the cannibals and vampires among us, lots of the crime against citizens in this country could be quickly eliminated.

Why does government seem not to care about crimes against the citizen? Because it is more concerned about crimes against the state, in particular the state's prohibition of popular vices. It is by such anti-self-abuse laws that the citizen who has committed acts against no one can be reduced nonetheless to a controllable criminal, where a free citizen could not be so subjected. It is clearly in the best interests of a control-motivated state that every citizen should be placed into the status of a criminal, where all of the rights of the free citizen are suspended. It is in effect, a form of national house arrest. Citizens who express resentment of such criminalization for control's sake are perceived as a threat to those centralizing and maximizing power. Why does US want to make it illegal for us to defend ourselves? Is anyone really so brainwashed they do not see it is because they do not want us able to defend ourselves from THEM?

The right to defend oneself is self-evident, as well as Constitutional. Every form of life does it. When one's life is at stake, the opinion of anyone else is meaningless. Though it be illegal, I will defend myself in flagrant violation, as the alternative is to let the lawyers and reporters talk about my rights after my funeral. Anyone who for any reason denies my right to defend myself, and forces me to accept vulnerability, is a threat to my life, an obstacle to my survival, and so my enemy. If I am killed where I could have defended myself, then the one who has denied my right of self-defense has murdered me no less than the mugger with the meat-cleaver I might have cleansed from my city's streets instead.

Though having lived among outlaws much of my life I have little personal experience with the people behind the badges, I believe most police are very good people, with the best intentions. I would like to believe most are not closet goons who thrive on making others grovel (in spite of exceptions like the schoolyard badge-bully and his handler the Dean my kids and I endured). I hope none are brain-washed zealot stormtroopers seeking to impose Imperial control over the security of their population. Even so, I wish I could say I thought most police, many, or even some police would refuse to enforce a blatantly unconstitutional, cruel, unjust, immoral, and clearly destructive policy against the citizens they claim to protect and serve. When they do not refuse orders from their lawful rulers which so command them, then they protect only the powerful, and serve only the state. Once a person in uniform has obeyed an order to conduct an act against a citizen he knows was not righteous, then he has moved beyond morality for his justification, and unless redeemed, might thereafter obey any command without regard for its righteousness. He has, at that point "turned to the dark side" and become part of the power and might of the Empire. Though he may deceive himself by such devices as attending rituals of forgiveness, and agreeing that his Ruler's proclaimed good objectives justify whatever evil steps he might be ordered to take, he has become the will-less minion of the soul-less state, a pistol-packing deadly cell in the body of The Beast.

Who Pays Dub's Tax?

No government employee should pay income tax. Why? Because the private sector supports the wage in the first place. Think. The productive worker, whose efforts produce a profit-making product or service, is paid a wage, from which she must pay a tax. Though various arrangements between government and her employer determine and disguise how much she must pay, it is her actual take-home pay which is her true wage. The government has no profit-making product or service. Every dollar it spends or gives away comes from the same place: the productive worker's tax. Every government worker's salary all comes from the productive worker's tax, ALL of it, which includes the worker's true take-home wage AND that worker's burden of tax. Where does the money come from to pay that government worker's tax? From the productive worker's tax. To create the ILLUSION of fair taxation, the productive worker is obligated not only to pay his own taxes so as to pay the wages of the government guy, but also to pay the taxes of that government worker too. Being tax supported, the government worker has no productive income to tax, and so should be paid only that amount which would be his take-home pay after tax. Then the productive worker's tax can be reduced by the amount that would have been paid to the government worker. (The problem is of course that the government, even if caught in the act of its double-tax ripoff, will never justify taking less when it can get away with taking more.)

In any fair and open competition, it is likely some individuals, or some groups, will gain a noticeable advantage. If rewards are based upon success, then inequities will be inevitable. In a free market, this is taken for granted, for better or for worse. I think there is not yet a word for the form of socialist thinking that believes everyone should not only have the same size piece of cake, but all should wear the same blue "Winner!" ribbon, no matter who got to the finish line first. It is a kind of mental communism of essential worth, the notion that no matter what our gifts of birth might be, or what our accomplishments or limitations, we all "deserve" the same. It is the kind of thinking that tells the winner not only must he acknowledge everybody else won too, he must pay for the cake. It is the thinking that makes him take polite applause at the awards banquet, while the cheers are saved for the guy on crutches who made it halfway around the track. Why should government jobs pay wages commensurate with the private sector's? Because all workers deserve to be equally rewarded for equal effort, productivity notwithstanding. To further disguise this moral leveling of the mass mind, we have the celebrity. The equivalent of carnival shills, they strut about the game joints displaying the biggest prizes, letting us all know that we too can reach the heights. These are usually product models from the ranks of delightful but fundamentally pointless activities, such as ball players and actresses. If Michael or Julia can get twenty million bucks for a ball game or a movie, doing the same thing the rest of us are doing for stipends or for nothing in the minor leagues and community theaters, then surely there is hope for us all, and we each will certainly achieve the American Dream we all deserve, and keep on working.

What will solve the situation? Put all government workers on the minimum wage. If the correct job of government is to manage for the individual those functions most efficiently done collectively, and to responsibly manage the resources it is permitted to take as tax, then its reward should be commensurate with its performance. If government is running our collective checkbook into the red, and then putting the bite on us to cover the overdrafts, it is not providing competent service to the individual citizen it exists to serve. (There is no such thing as "a group" by the way, no such thing as "the people." Far as I can see there's nobody here but us individuals.) Worse, if government's biggest expense is maintenance of its own huge internal machine, then it can no longer be called a servant of the productive citizen. It is a parasite. Put every government job from Dub down on the minimum wage. They do not deserve the same wage as the productive if they are not keeping our affairs in order. Don't feel sorry, they all insist we can live on it, and pay taxes too. First off, I'd bet the quality of low-cost housing in DC would go up. Thousands would just quit and go looking for real jobs. The deadwood would jump ship in a second. Eventually the only ones left would be those dedicated enough to stick it out, even if at their own expense. Lots of jobs would cease to exist, maybe even entire agencies. Apart from the collectors of revenue and the compliance enforcers, who among us would miss DMV, IRS, or DEA? Who would employ their "services," if it were a choice?

Virtual Money To End Crime?

Having been raised among research engineers and science fiction writers, I am no Luddite, and I was encouraged when young to learn social extrapolation of technological advance. Having long written about the increased socialization and loss of privacy due to advances in information technology, one of my pet horrors has always been the supplanting of bearer-paper specie with abstract electronic or virtual money. As a thirty-year veteran of the Drug War, an outlaw, I long ago recognized the war is promulgated in spite of clear evidence it causes more damage than the drugs it prohibits because it entitles government to impose surveillance and control over our personal transactions, and upon global transactions influencing the economy of nations. It is a war on privacy of person, privacy of possession, and privacy of transaction.

Proponents of the increased use of electronic transactions point out that credit card transactions are accountable and trackable, whereas cash can be used for illegal trade, as it leaves records only when traded with a government-accountable financial institution, which practice is called money laundering. Among proposals offered by those writing software for the highly secure accountable virtual money is the establishment of a cybernetic Federal treasury and the exclusive use of its "universal bank account" for all transactions larger than pocket change. Everyone would have a FedCard number, and the Federal Reserve Note would be abolished. An IRS audit of our affairs could be had at the touch of an enter key, daily, by those so authorized. The system probably would look good to those who are very close to people in high offices. Because they know them personally as intelligent, trained, dutiful, sensitive, honest, clean, and reverent individuals, they are more inclined than the man on the street to trust that the system they administer will benefit the masses they "represent." It would look good, and quite certainly BE good for the great majority of legitimate businessmen, and the worker masses they employ. It would certainly look good to anyone who believes law enforcement should have the best, as the power to "follow the money" is the best tool law enforcement can have. It seems clear to me, however, if any agency had the power to observe and control everyone's every transaction, then everything would effectively belong to that agency, to do with as its policy dictated. The elimination of free exchange of personal assets in favor of the "crime-proof" universal-bank-account system would immediately make its trustees the de facto rulers of the world, and would create a huge, hostile, and of necessity resourceful underground.

The virtual money of FedCard would be wonderful IF it were possible to make its accounts anonymous, and IF it were not the tool of tax collection, and IF it were not the tool of law enforcement. If spending e-money entails identifying yourself and your location, then no one wanted for anything, behind on payments, fitting a profile, etc, could use a FedCard without thereby giving himself up to the law. Though it is easy to say administratively that their debts are lawfully collectable and their accounts in suspension or whatever, people do not stop eating when their case file is closed by the apparatchiks or by subroutine 86-U2. The "unaccountables" will find some way to survive. Far from eliminating all the criminals, this policy (like Deadbeat Dads) would force people into the criminal underground who might otherwise be leading productive even if furtive lives.

For small transactions, we would clearly still require some kind of "coin of the realm." This would be of greater worth in the underground than as the pocket change of the regulated and socialized class. This dichotomy would create the opportunity for lawful citizens, that is, those with accounts in order, to get more for their pocket money by trading with outlaws, who might thus be encouraged to steal things. It would also create an incentive for the otherwise peaceful outlaw to rob the accounted citizen of her coffee money.

Barter media would be spontaneously created, and like the stock market, would be faddish. Lots of things would quickly become media, perhaps like Beanie Babies, baseball cards, or CD's. Among the hippies, beadwork, embroidery, hash-pipes, and the like often took the place of FRN dollars that required somebody get straight employment. At one time many cocaine dealers were using Indian jewelry as a kind of medium to avoid having to carry cash.

Highly desired illegal drugs become a kind of medium of themselves, even though consumable. This is one of the principal factors in their successful distribution even under Federal persecution. Guns and ammunition are better than gold, because the underground will constantly be persecuted by law enforcement, by virtue of being hated and feared by the successfully-lawful class, and violent confrontations are likely to be common.

Another group of outlaws would be those among the accounted

who chose to trade in something prohibited by the legislators, regulators, policy makers, executives, boards, committees, parliaments, and consultants with the authority to input the FedCard program. It would be a very large group, from gutter scum to Trustee. The vices have always thrived, and it has always been in the interest of some who proclaim them vices to see that they do. Even in prison, there is a thriving market for most of the common drugs. What fifty million Americans want, someone will find a way to sell to them.

As we are seeing in Russia today, those who are experienced in dealing forbidden products, that is, the criminals, may know best how to operate in a free market, which happens (only?) when the structure collapses. Those who are experts in the protectionist rules of a regulated market may be disadvantaged when their system of regulation fails, just as those who have all their lives enjoyed the services of the pharmacist may be disadvantaged when the drug kingpins ...I mean, the pharmaceutical manufacturers... fail, and folks are left to cope with whatever personal immune system they have developed growing up dependent on the state's patent medicine. A widening schism would be created between business/government/police folks, for whom the system would be the fulfillment of their dreams, and the millions at the bottom of the pyramid who already struggle pragmatically with the reality of living outside the law in order to survive, for whom the FedCard system creates a police state.

The advantage in that survivalist underground economy would be with one who understood the marijuana market, and had succeeded in operating a multi-level product distribution system. His motivation would have to be altruistic, the distribution of needed and desired products, and the result would be market communities like secret clubs, adept at sleight of hand. However, the need for someone in the underground to interface with the accounted economy through illicit accounts at FedCard, that is, to launder the money, would give the advantage at the top of the pyramid to the most self-serving and deceitful.

The notion that totalitarian accounting of everyone's transactions and properties, and control thereof by regulation may fairly be called "free enterprise" is like saying even in prison there is freedom to obey the rules. It "levels the field" by prostrating all. If government, at the point of an officer's gun, can declare what you may possess, which assets you may trade, what the price must be, and how much you must pay in tax for the privilege of trading (as it does today), then the only free enterprise is the underground. Only there can two private citizens agree upon the relative worth of their assets and contract to exchange them freely, without a government agent standing in the middle dictating the terms of the deal for a fee.

The way into The Empire Bank opens with the big sign that says TAX. If the system is used to collect the tax, then the government may legislate how the FedCard software treats its account holders. If taxation were to continue to be item-specific and regional-specific, then every possible product or service would require an identifier code, a location code, and a tax rate. The resulting World Blue Book would be the equivalent of a global price-fixing tool. It would necessarily have to be very fluid, with perhaps thousands of authorized terminals constantly updating the values of some category or other, or the consequences of some new legislation, or the recalculation of some index. Even with cross-tracked mirror sites as a safeguard, somebody must be able to enter "legitimate" changes to the database. The right or ability to access the database for selective marketing purposes would be more valuable than blood, and black-market FedCard data might itself become a medium of illicit exchange at a certain level of society. The power to input that program is to drink from the Holy Grail while wearing the Ring of the Niebelung, wrapped in Superman's cape. People will kill for that power to bankrupt competitors and topple governments. The opportunity to trade an important oil evaluation fix for a crop of cocaine to distribute for the swing vote of a demographic group might make a kingpin of Colombia's elected and trusted delegate to the Board of Trustees, and a President of its Chairman, and not leave a track for the bean-counter robots to follow.

The door slams shut with the big sign that says ILLEGAL. Once the system is in place for taxation, its potential for use by enforced authority makes the word totalitarian seem pale. Gum is illegal in Singapore, raw eggs in California. The gun you bought at Sears last year is illegal now and must be surrendered. City Ordinance has declared that book obscene, and the cash registers in this town won't sell it. It is not forbidden to publish it, but it is impossible to buy it. Everything in the WBB (and every imaginable illegal thing) would require a legal category identifier, and every person's legal category would be checked with every purchase. Felon? Can't buy a gun. DWI? Can't buy beer. Driver's license expired? Can't buy gasoline. Business license expired? The Master Control Program will not permit deposits to your account.

Today's Internet market is evolving many systems to do something like virtual money, but without eliminating national bearer-paper specie, based on those usurious wonders of the 20th century, credit card accounts. Science fiction paranoia aside, it is clear we will use it more and more in this century. I think also that we will all soon have a telephone with a global-locator and bankcard we carry like a driver's license (or wear like glasses), and its built-in skin-resistivity meter will tell the ATM, or the ATF, how we feel about the questions it asks us... and you can't lie to it. That'll stop crime for sure, and then we can enjoy a little peace and free trade around here.

Who Protects Us From The Protectors?

We watch the US Federal government grow like a beast. The Civil War was not between states, but between a group of states and the Fed. The Fed won, and has been consolidating power since. Arguing State vs. Federal power does not change the fact government at all levels in America has taken power over things neither rightfully nor Constitutionally its business. These largely have to do with government's presumption that our bodies are its property, and their safety and maintenance thus its prerogative, conducted at the point of law enforcement's gun. Other such unrighteous intrusions into our lives are the so-called blue laws, which use law enforcement to prohibit activities deemed morally tempting by the prevailing religions. All laws against self-abuse should be repealed outright, and likewise laws forbidding marketing of anything just because a particular religion declares it immoral. There should be no law against killing yourself, and no law against assisting another (be damn sure it was assistance). If some Joe wants to shoot junk until it kills him, well, let him go. We have a serious population problem, according to some. People who are here have a right to live, and keep on breeding too, so I can't say we should go around killing people, but we shouldn't waste a second trying to enforce laws which prevent people from doing things just because they are likely to get killed. Laws forbidding risk, or blaming those who offer risky products and services? It's your ass, and insurance is private business, so smoke, jump, or gamble it any way you want. Games with high death risk, even lethal combat? Long as it is voluntary, go for it. Abortion? On demand, for the cost of an office visit. Abortion pills? At the supermarket, with the stuff for your occasional lice. Sterilization of males? On demand, with a $50 bonus given, at any state clinic. Sterilization of females? On demand, at cost. Assisted suicide? On demand, at the cost of disposal of the body. What about bodies? If people want to pay private business to process bodies some particular way, they should have the right, including cremation, burial, taxidermy, or pickling. If they want to display Grandpa's mummy in the living room, why not? The unclaimed bodies, and all the donated ones are a recyclable resource. In addition to their value as a source of transplant parts, they could provide such assets as a skeleton in every biology and art classroom in the country. An agency of government could simply pick up any dead body its executors want picked up. The body would be processed by whatever is most to the advantage of the agency, whether that is burning it to run the steam boilers to heat the building, recycling its parts for medical and educational purposes, or just grinding it into generic meat paste. Abolish the DEA. Immediately free all prisoners in jail for crimes of possession, use, or distribution of a controlled substance. Discontinue all activity by government to detect, observe, or apprehend any individual or group for use, distribution or production of nonpatented or natural drugs. Abolish the Bureau of Alcohol, Tobacco, and Firearms. None of those require regulation by the government. Tobacco is just another plant, and government should revoke all laws which define it as something apart so as to regulate its growth, use, or sale ... along with marijuana, opium, coca, peyote, psilocybin, comfrey, or vitamin Z. Alcohol can be made by anyone who wants to learn the recipe, and should be unregulated. No more liquor licenses. If it is OK for one American to sell beer, then any should be free to sell beer, out of his basement like Amway soap, if he likes. If it is OK to sell beer Saturday afternoon, it is OK to sell it Sunday morning, and if it is OK down the street, it is OK next to the church, or the gun store. The Constitution forbids laws restricting our right to arm ourselves. All laws limiting our right to own any weapon should be revoked. If an American wants to pack an Uzi, or land-mine his property to kill burglars, that should be cool. The right to use any level of force defending your person or property should be absolute. However, punishment for unrighteously initiating force against another should be huge. Kill somebody in a robbery, Charlie, you have screwed the pooch, and we weed the gene pool of you, now. Threaten deadly force to compel submission, you're in the cage with the boogeyman, bozo, and we put the videos on late-night TV. We are most free when we respect and protect each other's rights and freedoms, punish those who violate our own and others' freedoms, and confine government to its correct judiciary, fiduciary, and military purposes. That is how America was conceived to be. We are least free when ubiquitous government takes unlimited power over us to protect us from ourselves. I hope I do not make myself an enemy of the state for saying so, but my free white American ass is not Federal property, and I can take care of it or consume it just fine by myself.

Freedom From Power Groups

Many Americans seem to think WTC911 was a tragedy producing at least one result taken to be an improvement in America, that is, a renewed sense of patriotism and respect for government. I would agree that is an improvement, but for one small matter. My sense of patriotism lies not merely in ball-team nationalist loyalty to the coincidence of my birth here, but in my personal support of the fundamental belief that by law here all persons who make up our nation should be granted certain respect and liberty, by one another and by the state, the structure of government administration and power. What I see happening in government and among the masses, is the ad-agency-style creation of iconic enemies, and the manipulation of fear and anger toward those icons to justify the government's taking greater and greater exception to those protections of our liberty and privacy from each other and the state. Not only are greater measures against the citizen's freedom and privacy being taken in the name of protection from such actions as were used by the terrorists, but others also are taken in the name of protection against anything that can be imagined a terrorist might do, and which might frighten folks to think about.

Serious, resolved, and confident of their righteousness, such protectors of the state's flocks as AG "Cotton" Ashcroft feel their responsibility as God's anointed shepherds to the faithful, and God's appointed wardens to the uncontrite imposes upon them their duty to rule by force of law. In the long run even their good and pious intentions cannot change the fact that once the state has found reason to take freedoms and protections away from us, they are gone forever. In my sketchy knowledge of history, no government has ever without violence given back to its people any right or power it once found reason to take away. If those great principles of liberty, personal sovereignty, and protection from intrusive government expressed in our Constitution are taken away, then surely "the salt hath lost its savor," and we shall have given away that which is most precious to us. Those whose free choices may be uncommon and disapproved by the majority suffer the same problem as those who desire democratic freedom but prefer not to be involved in group political action. How do you organize anarchists so they have the ability to keep themselves individually independent of organized power groups? Power groups believe their ability to use social power to structure the lives of their members, in accordance with voluntary agreement, should also extend to structuring the lives of others whether voluntary or not. A big one, for example, is the political machine in DC. It is certainly not a group of evil people, but an organic structure of authority, money flows, associations, and interests, its panels and pedals staffed by the good people of our nation. It is also an organic structure with objectives and needs independent of those of any of its people, and it has direction and momentum, like a great beast in motion. It is not always in the interest of that beast to protect the individual rights or resources of its people, in fact often quite the opposite. Many a regime has become a beast which destroyed a fine people by consuming them to keep itself alive. If we believe government should rightly exist specifically for the purpose of protecting those individual rights, then inevitably we must take issue with some behavior of the government toward the people, regardless of the inviolate nature of the objective touted as justification.

I did the terrible drugs, and I know most are shit, legal and illegal, but none bad enough to justify shooting people to keep them from using it. None. Not all of them together is bad enough to justify the earthly Hell of our global War On Drugs, the stupidest and cruelest chapter in our history... so far. The fact that the power structure knows the hypocrisy of it, but finds it expedient and profitable to keep it going makes respect for it difficult. We have freedom to practice religion, but no way to protect people from abdicating their freedom to religious power groups. If the momentum of the state beast is governed by a religious agenda, how do we protect the rights of the free from those who vote to use the law to promote the predatory thought-forms of the soul-collectors? The best defenses we have are an absolutely free press, and the guts to use it, the principle that government shall not pass laws granting religious precedence, and the guts to enforce it, and the stipulation public education be a non-discriminatory course in practical intellectual skills, empirical sciences, and objective history, all political, theological, and sociological considerations notwithstanding. We do not have to fight to *obtain* these defenses against political or religious power groups, or others. We must fight to *preserve* them, and make full use of them, however, or they will become curiosities quietly removed from popular history.

The War On Drugs Is Over. We Lost.

"A marijuana OD is when I get so stoned I can't find my beer." History has yet to record a death known to be caused by the ingestion of marijuana. How can I say that so confidently? Because if one were known, his name would be a household word in the homes of the propaganda-re-bleating obediently ignorant classes. The number of persons killed by using illegal drugs is in the order of 1000 per year. Most of these are from accidental overdoses of heroin, contaminated homemade speed, or from black market pharmaceutical depressants, and not the natural herbs. The number of persons killed by police in the prosecution of the War On Drugs, or killed by outlaws as a result of betrayal coerced by police forced-fink tactics is on the order of 10,000. The number of persons killed by taking drugs prescribed to them legally is on the order of 100,000 per year. The number of persons killed by diseases resulting from using tobacco and alcohol products is several times that, and both are not only legal, but subsidized and highly taxed (that is, marketed) by the government. Where lies the clear reasoning behind the cruel, destructive, unrighteous, and unconstitutional War On Drugs? There is none which acknowledges that the War causes many times more death, destruction of lives, and damage to our society than the forbidden substances.

The War On Drugs is over. Who lost? Millions of us are now in jail, or otherwise under government surveillance and control, unable to vote, to own defensive firearms, or to obtain security clearance for employment. The Constitution has been rendered no more than a hemp linen rag used by law enforcement to wipe the blood from its boots and badges. We have no level of privacy the government cannot invade upon even one coerced secret witness's unsubstantiated accusation, or any officer or his dog whispering the word "drugs" before plumbing your body cavities, disassembling your airplane, or seizing your farm. The governments of many countries have been destroyed and replaced by military police regimes loyal to Washington in order to control their own populations by force to prevent them from freely growing herbal drugs, or refusing to grow them for the corrupt governments. Two generations of Americans have been raised to see law enforcement as an oppressive enemy working for a government usurped by greedy and ruthless corporate gangsters.

So who won the War On Drugs? The pharmaceutical companies, big oil, and the Federal Nazis. Marijuana is not self-prescribed for terminal glaucoma, but for a sense of mild euphoria and well-being, the "high" effect. There is a class of synthetic patentable chemicals which attempt a similar effect, but they don't talk about admitting marijuana to that class. The fourteen-letter equivalent of high is anti-depressant, and the whole class of such synthetics is sold as "medicine" though they do not cure any disease, and must be used continuously to keep up the Dr.Feelgood effect, so as to deserve the appellation "miracle drugs" as opposed to the dangerous and immoral criminally addictive evil drugs obtained without the permission of the doctors and their lawyers and stockholders. There is a curious difference between marijuana and all of those legal "medicines" – they are all so dangerous that they cannot be sold on the open market, but only by the explicit permission of a doctor. If they were harmless, then the doctors could not justify their fees for prescribing them to protect us from overdosing ourselves. Unlike harmless marijuana, they are all lethal if you take too much. Other winners: petro-chemical fabric, paint, and paper makers, the producers of water pollution and acid rain. Police state power freaks. The IRS.

The War On Drugs is over. Now we have the War On Terror to justify the increasingly totalitarian imposition of Federal surveillance and control over us, and even if they gave us back the natural herbs that were once the gift of God to all of us (and as long as there is an AMA, they will not give up their forced exclusive market), they will never give us back the rights they took away in the name of protecting us from those herbs. Ending the persecution of dopers would not mean we get any of the rights back, and the Czars will still persecute us to protect us from something, so as to justify their high levels of surveillance and control over us. That being the case, there is little point in seeking drug legalization so as to get our rights back. Drug legalization is still the sensible and righteous thing to do, but should be pursued for its own sake apart from such considerations as reversing the many violations of the Constitutional Amendments guarantying our rights and freedoms. Face it, those rights and freedoms are gone, and barring a global epiphany and a worldwide Libertarian revolution, gone forever.

Who lost in the War On Drugs? You did.

More Drug War Victims: Our Good Cops

One of the most destructive effects of the idiotic, unrighteous, and tragic War On Drugs has been the demonization of our police, in reputation and in practice. In a libertarian society as envisioned and enabled by the US Constitution, an empowered police would protect each individual from the initiation of force by another, and would respect and protect each citizen's right to privacy of person and property, but could not be employed by the state against an armed united citizenry. Having such power and such limitation, police would be the people's trusted and respected allies, the first to whom to turn for common assistance, the last to fear will invade your life and violate your rights. The War On Drugs has tragically turned our police into something very different from that wholesome ideal.

It is uncomfortable truth that the last word in any structure of social interaction from the sandbox to the Supreme Court is force. Mao had it right: "Political power issues from the barrel of a gun." The law is a subtle abstract of motivations which serves only one function, and that is to direct the use of force. Look at it this way: how many of us would stand in court and let some puffed up Beavis in a choir robe bang his little hammer and tell us how much of our money, time, or life he was going to take away from us if he did not have Officer Butthead at the back of the room with permission to kick ass or shoot if we tried to leave? None of us would waste a breath laughing at him on the way out. Without superior force to impose it, the law is just a curiosity, and the judge a joke. Is this wrong? No, it is simply acknowledgment of a fundamental fact of human nature. No society free or oppressive can exist without someone having the power to control that last word. That is to say, the most essential organ of state is an effective police force. Without that, the Congress is just a chat club.

A nation's police must have unquestionable superiority of force. That is not the same as having a monopoly of force, as the anti-gun loonies would impose on us. An armed people can rise up and resist if they agree lawmakers are misusing the force of police against them. When the people are disarmed in the name of protecting us from the horrors of communism, drugs, and terrorists, and the police are armed and authorized like storm troopers, then the ability of the citizenry to collectively resist the force employed by the government is lost. It is precisely at that point that a country ceases to be a democracy and becomes an authoritarian state of some kind. It is neither prophecy nor indictment, I believe, to say that point was passed some time ago, and whatever might be granted or denied by law with respect to drug or gun possession has become moot. The rights are gone, to save us from drugs, and even if we are given legalized dope, the rights will still be gone, to save us from terror, and no doubt someday from sin.

Lots of young people today would never approach a cop for help, no matter what their problem. These include the kids with jewelry on their faces, colored hair or shaved heads, "Satanic" entertainers' logos on their clothes, gangsta pants, ball caps, Hispanic ethnic tattoos, slutty skirts, or too much skin showing, all of whom would expect to be treated the same if they spoke to a cop at all. They would expect to be stood up, ID'd, questioned like suspects in a refugee camp, sniff-searched, and patted down for drugs and weapons... for the safety of the officer, they say in court. With the addition of new "questionable person" profiles, those kids who happen to come from Arab-looking Muslim families are not likely to see a cop as a potential protector and friend either. This is not written as an indictment of police, but a lament for the tragedy it represents about our country. As a result of the War On Drugs, at least two generations of Americans have been raised to see the police not as they should be, our protectors and champions, but instead as smugly sinister and ruthless predators, or obedient minions of the state mindlessly enforcing absurd and unjust laws, all persons you pray will never see the inside of your home, or know your name. How much more tragic that for those millions whom the government identifies to its police as the enemy, the United States itself is not a trusted benefactor, but the oppressive Evil Empire.

The image of a dozen men in black armor, with machine guns, electric jolters and microwave rayguns, eyes behind infrared goggles, megaphone voices barking commands, blasting the door of my home open, slamming me to the ground, chaining and beating me, then dragging me half naked to a helicopter to be swept away in the night, all my property seized, my life ruined, and thrown into a cell... to protect my children from smoking marijuana? It could only happen in an insane sci-fi horror story of a nanny-state government gone terribly, evilly wrong. It happens every day in America. It is happening now.

Who Is Using The Dark Side?

When Darth Vader speaks of "turning to the dark side" as a tool of statehood, just what tactics and techniques are being spoken of? Secret rule, omniscient surveillance, ubiquitous presence of invincible police troops given unlimited license, summary courts without public accountability or representation, propaganda by misinformation, justification of oppression by use of agent provocateurs, predatory prosecution and delay or denial of process, persecution by prosecution for common practices or ethnic characteristics, false witness, denial of the means to resist, such as civil disarmament, disassembly of local militia, disbanding citizens groups as conspiracies, monolithic control of media, child brainwashing in forced state programs, abolition of privacy, warrantless search, capricious seizure of property, imposition of moral mandate by forced obeisance to state-affiliated religious cults, assassination, genocide, and maintenance of Imperial power by fomenting discord among factions, to name a few things that are easily observable in the media today, even with its many peculiar biases. To some extent, the above are all overtly expressed and openly manifested practices approved and conducted by the United States government, in the name of its Wars On Communism, Drugism, Terrorism, Evilism, and Etcism.

Media is not a propaganda tool. It is itself highly propagandized, and rigorously self-censoring. Schoolteachers are last to see that schools are statist propaganda brainwashing mills, because they are the most effectively programmed believers. Judeo-Christians are last to see how far in their devotion to their idolatrous cult they have removed themselves from the spirit of God who loves all of his children and all of creation. Old veterans rallying round the Flag are last to notice that the form of government that banner once stood for has been usurped by those calling most loudly for loyalty and obedience, and is being replaced by the attitudes and practices of the most villainous regimes we ever fought to defeat.

The US government has actually announced it has an Office of Misinformation. A three-letter word for "misinformation," which means believable but deniable non-factual intelligence data released to our enemies (and only them, we promise) to confuse them, is LIE. Likewise, a three-letter word for "covert informant" is SPY, or also RAT, CON, and the longer but equally appropriate fink, squealer, traitor, betrayer, and stool-pigeon. To justify doing it does not change what it is. Does no one remember that Gestapo was an acronym for Geheime Stadts Policei? It means "covert government police". Whatever notion of honor he thinks he is serving, an undercover cop is tasked with pretending to be an honest person and a friend so as to gain entrance to places his badge is forbidden to go, so as to obtain information to which he is otherwise not entitled, so as to bring the pain of punishment to those so deceived, presumably taking the name of God and love of Country as justification. Whether he is there to disclose their use of drugs, possession of arms, their sexual practices, their race, or their religion, it is still an act which would be called premeditated fraud and personal betrayal if done by anyone lacking the hidden badge to give them claim to moral superiority, and the self-righteousness that engenders.

Shall we each some day be a secret agent of some department, living a covert role to report the activities of our neighbors? To curry favor with our seniors in the agencies we report to then, we each must find something for which to narc out our neighbors. I once asked my six year old if I had his permission to spank his sister when they were quarreling. When he agreed, I asked her if I could spank him, and she also agreed. I pointed out they had sold each other out, when they should be protecting each other. Likewise, good neighbors look out for each other, and protect each other's rights. They do not spy on each other in order to perpetuate the power of the Big Daddy State.

President George Whatmeworryletsroll Bush praises the unseen behind the powerful, thereby acknowledging himself the tool of unknown masters. To keep the enemy from exploiting the news, media are now kept out of military events, and instead provided with the grist of pleasing reports. If the factual intelligence data on which decisions are made -- that is, the truth -- is so secret that to know it and to reveal it would be treason, does it not inescapably follow that whatever they tell us officially must be something other than the truth? Does it not then follow that the job of White House spokesman Ari Fleisher is to present the official non-truth in a manner that makes it easy for us to agree to believe it? What has been done to the American mind, such that we love to believe it, even knowing they have told us it is misinformation? Is it a Jedi mind trick?

Lord Vader's Kids

What if you were one of Luke Skywalker's pals, defenders of responsible freedom and free trade from an authoritarian Empire more interested in the wealth of subjected planets than the lives of independent people, and one day you find yourself in a bar with a bunch of Imperial troopers off-duty, and you see that "Vader's Raiders" are warm, clean, sincere men and women, dedicated and obedient patriots, obviously good people, the best, but astonishingly naive. They love their laws and flag, and are prepared to lay down their lives for them, convinced they are champions of the moral high ground, eager to lay waste the wicked lawless, as defined by their training manuals. What do you say to them when it is abundantly clear that though they can expertly repeat the definitions and descriptions provided to them by their authorities, and they are satisfied with those, they have little sense of the reality among those who must face the robot enforcement units they operate on the job? If you attempt to speak of that to them, how do you relate politely and civilly to them, as they personally deserve, and at the same time express the rage and frustration you feel in attempting to defend your free way of life from the terrible destructive practices of The Empire they professionally serve? If it is illegal to obtain the experience you would share knowledge of with them, how do you speak to them at all?

We hear a good deal about, "how to talk to your kids about drugs," ("No-no, no-no, whackee pee-pee, doodie-doodie, spankee baby.") but how do you talk to an innocent and ignorant adult about drugs? How do you tell someone who is obviously a good person, intelligent, well-wishing perhaps to the point of fanaticism, responsible, dutiful, patriotic, and pious that the activity to which they are loyally devoting their good service is a scourge, an abomination on the earth? How do you respond to their politely magnanimous first line of response, "Well (sniff), you are entitled to your opinion (though as the experts, we know better), and let's not talk about It."? How do you tell them that their expertise is often as not standing (deliberately placed, it might seem) between them and any knowledge that might change their opinion? For an example of how training can obfuscate one's view of reality, consider the young Mormon boys who spend two years knocking on the doors of strangers and addressing all of their questions about the dogma and doctrine of their cult. By the time they are done, they have the answers to all the questions down so pat they cannot even think of a new question to ask. Give them a degree in the subject, and a point occurs where the dogma becomes more real to them than even the most persuasive empirical evidence to the contrary. If you then give them badges and tell them to impose doctrine on everyone by force, it is tough to reach them with reason, righteousness, or reality to object.

It takes very little personal exploration in the field to observe that the government's official definitions and axioms are far from reality, when it comes to drugs, both legal and forbidden. Worse is seeing personal knowledge taken as reason to disqualify candidates for high office. Suppose a very fine administrative person, perhaps a lawyer, who had never lived in a war zone or on a military base, never seen combat, never been an officer, never went through boot camp, was given a Congressional briefing package on War and made Secretary of Defense? At the least, the retired officers in the opposition party might suggest he was ill prepared for the job. Yet when it comes to the Drugwar, one of the quickest ways to lose your chance at high office is to admit personal knowledge of the subject. As with the mind-crippling notion that empirical evidence which confounds Scripture is Satan's clever lie, the notion exists that personal use of drugs (like reading Marx?) so distorts the mind as to make one's thinking ever thereafter faulty, so the testimony of anyone who says he did it may be summarily discounted.

Many of the oppressed classes who suffer most at the hands of the various armed alphabet agencies of the Empire have no clear image of the wholesome lives and well-wishing attitudes of those good people who wear the armored suits and drive the Imperial cruisers. Trouble is, when you're being hunted down, held down, tagged and numbered, squeezed for your money, your time, or your life, it gets hard to remember that K-9 Unit Shepherd is a beautiful animal, a loving, loyal, wonderful dog for which you have nothing but respect. There comes a time, when Darth sends him out to get you, you must choose. If you will not roll over and wag your tail, then you must let him tear out your throat, or you must shoot the dog.

Dirty Laundry

I am a combat veteran and a lifetime patriot, but I can no longer "pledge allegiance to the flag". I still hold the principles for which that flag was created to stand as the highest aspirations of humankind. I pledge allegiance to those principles, and to the Republic defined by those principles in our founding documents of law. I still believe the Bill of Rights is the greatest and most important political document ever created by humankind. But.... when our leaders say "pledge allegiance to the flag", it is all too clear by their behavior they only mean "promise to obey whoever waves it", no matter what he (or she) orders you to do, or not to do. Every Constitutional Amendment in the Bill of Rights is daily violated by the government of the United States of America. The oppression of our government's domestic War On Drugs (and yes, yes, we all know drugs are bad stuff) has turned our Constitution into a hemp linen rag used to shine badges, boots, and bullets, and has turned our police force (some of the best people we have, and the best police in the world) into a modern Gestapo given license to violate every protection against statist tyranny written into our Constitution. In addition, the aggression of its global drugwar has created a phalanx of overt and covert organs of power conducting national foreign policy built around the world drug market to manipulate the internal affairs of other countries. The effect is 1000% more destructive to America than the combined effect of every drug every made, grown, or used. Millions of Americans may not vote because they are felons for the alleged crime of "self-abuse". This presumptuous policy is nothing less than a litmus test for fundamental obedience, and the dissident is being systematically disenfranchised, without having made even the smallest overt move to harm the government, the country, or any other person. Search and seizure protection? Just let officer, dog, or a coerced snitch whisper the word "drugs" and anything goes, everything goes, from your body fluids to the deed to the farm to your life if you object loudly enough. How can we be expected to trust anyone in government -- or trust each other — when you know every pot-puffer popped packing his pipe might be coerced by extreme difference in sentencing for "cooperative action" to become a covert spy for the state, and sent out wired to DRUM UP some betrayal-worthy business in hard drugs, guns, hookers and alley-wankers, mad bombers, bet runners, Hanuman worshipers, who knows what all of them are looking for – in any case it is an activity for which one might be killed. The killings are not drug-related, gang-related, or sex-related. They are the direct result of the forced-fink policy long popular with tyrants, terrorists, government torture-chamber-testimony enthusiasts, and other such extreme-control freaks. This is not the way to create the voluntary unity that makes democracy possible, but instead creates the "snitch state" where not just Big Brother, but every brother is watching you. Must we register guns to own them? Here is the fact: every gun registered becomes property of the State, and when they send the Waco vets around to get yours, they won't take no for an answer, even if it means calling in the B-52's (and I don't mean Fred Schneider's band). If you don't believe in owning guns, give yours up, and tell it to the next thug that mugs you. If you do believe in keeping and bearing arms, it is probably a good idea to keep it to yourself. Do we need an anti- flag-burning law? Should it be a crime to MOON the flag? When to protect a symbol of freedom, your freedom is taken away from you, then that symbol is truly tarnished. When a politician calls for a flag protection law, and then wraps himself in the flag, I'd say he is trying to protect himself.

I love GOD AND COUNTRY but the Cult of Power in Washington would have me believe CHURCH AND STATE mean the same. The State does not own my body, so as to "protect" it from my abuse. The Church does not own my soul, so as to seize state power to "protect" it from damnation by their idol for my violations of their taboos. Both are unconstitutional usurpations of that which God has given to ME. The way things are today, it looks to me like all the hallowed dead who gave their lives to protect what that Star Spangled Banner once stood for have died in vain. I am reminded by history that whenever people have had to fight for freedom, it is against their own government (or an equally self-righteous neighbor's government) they have had to struggle. Wake up. Your flag-waving government is stuffing your neighbors' kids into indoctrination camps. You are next, and likely for something you think is legal -- and maybe it is, today, which will not stop them tomorrow. I shall always be a patriot. I shall always strive to protect those precious rights upon which our nation was founded. As a consequence, I might likely be regarded by many a government agency of today as an enemy of the state.

Would It Be OK To Call Black Terrorists Niggers?

Arabs and Muslims of the world might be correct in their accusation Americans are bigoted racists prejudiced against them. Look at it this way: suppose the hijackers had all been black Nigerians objecting to our foreign policy. Would it now be all right to call all foreign and domestic blacks niggers again, and to call for all niggers to be "profiled," kept from airline flights, rounded up and interrogated, denied security clearance, and their assets seized, like the ragheads? Would we feel justified ordering all Africa to be bombed if they don't give us up the one nigger whose name we know? If folks started wearing Confederate Flag T-shirts saying "Jeff Davis was right," would it be patriotic to hawk them on the streets? Speaking of blacks and Muslims, why have we heard nothing from Ayatollah Farrakhan? Is he still a Muslim extremist preaching racism and anti-American sedition, or is he suddenly a patriot too? If it happened to be believed by the FBI that the Nation Of Islam were harboring suspected Arabs in temples of their cult, would it be all right for the Air Force to bomb Harlem and Detroit? I don't want to arouse suspicion that I am pro-terrorist by suggesting maybe all Arabs and Muslims should not be knee-jerk kicked in the balls here, but I may be hinting at a parallel. Likewise, suppose the next act of religion-motivated violence against Americans was a small tactical nuclear weapon, a suitcase bomb, set off in anthrophobic right-wing Reverend Jerry Falwell's church by fanatical anti-Christian Zionists, using a warhead misplaced by the Israeli Army? Would we Americans suddenly rise up to become rabid flag-waving anti-Semites calling for the government of Israel to surrender all the Ashkenazi and the nuclear arsenal they "don't have" to Our President George W. Bush or submit to the pounding of Operation Bomb Schalomb? Would we send our F-22's to Israel to fight the F-15's we sold them to defend themselves from the F-4's of our allies in the Muslim oil lands, whose product is fueling all three? If we put up big posters of Our President Thanks To God George W. Bush scolding the evil terrorist mad-bomber Zionist fanatic Moshe ben Levin, would it become all right to send the B-2's to Megiddo?

In my lifetime we Americans have made huge strides in freeing ourselves of the mind-cages of racism and religious prejudice. We obviously have a long way to go, but lets try not to forget what we have learned. If someone offends you, it is not justice to kill an innocent person who happens to be of the same race, nationality, or religion. What goes around comes around. That's one Law of God even the physicists agree on. If you don't want political and religious violence coming around, it's a good idea to avoid sending it around. I see Americans being deliberately aroused to jingoist fervor to support acts likely to cause anti-American feeling among a third of mankind. That looks stupid, and whatever their faults, I don't think our leaders are stupid, which means I have to believe there is something important they are not telling me. After Desert Storm happened on live TV, permitting rocketeers to correct their coordinates by watching CNN, the Army swore they would never let a journalist on a battlefield again. That means any war we fight from now on must be a covert war, that is, kept secret from the American people. TV functions as national cheerleader and counselor, arousing the people to patriotic fervor with heart-touching stories about Our Heroes, keeping them frightened with stories of bogeymen in the candy stores, and comforting them with reports of victory and promises they will still have all their favorite products. Some of us may envy those able to trust what the smiling spokesmodels say, whether they are selling world war, basketball shoes, or non-stick bubble gum. Some of us must endure knowing we cannot even make a reasoned judgment of our "democratic" government's acts, being kept from knowledge of the true nature and motivation of those acts. So we must trust them. With new laws to protect our security, we can trust that sooner or later, agents of government will examine every part of our lives, to our neighbors' cheers and jeers, and whatever it is they seek, they will act upon whatever they find. God Bless America, and shed His Grace upon Our President the oil man, his Defense Czar the pillmaker, his State Department general, his Drug Czar, his Terrorism Czar, his Holy Grand Inquisitor our Attorney General, and the horse he rode in on. And God help us all.

Don't Call Me Skinhead Just Because I've Got No Hair

A letter was forwarded to me from the reader of an online newsletter which carries my column, and an ad for the book collection of the first forty such essays, titled GOOD NAZIS IN OFFICE, GOOD NIGGERS IN JAIL. "Your newsletter is quite interesting and I found many opinions coinciding with my own. However, your plug for "Good Nazis in Office..." concerns me. I love my privacy, and fear the intrusiveness of the government, but I do not wish to be associated with white supremacism, Nazi-ism, Neo-Paganism, or any other group that supports the theory that the members of any one race are inherently superior to those of any other race." If I may be forgiven for the crass commercialism of making my reply to her thoughtful comment into a column advertising the book, I think the issue worth addressing. Of course I expected negative responses to my title, which reaction I confess I prefer to being ignored. I assure you, this book does not support any kind of demographically specific hatred, nor does it support authoritarian police-statism. Quite the opposite. The title is an ironic reference to one of several column essays in the book concerning the use of penal-system security modalities as the operative format of our public schools, the result of which is to train "jailhouse mentality" into our children, such that they grow up to be members of two groups, the " good guards" and the "good inmates," both of whom live and work inside the walls. Using emotion-loaded words for those roles is hopefully mind-opening to those who read far enough to understand it. The line from the column says, "Anyone who thinks I mean goose-stepping Aryans and African-Americans has missed the point. I would expect old Jews and young Blacks to be first to know what I'm talking about." (Maybe not, as I'm a middle-aged Anglo-American from the Southwest, at home with Mexicans and Hispanics.) The unmentioned third group in the schools is those who do not take the program, and either survive it to be the "outlaw free" or are destroyed by driving themselves against the bars. If guns and free thought are outlawed, then only outlaws have guns and think. That doesn't make the outlaw a bad guy, even if there is no word which makes the distinction. (Some outlaws and inlaws are bad guys, but that's a different problem.)

The downside of course is that some people find the word association GOOD NAZI, and the mere existence of the word NIGGER to be so racist as to make it impossible for them not only to say it in any context, but even to see it willingly without feeling some guilt, and the consequent urge to prove themselves not so guilty by rejecting the book, flaming the author in e-ffigy, or the like. The word has many cultural connotations, positive and negative, some race-specific, and some not, and it is always situation-sensitive, that is, its meaning depends on who says it to whom and why. (Warren Beatty's under-appreciated film "Bulworth" deals with this, a bit clumsily but with sincerity.) Banning such a commonly used word by presuming it is hateful in all situations, and thus presuming racial hate in anyone who uses it in any context, is not merely unrealistic, it is certain to cause personal emotional problems and social discord. Like FUCK and SATAN, such words are given great "dark power" when they are made taboo. Making a show of banning words used by racists only gives those words greater power to do harm, by forcing people to mask their feelings with socially controlled politically-correct speech, behavior, and thought. It does nothing to address the causes or cures of racism in people, but instead adds to those ills whatever resentment they might feel toward others for having to go through the little no-sah-mistah-boss-I-nev'-even-think-the-N-word social minuets expected of them in the presence of N-persons. Personally, I think the best medicine for that kind of thinking is comedy (a form of social commentary I deeply respect and have two left thumbs for). From Lenny Bruce to the Wayans family to Spike Lee's brilliant "Bamboozled," it is the reduction of racism to its true absurdity that enables us all to take off the masks and laugh at each other with each other. And once it's an old joke, then it's no big thing at all. Vis: "You're telling a Polack joke? Man, that's so old and dumb only a Polack would tell one." Ta-da-dump.

Racism, A Favorite American Insanity

Reflections on OJ and Rodney, et al, not to re-argue the cases, but their social context in the light of today's increasing racial dissatisfaction, like the addition of Muslim hatred to our social milieu.

If the Simpsons had been an ordinary working interracial couple, divorced, with a record of domestic violence, with the same physical and circumstantial evidence, it has always been conceded even if ruefully that conviction in any court would have been quick and routine. Considering the collateral murder of victimized bystander Ron Goldman, likelihood of death sentence would have been high. If Ron had been the black celebrity instead of OJ, conviction would have been celebrated in the streets, and OJ sent to death row.

Suppose Joe Montana had married a black showgirl, and the same evidence existed that he hacked her head off with a jackknife. Would it be unreasonable to believe blacks would insist if the jury were members of the defendant's white race, then the victim would have no chance of justice? To believe they would cry that the prosecution's refusal to seek the death penalty was proof Joe's fame and millions were buying the court? If Joe had walked out of the courtroom with a big smile and a ten million dollar publishing contract, would not the black community have rioted in the streets protesting blatant injustice?

It was clear from the beginning the question was not whether or not he did it, but whether or not convicting him was an act of justice, considering his stature among his race, and the record of American justice to others of his race in other courts at other times. The system was put on trial and successfully prosecuted for racism (and incompetence), and thus the acquittal of a black icon guilty or not was taken as justice for the innocent black men convicted in routine cases since the first slave boat hit the beach. The issue was not one man's murder, but that murder's significance in the context of racism in America.

What about Nicole's justice? Why no outcry on her behalf? Could that be because so many Americans think her suffering was simply part of that justice? For many blacks, and those who agree blacks have suffered injustice in and out of American courts, particularly those who feel black women have suffered the greatest, the death of Nicole was just whitey getting a taste long overdue of what the negress has been dealt some three hundred years — just some dues getting paid. For all too many whites, perhaps most tragically, Nicole deserved what she got for whoring herself out to that gold-plated puffed-up jockstrap jungle bunny in the first place. She is thus the victim of racism of both blacks and whites.

Nobody deserves to be beaten capriciously by police, but the Rodney King trial was about whether or not the beating could be claimed as unjust because Rodney was black. Had he been white and the cops black, and he had violently resisted, called them racial insults, he would have been tried for his offenses, and also for his verbal and physical assault of the officers. In the ten years before that case, some 20 police in America were killed with assault rifles or such forbidden guns, over 120 killed with their own weapons taken from them, and over 700 officers killed in high-speed pursuits. If Rodney had threatened those cops' lives with an assault rifle, he would not have been beaten into submission, but shot dead in an instant. The danger to which he had just submitted those officers was 3500% more likely to kill them than an attacker with a forbidden gun. Yet guns are outlawed, and Rodney is a black icon.

Reactionary racist blacks sadly too often to adopt about their color the same attitudes they condemned in whites, the extreme among them being blacks for whom freedom is not enough, and who will not be satisfied until whitey is in chains on the block. The call for reparation is such thinking. Whatever might be said about the price of justice, the desire for such satisfaction cannot be fulfilled as long as the plaintiff can imagine something done to one of his kind which is more horrible than what he is permitted to do to one of the kind he hates.

Whether practiced by white Anglo-Franco-Italo-Slavo-Semito-Etcetero-Americans who credit themselves with creating everything the other races demand to be given, African-Americans whining about nineteenth century slavery, Mexican-Spanish-Americans echoing the blacks' case for discrimination, or Native Americans protesting two hundred years of decimation by the Spanish before the gringos showed up to finish off the job, racism is a mental and cultural disease with its subconscious roots in our long past. Rising above it is among the most important things the human race – all of us – must do to survive the next millennium.

Yo, Bro, Do I Owe Yo?

Should the IRS be empowered by enforced law to take money at gunpoint from white people (that is, to selectively tax them) to pay reparations to American black people because their black ancestors were enslaved and then brought to America? No way, bro. Consider the lives and circumstances today of those black people who did not suffer the alleged disadvantage of becoming slaves, and who instead remained in Africa. I think it neither racist nor deprecatory to state the historical fact that until contact with white cultures only a few hundred years ago, African black culture was still in the Stone Age, not metaphorically, but literally. I certainly do not contend that makes black people, Africans, or Stone Age life inferior to the urban jungle we 21st Century Americans have all inherited. It is my impression nonetheless that of all the many black cultures of the world today, those suffering most the hardships of primitive life are those who remain today in the regions of Africa from which the ancestors of American black people were taken. The worst off are those left behind. You can see it coming. Where might we look to find that culture of black people who have it best of all? C'maaaaahn. In all of the world, there is no culture of black people who have greater freedom than American black people, nor any who have more personal wealth, more support from the government, more education, access to knowledge, ability to move and communicate, nor more opportunity for success financially, professionally, artistically, or politically. I cannot offhand think of any culture of black people anywhere in the world that has more of ANYTHING than American black people. I don't want to upset any of my relatives with tales of who been doing who all these years, but it is also a demographically measurable fact that most American black people today even enjoy whatever advantage might lie in having a white bloodline somewhere in the family. White people have even happily gone swimming in the gene pool with black people in America, with results that should be making both feel damn proud. The most fortunate group of blacks on the planet are the descendants of those Africans who were enslaved by others their own color, bought and sold by white Hispanics and other Europeans to white people of Anglo and other ethnicity. Those American white people were eventually so moved by their exposure to the powerful humanness and depth of spirit of mankind's most ancient bloodline, that they rose above their own cultural prejudice to declare mankind one race, and to make even declaration of any race's superiority to be a blasphemy, and if spoken in anger, a crime of hate, against mankind.

Nobody says it was a cakewalk for those first black immigrants in chains, or that it has been easy for their generations. So welcome to Club America, bro, not to shake up that victim image you're panhandling with, but lots of white people came here in chains too, to penal colonies, labor gangs, or just to poverty, enslaved by one puffed-up Mr. King Man or other, and lots of white people sweated their lives out in the mills and mines in jobs that were hell compared to the bucolic paradise of the cotton fields back home. "Here's your Irish banjo, McCoon. You scoop up coal with it." Lemme put it this way. In accordance with the law of NAACP, "Niggers Ain't All Colored People" (which is a corollary of WALLNUTS: "We All Look Like Niggers Under The Skin").

Rightly or not, until very recently ALL high offices of the United States government were held by white men, and most still are. It is fair to say then, that all which has been accomplished through acts of government to improve the lives of black people in America over the last two hundred years has been done by white men. White men fought a war against other white men to free black people from slavery (and a bunch of other reasons). White men wrote and passed laws granting black people full citizenship. White men allotted public money to grant black people full access to education, military service, to ownership of property, the right to vote, and even to hold public office. My knowledge is not great, but show me anywhere else in the history of the world where a race of people has inherited a tradition of slavery, and has elevated men and women of another race they themselves held enslaved to full citizenship, embracing them into their religions, institutions, and families as full brethren in a land of multi-cultural enlightenment. Where? In a mere three hundred years, the American black culture, by whatever name it is polite this year to call it, has been bootstrapped from the stone age to the space age, and has proved the right and wisdom of being here. And for that fact, should white men raise their children in shame of their color, and pay taxes in forced tribute to other Americans because they are black? Show a little dignity, a little self respect, bro. Some folks might even think gratitude is in order.

No Slave Mentality, Please

"Plymouth Rock landed on us..." one reader said, protesting my opposition to so-called reparation payments. Aww, that's cute, I reply, and it rhymes with "back of the bus." I presume you are African-American, and when you use the label "...my community..." you mean others of your own race. To my way of thinking, making color your first line of self-identification is basic racism. "...all white men get mad..." The stereotyping of individuals into a color group is also the basic mental bad hygiene of racism. Come on, Wood, you know this stuff. Intelligent blacks have been saying it for decades. Presuming whites all to be race-obsessed goons who want only to hold blacks down is not only an injustice to the millions of white Americans who have risen above such narrow-mindedness, who champion equality of opportunity, who abhor racism in all colors, and who would love to give you an honest break, it keeps you seeing yourself as a victim, one who is down, whether held down or staying down so as to be given victim's benefits by a socialist state looking to buy cheap votes. It is worse than slave mentality, your own racism turned against yourself, like panhandling with a sign that says "black" instead of "blind" and believing you are truly handicapped.

I am writing about 21st Century Americans, but the article you quoted is about 19th Century America. I notice it is written, and in excellent English. Perhaps you will fill in my limited knowledge and remind me which black African culture created a written language. I confess I know of none, but it is clear from such members of "my community" (that is, literate freedomists) as Frederick Douglas, James Baldwin, and Thomas Sowell that given the tool, the descendants of African black men are as intelligent and able in its use as anybody else. It points out eloquently that slavery sucked. Notice I did not use the default subjunctive characteristic of Ebonics, vis, "Slav'ry suck, yo." I completely agree with the sentiment, but I said it sucked, as in past tense. Perhaps I missed a history lesson, but it is my impression there is no living American who was a slave, or who owned one. Slavery has been a fact of human life as far back as we have records, and all of us, I say again, all of us have ancestors who suffered nasty shit at the hands of somebody else. It would take an army of accountants and lawyers armed with the Mormons' genealogy records to figure out just who owes what to whom because of what their ancestors did to somebody else's ancestors, or other persons of the same color. Because Hitler was white, and most Americans are white, do we all owe reparation to the

Jews? Should black Americans then be spared from taxation that supports Israel? Or do we all owe the Jews because they were slaves in Egypt? If having an ancestor who owned a slave qualifies one as owing something to anyone who had an ancestor who was a slave, then whom does the American of mixed race owe? What about the descendants of free blacks who owned slaves? If the whites of Custer's 7th Cavalry owe the Indian, do not the blacks of the 10th Cavalry? Does nobody owe the Irish, the Chinese, the Polish, or Asian Americans whose ancestors lived and died like slaves here?

I know of no whites bringing slavery from the countries of their origin. Slavery has been common among African tribes since antiquity, and other Africans enslaved most slaves sold to American whites. It is fair then to say that slavery itself was a practice exported from black Africa to white America, and we white and black Americans have risen above it together. It took time, and we who have so succeeded in rising above the cruel murk of slavery and racism are not the men and women of the 19th Century, white or black.

So get up off your knees, fellow free 21st Century American, and hopefully not just to get in somebody's face and trash the hood to show how ignorant the white man is. Quit crying about how Massa Washington has to improve your molasses ration, and build something good for yourself and those you love. My favorite Libertarian dicho: "The price of freedom is paying your own way."

I don't like victim mentality, whether couched in race, sex, or some other allegedly disadvantaged factor. I think it produces self-crippled crybabies, and the cynical lawyers and politicians who exploit them. That is just one man's opinion, but my opinion is what my column is about. My bet is if you can turn one out from your viewpoint, The Valley Explorer would be glad to publish it, whether they "endorsed" it or not.

Our Unholy Holy War

Were the Founders wrong, to include in the First Amendment the phrase, "...shall make no law respecting an establishment of religion..."? Should we have given the Christian institution then in predominance the power of the state to impose dogma, doctrine, and justice, and to collect a national tithe in lieu of taxes? Would it be better now if the religious diversity which has been the American experience had not happened? Will it be better if we let the Christians now in power now correct their mistake? Maybe so. Is there really something sacred about the principle that state power shall not be vested in a religion? Should revolutionary patriots do nothing about its passing, perhaps just join the church?

Today members of an extremist mystical movement among Christian sects have effectively seized control of the government of the United States, and control of significant industries, including oil and weaponry. Our President is running gleefully through the halls of power, drunk on the spirits of his dominionist exaltation, like Jim Bakker showering himself with Krugerrands in Jesus' treasury. Behind him lurks the dark-countenanced commander of his ubiquitous and omnipotent domestic security forces, the Reverend Darth Ashcroft. With the passing of the brutally ironically named PATRIOT ACT, we are now subject beyond our ability to lawfully resist to a cabal of billionaire Jesus-nuts with their fingers on the triggers of the biggest nuclear arsenal in the world, and an intelligence-gathering technology second only to God's. Worse, they believe because of their willingness to declare themselves participants in the ritual human sacrifice of an innocent man two thousand years ago, their totalitarian idol of God commands them to use that power to take dominion over the world, and to weed His garden of all who refuse to so participate. It looks like about eighty percent of America is banging their Bibles, waving the flag, and hooting Hallelujah like roosters at a monster-truck rally.

They have allied themselves, again ironically, to the nation of Israel, a race and religion discriminating police state claiming to represent the cause of the Jews of the world. It is expedient and theologically correct for them to gang up on the Muslims, who like themselves lay claim to being the true heir of God's promise to Abraham. It is a duplicitous alliance on both parts, as the Zionist extremist "Jewish fundamentalists" believe like the Christians that when the War On Evil is finally fought, only they themselves will remain, and Man and God will be One again.

The truth is, of course, that Man and God are One, and have always been, and ever shall be, Abraham's cult of guilt notwithstanding. Until now, teaching that people are born guilty in the eyes of God, frightening them with their own imagination of punishment, then selling them redemption has been the most successful racket in the history of mankind. It is not important that it be revealed as a great hoax to exploit the masses these five millennia. As P.T.Barnum said, "If He had not intended them shorn, He would not have made them sheep." But we are not talking about shucking people for their pocket change. Now, because half the world is acting as though Abraham's bizarre Xenuvian fantasy were true, its dreadful self-fulfilling prophecies are but a mad instant away. Fundamentalist Christian, Jew, and Muslim political states, all armed with atom bombs, all with overt and covert networks of alliance all over the world, are prepared to commit the billions of people their states represent to global war, each fighting for the power and wealth to bring to its own idol's altar the victory of its own version of the dark prophecy.

Is it possible some global epiphany might bring to the billions so aligned the awareness that we are all fighting over the details of an ancient historical fiction invented to herd people? Would we so enlightened citizens of all political states demand our governments cease and desist all activity based upon the premise that war in pursuit of any religion's advantage is the will of God? If we could so stop the impending Apocalypse, would we also demand an end to all laws based upon the premise that state power should be used to oppose that which any religion declares to be against the will of God, as defined in any occult, historical, secular, or spiritually channeled text?

What if we were the 100th generation of Star Wars fans, about to fight the Empire seizing power through the Dark Side, a revolution that could consume our planet? What if you knew the only thing that could save us all was to acknowledge that two thousand years of Jedi history was all just a bloody free-for-all at a fan club meeting? What if you knew just saying that could get you killed by millions of believers, and those who exploit them?

Don't Blame Me, It's In The Book

Though I may refer to the Bible in my writing, I do not often quote it. When one begins to argue the relative truth of some fine point of dogma versus some other fine point, he has already bought into the notion that one point or the other carries the weight of authority. When fundamentalists and dominionists take their divine mandate from some arcane Bible quotation or other to seize power to impose God's will by force of arms, it becomes important to recognize just what that will is fundamentally declared to be.

For example, when someone tries to defend the homosexual lifestyle, you might simply remind him that Leviticus 18:22 clearly states it to be an abomination. For a fundamentalist, that is the end of debate. Swapping semen will get you eternally reamed by a team of demons, God said it, and you better believe it, amen. For the fundamentalist, God's prohibition is absolute, as in Zero Tolerance. The matter is not up to a board of mincing shrinks, or college boy lawyers with degrees from Bible schools. Some other very specific Biblical declarations might be even harder to reconcile with modern lifestyles. When I choose to exercise my Constitutional right to free religious practice by burning a bull as a holy sacrifice on the high altar I have constructed in my back yard, I know it creates a pleasing odor for the Lord, as I am assured by Leviticus 1:9. The problem is my neighbors, who claim the odor is not pleasing to them, and who call the Empire's centurions, who come to defile my sacrifice, and to demand I pay tribute to their idols of power. Worse, those same neighbors thereafter burns scraps of taurine flesh in their own yards, and then eat the sacred host themselves, in the most lascivious sacrilege. Leviticus 25:44 states that I may buy slaves from the nations around us. A friend of mine with contacts in the trade claims that this applies to Mexicans but not Canadians. Personally, I prefer the domestic market, as American slaves will do anything if you give them a mortgaged shack with a TV set and a pickup truck, and let them vote for which of Massa Washington's boys gets to wear the big hat this year. In spite of the very limited market for slaves today, I would like to act upon the wisdom of Exodus 21:7, and offer my daughter for sale as a slave. OK, so she's no virgin, and I might have to arrange for her husband to be drafted into military service and sent to a faraway war, but that wouldn't be the first time that trick has been used. Again, I find I get a lot of flak from many elements of our American society for even trying to get a fair market price quote. As if the women of my own household aren't enough trouble, I know that I am allowed no contact with a woman while she is in her period of menstrual uncleanliness, as Leviticus 15:19-24 makes bloody damn clear. The problem is, how do I tell? I have tried asking, but most women take offense, and the Empire's centurions threaten to put me in a cage with refugees from Sodom just for mentioning it. Sometimes I think the only way to be sure is just stay away from women all the time, but that is no way to raise up a line, or rise in middle management. So I bathe a lot, and I have been looking for somebody who knows how to train those dogs that tell cops when people have dope in their shorts. You see where I'm going with that, I'm sure. Leviticus 20:20 says clearly that none may approach the altar of God with a defect in sight. There is no question that means the blind should be kept out of church, but does vision have to be perfect, or is there some wiggle room here for the Christian in contact lenses? Fundamentally speaking, 20:20 means 20/20, and the one-eyed guys and the coke bottle lenses should be driven from the temples, and their little dogs, too. As much as I like eating shellfish, from rock lobster to bearded clam, Leviticus 10:10 makes it abundantly clear my indulgence is an abomination. What is not clear is whether there are different degrees of abomination. Is eating shellfish a lesser abomination than homosexuality? Is the abomination of an oyster-slurping carpetmuncher, or a mussel-munching queen the same as any other's, or is it doubled? We all know that witches should not be suffered to live, but I have a neighbor who insists on working on the Sabbath. Exodus 35:2 clearly states he should be put to death. I don't have a problem with that, but I wonder if I am morally obligated to kill him myself. Oh, Lord, Thy yoke is heavy, but if that heathen devil shows up to mow my lawn Sunday morning again, Thy will be done, bidda-boom, budda-bam.

If Not Santa, Then Why Me?

Wouldn't it be fun to write a sweet bit of Holiday Froth and take a break from the usual gadfly shtick to talk about the prospects for world peace, the celebration of good times, and about how our nation has become the champion of Constitutional freedom we old hippies and hardcorps patriots alike have so long hoped it would be, and about how America is beloved and respected the world over for bringing the Bill Of Rights to the citizens of post-WWII nations friend and foe alike, and to the peoples of the Third World? Wouldn't it be wonderful to point out joyfully that Judaism, Christianity, and Islam are three versions of the same religion, and all should therefore be pleased to celebrate each others' devotions, in accordance with our Constitutional policy of religious freedom and tolerance?

Now the goofiest thing is happening in Lexington, the very birthplace of our nation, and in other communities. The Santa Claus riots. A small number of Jewish citizens stood upon the Constitutional phrase "....shall not pass any law respecting an establishment of religion...." and called for the removal of Santa Claus from a town Holiday event. In protest, a group of people showed up in Santa Claus suits. Libertarian socialist Bill White displayed a sign saying, "If Jews can ban Santa Claus, why can't we ban Jews?" The war was on. A group of aging bikers converted to Judaism proclaiming themselves the Chosen Sons of God took issue with White's First Amendment rights, and the town cops permitted them to assault him, being unwilling to defend his allegedly-anti-Semitic sign. To their misfortune, he turned out to be a sport fighter, and laid waste to a couple of them. In Lexington, the right of the Knights of Columbus to display their nativity crèche as they have done for centuries has been challenged. Curiously, those who call for the prohibition of any particular religion's public celebration on Constitutional grounds most often take the stand that the government must purge itself of all that might be seen as supporting any religion. Everyone seems to overlook the second part of the Amendment: "Congress shall make no law respecting an establishment of religion, or **prohibiting the free exercise thereof....**" We have a majority religion in America openly using its plurality to obtain high office and thereby impose its notions of morality and truth by enforced law. Others call for the power of government to be exercised to remove from any "public" place any display of the symbols or celebrations of that particularly predatory sect, and all others as well. Both seek greater government license to pass laws respecting that establishment of religion, one for it, the other against. Both have missed the point. The point of religious freedom without respect for any establishment is that all religions might flourish without any sect seizing secular power, or anyone being prevented by government from openly celebrating his faith, especially on public property. Though I decry and rebuke the sectarian cabal which so proudly and publicly wears its robes in the halls of Congress, I must still object to prohibition of their colors. No Christmas in Town Hall? Run the carolers off the Court House steps with riot control troopers? Oy! Jesus, Moses, and Mohammed's camel, will you gimme a break!

Lots of Americans and others are pissed off at the Muslim fanatics waging Holy War on America and the West. They are right, the mujahidin deserve it. People are pissed off at Israel and the American Jews who support it no matter what, and they are right, the Zionists deserve it. People are pissed off at the Christians who have seized the Capitol and are waging the New Order Crusade, and they are right, the Dominionists deserve it. Now we have three groups of nations, each the result of one of those religions' fanatical devotees gaining control of the machine of state, and using its power and might to assert its dominion over the others as the true heir to the estate of the one God all claim to believe in. All sides feel justified by their religious presumptions in using the most despicable tactics, covert atrocities, and acts of overt terrorism against the others. All sides feel justified by their nationalist presumptions in using penal statism to control their own populations. All share tenuous alliances with other world powers, and all are armed with atomic bombs, and different clever ways of delivering their Holiday packages.

If Santa Claus were drafted, would it be the American thing for him to shoot Osama bin Laden? Should Santa make his peace with God and shoulder the rifle for the Stars and Stripes against the evil terrorists of Islam? Would it be moral, a patriotic act in support of our Christian values? If it would be immoral for Santa Claus to do it, then why should any American?

The Uncomfortable Truth

Christian extremists like Pat Robertson and Jerry Falwell correctly point out that The Bible is explicitly against male homosexuality. In a time when the idea is widespread that perhaps God might not actually be so intolerant of our personal relationships and erotic behavior, and mainstream church-goers are stretching the faith to accommodate gay pastors and congregations, that is an uncomfortable truth. To take the fundamentalist position, it is necessary to confront many such uncomfortable truths. The Bible is also explicitly male-supremist, beginning with the declaration that God is Male, Man is God's work and woman a helper (taken out of his body!) who should serve husband as Lord. This idea is further developed in the Eden fable where it is Eve who first submits to Evil, disobeys God, and then tempts Adam, but as she is chattel of his house, it is not held against mankind until The Man uses his free will to disobey, and it is thereafter called Adam's Fall. She is his domestic tool, his reproductive tool, and the tool of his fall into God's debt. If she were truly a person, and her own woman, it would be called Eve's Fall, and Adam her first disciple. The existence of ordained Lesbian Christian Ministers not withstanding, The Bible says women should not even speak in church. Though we use her name to imply shameless sexual manipulation, Jezebel's crime was to be a Priestess who proclaimed femininity to be rightly a Divine characteristic. That is to say, through and through, The Bible is fundamentally sexist. I do not write this in judgment, neither in protest nor agreement, but in simple recognition of another uncomfortable truth.

The basic Bible plot line says God made a promise to Abraham if he and his descendants and their dependents would obey Him, they would suffer a lot, but in the end God will destroy everybody else and they will inherit all of heaven and earth, such a deal. Christianity and Islam have each laid claim to this Zionist promise, some sects admitting adoption or conversion by sacrifice, some not, but all agree God has a favorite family line it is eternally important to belong to, and no patience for pretenders to the flock. That is to say, The Bible is fundamentally racist (the United Nations not withstanding this uncomfortable truth). It is most uncomfortable to recognize that its racist bias can be used to justify supporting or attacking many different groups. In times past Christians have believed that only themselves, the branch grafted onto the root of Abraham and David, were participants in the Sacrifice so dear to God that they should inherit all. They have believed therefore the Jews had damned themselves, presumably by executing Jesus instead of sacrificing Him, and their branches should rightly be pruned away. The same benighted belief that God likes one family better than everybody else has one cabal of nuclear-armed lay priests crouching in their bunkers today insisting only they are the true blood heirs, and another insisting the true blood is only that flowing from their own altar, and a horde of others claiming the true heir was driven into the desert for his mother's race, each now come to claim his own.

Many of our founders had strong anti-church views, and all agreed on free diversity of religion, and a minimum of influence of church upon state. Even so, many like right-wing patriot dominionist Pat Robertson and our President say America is a Christian nation. Not so. Even if the founders had all been ordained Apostles, the blueprint for a libertarian state which they created no way represents a Christian political structure. Biblical reign is not democracy, but monarchy imposed by a bureaucracy of the cassocked minions of a capricious authoritarian in absentia. For Adam's primal disobedience, all mankind is doomed to God's implacable judgment without appeal, subject to options of contrition and sacrifice, administered by a consecrated cadre whose will is more perfectly subjugated. That is, the Biblical world view is fundamentally totalitarian, and those who would take that view as absolute must eventually create a totalitarian administration on earth in their Name of God. That is another uncomfortable truth.

Churches today accede to whatever will keep the sheep in the fold, but those who call themselves Christian believers must confront the fact that The Bible literally and clearly proclaims a life very different from America's customs and laws. Likewise, the American who would serve the principles of freedom of thought, empirical truth, tolerance of diversity, personal morality, equality of sexes, equality of races, choice of lifestyle, choice of name of God, choice of sleeping company, and the application of reason to democratic rule should give careful consideration before voting for the Christian zealot who would take up the deadly sword of civil law to enforce the directives of his jealous, intolerant, sexist, racist, bloodthirsty, sinner-damning totalitarian image of God. That may be the most uncomfortable truth of all.

Choose Life, Or We'll Kill You.

Choose Life. I like that, as I am certainly pro-life (even if not Pro-Life), and I should wish that every fetus conceived lives long and prospers, unlikely as the ways of God's world seem to make that. I also like that it presumes I have the right to choose, as I am certainly pro-choice in most matters of personal morality. I choose life. If the mother of my child, also having choice, decides to terminate her participation in our pregnancy, I may claim to have some right of ownership of the child. She might reply, "OK, as its owner then, you take it and carry it and deliver it yourself." If I CANNOT do that, whether the law says I MAY or not is moot. If only she can do that (in accordance with God's law that no man shall possess a uterus), then my rightful power to exert my choice has reached its limit. I have not the right to commit her personal resources against her will. She is, after all, not my property. Whatever claim I may have to "own" the child as its progenitor, my only option to protect my "investment" is to initiate force against her, and to compel her to commit herself to my desire that the child shall live. If instead of so kidnapping her, I gather around me others who agree with me, and we get a law written to empower us to send a man with a gun around to compel her by threat of prosecution and punishment to obey my desire, my act is no less a violation of her personal right of ownership of her body.

By calling her denial to the child of the personal resources of her body a murder, we are able to declare that as a criminal her person is the property of the state, and her abduction therefore just. At this point, we are no longer discussing whether her body is her own to commit or deny to the fetus, nor even if it is somehow construed to be the property of the father. We are talking only about the circumstances in which violence may be initiated by the state against one person in the defense of another. If the state has not the ability to provide for the fetus what only she can provide, then it cannot save the child, any more than I or any other man could. The only power it has is to use law enforcement to abuse the rights of the mother in punishment for disobedience to its demand she surrender her self to its official judgment, and commit herself to save the baby. If a woman's body is not her own to deny, even if denial means the death of a baby, but may be righteously taken from her by the state to protect the life of the baby, then what does any of us have that the state might not so righteously take, if to deny it to a child meant its death, and its death was declared a murder by negligence, and our crime? Since it is clear the state does not guarantee to provide for the child after parturition, or its mother before, then its proclamations of concern for either would seem hollow. We are speaking then of when violence may be initiated by the state against a pregnant woman, or against anyone else, for reasons based upon someone's judgment of her personal morality.

Personal morality, and in the end I think there is no other kind, is a matter of the soul's state of grace before God. That is to say, her morality is rightly between her and God, and my morality and its consequences are between me and God, and basically nobody else's freekin beezwax, particularly some puffed-up sheep-shucker with a state office telling me he is sending the guy with the badge and gun around to take over my life because he has decided to declare himself God's attorney and warden on behalf of my soul. Unless the soul has become Federal property, and its maintenance in God's grace therefore the prerogative of government, any argument based upon moral presumption for or against laws concerning such practices as abortion, homosexuality, or enforced definition of marriage is moot and should be disregarded. For example, the important consideration in legal marriage is whatever stature or civil rights and powers are granted to those married by law, and why those should be denied to any willing union of competent persons, number and gender being irrelevant. If three adults choose to enter into a legal contract of marriage, whatever its privileges and responsibilities, no law forbidding them should exist which is based upon the presumption their choice is immoral because, for example, more than one must be of the same sex. If it is truly immoral in the eyes of God, then surely God will have a way of dealing with that. I think it neither right nor righteous that we are forced to endure those who presume God's way of dealing with such things is to ordain them to judge the rest of us upon our morality, and having so taken the name of God unto themselves, to use the power and might of civil law enforcement to execute sentences of their own divination and pronouncement upon us. To my way of belief in America and God, doing that is unconstitutional, and a sacrilege.

Ready For The War On Sin?

Who will be persecuted under the fundamentalist representatives of President Jesus? Those who wield God's cleansing sword will make war upon sex criminals, which will include pornographers, that is, anyone who shows or describes to anyone else his or her own body, or that of any other person, through any medium of publication, and prostitutes, that is, anyone who engages in any activity intended, demonstrated, or alleged to be erotically stimulating to anyone, including show dancers, models, actors and actresses who portray people in erotic situations, and those who talk erotically over the phone. Massage practitioners, acupressurists, aura balancers, and other such persons who claim they can heal with their hands without invoking Jesus will be suspected of covert erotic practices. Male and female homosexuals, adulterers, temptresses, seducers, and other fornicators, masturbators, fellators, cunnilinguists, manufacturers or possessors of any erotic paraphernalia, and anyone who contracts a venereal disease, will be declared criminals or at the least social undesirables. Of course, rapists and persons engaged in any erotic activity with a virgin will be dealt with severely. Anyone accused of lustful acts by a child will carry an uncleansable stigma. Unmarried pregnant women, persons who perform abortions, and women who have them will be chastised, as well as persons who publicly promote abortion, contraception, or sterilization. Child-abuse and wife-abuse investigators, caseworkers advocating children's' rights, and civil liberties activists will be opposed. Members of cults — that is, of any cult but their own — will be declared the demon-possessed hordes of Satan. This group of God's enemies, and therefore the enemies of the State, will include witches, occultists, psychics, mediums, Astrologers, Scientologists, Pagans, Rosicrucians, Unitarians, and Ouija-board users, in addition to the Wiccans, Druids, Atheists, and of course the professing Satanists. Black Muslims, and others of Islam, members of the Native American heathen drug cult, Buddhists, Hare-Krishnas, Yogis, Taoists, Sikhs, Sufis, Hindus, Voodoos, and devotees of other such Godless false doctrines will be encouraged to go back to wherever they came from. Catholics, like the Jews, will be dealt with but never trusted. They will relentlessly strive to silence all heretics, that is, anyone who expresses a theological notion with which they disagree. They will persecute as moral degenerates all marijuana smokers, users of drugs not sold by prescription, and anyone who possesses any controlled substance without permission. Owners of handguns and other weapons, bikers, hippies, and longhairs in old Army jackets will suffer constant suspicion (though the Christians will be heavily armed with hunting weapons, and their police armed for battle with Satan himself). They will not tolerate vagrants, bums, or indigents, that is, any unemployed persons who have no permanent address, or who cannot name the pastor of the congregation to which they belong. They will gain legislative power by mobilizing the middle class against the horrors evoked by Rock and Roll musicians, and those who sell or buy their works, artists who paint demonic pictures, or who use demonic symbols such as inverted stars, astrology symbols, Hebrew letters, or persons with their tongues outthrust. Publishers, writers, producers of "non-J-rated" films and literature, will find it increasingly difficult to find work. Scientists will fall out of favor, pediatricians, evolutionists, psychologists, logicians, philosophers, theologians, and historians, most of whom will be accused of being among the most Godless of all, the dreaded Secular Humanists. Objective journalists will cease to exist. Another group which will feel the pressure severely are women. There are few so hated and feared among Christians as Feminists, that is, women who refuse covering (that is, domination) by a Christian male. They will oppose women in positions of power, including politicians, ordained ministers, and military officers, and denounce women body-builders as usurpers of male privilege. Anyone who opposes their regulations on the basis of restriction of civil freedom will be called a leftist, a communist, or anarchist. Those who stand upon the Constitution will be called subversives and traitors for attempting to pervert the meaning of the rights guaranteed by that document to condone evil. Anyone who opposes them by expressing anger will be called a terrorist. Anyone who opposes them on religious grounds will be called an agent of Satan, and a promulgator of the doctrines of demons. Anyone who takes a public position of leadership and opposes them successfully on any issue will be called Anti-Christ. I will be called a false prophet, heretic, or just a fool.

Moses' Myth, or DNA?

Ascending now in power and might, politicians of the Christian Right would tax the unbeliever upon penalty of law to pay the schools to teach his children the dogma of their establishment of religion, and they seem to think calling it a "faith-based organization" frees them from Constitutional restraint. Does it matter if the details of our religions are scientifically or historically true? Many argue that belief in the story is more important than whether or not it is precisely and empirically true, because it is allegedly the foundation of the moral structure of our culture. Setting aside the question of whether the bigotry of "one way only" religion is more "moral" than, for example, secular humanism, yes, the real history matters, even if it does refute the fanatic's illusion of spiritual security. If the faithful kept their religion to themselves, it might not matter at all. Who cares if someone chooses to believe Harry the Carrot God strew radish seeds in the Dead Sea to create mankind, or any such myth? But when believers base their social behavior upon Genesis, or any such occult text, and impose their belief upon others at gunpoint, the fiction becomes toxic. It is likely true that few of us really believe the details of the story of Adam and Eve, though most will glassy-eyed proclaim their "faith" in the belief, their education in science and history notwithstanding. Judeo-Christians defend the Eden myth not because they care about paleo-anthropology, but because that story also contains the only reference in literature or empirical study to support the notion that all mankind is born in debt to Abraham's family idol. Factions of that idol's ancient cult have warred upon, enslaved, and slaughtered millions in its 4000 or so years arguing which sect is the true heir to whatever Mohammed or Jesus or Joseph Smith said Moses said Abraham said God said He promised to those who would submit their flocks and their bloodlines to the patriarchal prophets. Without that absurd soap opera in the Garden of Eden, without that original sin of disobedience to motivate propitiation of guilt, there is no need for sacrifice of livestock, gold, virgin daughters, or problematic prophets. Without that single cruelly binding hook of guilt to justify it all, the entire theology and sacrament of Judaism, Christianity, and Islam is only sounding brass, and all those millions of dead, including the alleged human sacrifice of Jesus, and the millions arrayed for battle over the Holy Lands today are victims of belief in an ancient fantasy which science has long since revealed to be ludicrous as

Superman's origin on Krypton.

If millions were moved by faith in their belief to wage world war contesting the rule of Darth Vader, Daddy Warbucks, or any other such fictional character, the folly would be obvious, and revealing the misdirected faith of believers critical to human survival. Yes, it matters that such science as archaeology, genetics, and sub-atomic physics might truthfully reveal the mythic nature of all versions of Holy Scripture. Particularly in dealing with such world-moving matters as "faith-based" governments armed with atom bombs, there is no substitute for the truth.

Where mind and myth collide to impose a perspective, the reality quickly confirms belief. Flexibility of perspective is a talent which can reveal those illusions within which we might find some sense of security, but which in fact limit our vision of the options before us. Where many people share common illusions, and the fixed viewpoints which create them, people behave as though the illusions were real. For those who do not subscribe to their perspective, their behavior can be evidence of hell on earth. People whose behavior in the world is motivated by their interpretation of the books of Genesis or Revelation comprise a real threat to those who do not subscribe to their illusion, especially since they hold the seats of power in several nuclear-armed countries. For five thousand years the political/racial/religious illusion of Israel has seethed, as it's branches like the heads of a cannibal hydra battle each other over their respective claims to be the favorite son.

Perhaps it is impossible to "free" people from such an illusion box, if it is all they have known from birth. Though the particulars of the story are easily seen to be a kind of historical fiction or such literary device, billions of people today stand prepared to leap onto the field of Armageddon to decide once and for all who is the True Heir who stands on that ancient rubble-piled ridge in Jerusalem when the Great Referee blows the final whistle. Fiction or not, this box of images, this extended virtual-reality role-playing fantasy-game universe, is the driving force behind the destiny of nations, and as such is real as the holocaust, real as rock. The unavoidable result of such conflict is... well, read the book, it's no picnic.

Keep School Satan-Free.

As a Middle School student with a precocious interest in art, my son Alex decided to design a shirt for himself. Like many kids today, he appreciated then what might be called "dark, sinister, or Gothic" art — Halloween imagery, ghost comics, ancient cults, sorcerers, vampires, and the like. Among the common images from this genre is the inverted star, often associated with various proto-Semitic goat-deities — Baphomet, for example. To some, the goat pentacle is a symbol of Satan, a sinister idol from the mythology of the region. Curiously, a large number of people today actually believe in the existence of this spirit world boogieman, and are terrified of anything to which they associate the name. These same believers in Satan insist that everyone except themselves are subject to Satan's power, and are doomed to eternal torture in a Hell they envision in Gothic images. Surely if these people did not comprise the major religion in our country, such belief would be considered psychotic, and those who acted violently toward others because of it would be declared psychopathic. Stranger, instead of treating them for their delusional fixation on the characters of an ancient occult book, we fill the legislatures and school boards with them. There they feel their belief entitles and obligates them to use the power of church and state to oppose the influence of Satan in the world, as they perceive it. To my way of thinking, this is mass psychosis, and it's promulgation leads inescapably to the lawful persecution of the sane in the name of opposing Satanism.

So Alex drew an inverted star with horns, gaping fanged jaws, and fierce eyes, and paid the shirt shop to silkscreen it onto his shirt. When he wore it to school, he was told by a teacher (wearing a crucifix) that he could not wear the shirt at school, as it was "disruptive" because it was Satanist. To assure me as his parent that such was approved administrative and disciplinary policy, I was provided with a copy of the school's Board-approved dress code, which specifically forbids Satanist images as "gang-related".

As a Libertarian, I have no problem with either the teacher or Alex wearing the symbols of any religion, whether they subscribe to its beliefs or not. The First Amendment not only prohibits the government from making laws favoring one religion, but also keeps it from prohibiting religious practice, particularly on public property, I should think. I should therefore not wish to see the First Amendment taken as reason to ban display of any religious symbol from state property, much less all such symbols. The error occurs when the power of the state is used to promote the interests or beliefs of one particular religion, and to ban the expression of others. Clearly, that is exactly how the Satan's Shirt event could be taken: the school is permitted to behave as a Christianity-respecting state agency suppressing religious expression with which it takes issue. However, the consequences of seeing it that way, and attempting to call the school, the state, and the court to accountability for it could be less desirable than enduring it. He and I discussed the matter at the time, and concluded making a public issue of it was not in his best interest, nor would it improve our school's ability to get some teaching done in spite of all, nor would it be the substance of a good case for Constitutional approach to religion.

If we made a Constitutional attack, what would be our objective? (a) force the Board to rewrite the dress code to admit Satanist imagery? (b) force the Board to attempt forbidding all religious images, including Christian? (c) obtain damage settlement money from the school for violation of Alex's rights? (d) take the case for Satan to CNN? What would be our grounds? To gain the Constitution's protection of the allegedly Satanist symbol, must we profess to be Satanists practicing our religion? Not subscribers to Biblical dogma, we consider the Satan story mythological fiction, and Satan a character like Darth Vader or Freddie Kreuger, having no reality other than on the pages of a book, and in the minds of its readers. In attempting to defend the symbol as religious expression, however, we would appear to promote the extortionate myth as reality, and thus produce a result contrary to our own spiritual beliefs. If we attempted to defend the work with artistic freedom, their objection that like yelling "Fire" the symbol destructively effects the behavior of other students would likely be upheld in Court —as it would if his shirt bore a Tantric yoni-lingham. The unfortunate result of banning all that might be disruptive from school is the creation of mandatory institutions where children are behaviorally manipulated to participate in a rigidly enforced illusion, with zero tolerance for bad images, bad words, bad clothes, bad habits, and bad ideas, and everybody has three fingers and no penis, and goes to church at least once a week.

Too Late For School?

Can the American school system be fixed? No. Its problems are fundamental. Public school is now a mandatory term of incarceration in a state institution, under armed guard with physical and mental duress. While being presented technical skills and historical indoctrination, students are subject to behavioral regimentation to enforce the primary datum of the syllabus, that is, the rightness of obedience to the authority of the institutions of state. Those who do not easily conform may be placed on mood-altering medication. Practiced by other governments, placing youth in mandatory conditioning camps and using force, drugs, and propaganda to get them to follow the leader is commonly called brainwashing.

Measures our legislators direct toward reform are well motivated, but frankly appear to me like well-wishing sorcerers' spells for sunshine uttered into the teeth of a storm. Though worthy, they do not address the true root causes of breakdown in the American education system. Nor can they, because so much of the truth is politically unspeakable, and the solutions far outside the range of options given within the existing structures. Since I enjoy the advantage of being neither an educated authority nor holder of office, I am able to express what observations may occur to me without risking more than making a fool of myself. It is my hope that from considering these viewpoints, someone may gain something of use.

To begin with, no solution can be made until we become honest about the purpose of public education. When attendance behind locked doors is mandatory, dress and behavior codes rigidly enforced to impose a uniform puritanical image, and safety concerns motivate penal-science methods of security and discipline, it becomes difficult to accept the rhetoric that public education is a benefit program operated at taxpayers expense for the good of the children. Every teacher, administrator, and security officer on every campus will quickly affirm (with hand on heart and eyes glazed over) that the formal education, intellectual development, and personal growth of each individual student is the sole purpose of the entire system. For all of their desire or belief, it is simply not true.

I believe it not indictment but observation to say the school system is strongly influenced by such other motivations as "Robotizing," that is, turning children into employable "worker units" trained to fill certain roles in other industry. Whether seen as socialist horror or as generation-transcending perpetuation of productive order, it is clear no industrial society can long perpetuate itself without instilling in the young the skill, discipline, and reward-motivation which enable them to be used in structured service by industry. This fact supports a certain logic that children are in some measure the property of the industrial state, "raw material" without which it cannot function. It is my personal libertarian opinion that educated free people engaged in professions they honor, proud members of guilds and unions, will not have to be forced by government troops to teach their children the ways of honest employment and hard work.

Likewise, schools in fact perform a certain "Toilet training," that is, teaching basic rules of social behavior: punctuality, civility, respect, cleanliness, obedience, conformity, and taboo. Though some might argue these are matters which should be instilled in the home, it is clear our society does not consist only of families who know and practice these principles. If, however, in the name of these behavioral concerns, the schools in actual practice impose the same "safety and security" modalities used in correctional institutions, then the basic rules of social behavior the children actually learn will be those of the prison, and not of the voluntarily cooperative democratic free country we keep telling those school children they are growing up in.

Schools are responsible for keeping employable youth out of the labor market, yet off the streets, that is, for "Warehousing" them. Without such protective incarceration, adolescents would probably be a far more visible part of society as they work out the issues that naturally matter to them: self-discovery, pecking order, sexual stature, and the formation of protective alliances. Whether correctly or not, the school system rigidly inhibits all of these motivations.

Another consideration that has nothing to do with the children is the school system's role as an organ of "working welfare" in which a huge number of people are employed at public expense serving the children as a social services "Client group." Like the prison system, schools employ large numbers whose jobs and mortgaged lives depend on maintaining the status quo. Having identified school children as a client group, the children become clients of other agencies also. Their well being becomes motivation for further expansion of government power, more government jobs, and greater revenue flows. Among such programs are medical services (for refusing which, parents can lose children to other agencies), and the ever-more-efficacious drug interdiction services by which suspiciously-profiled students come to the helpful attention of various counselors and other inquisitive persons acting for their good.

Each of these influences brings its own problems, which may be destructive to the child, to the process of education, or to the society at large. The most destructive, it seems to me, certainly include the self-appointed moral police, drug warriors protecting the children from self-abuse, and self-righteous zealots protecting them from knowledge of and opportunity to sin. With them are the illusion bound Pollyannas who believe enforcing ignorance in the name of defending innocence is better for youth than helping them gain access to all of the truth, and the wisdom to use their right to make their own decisions about it. None can be held more accountable than parents willing to demand schools not only educate their children, but teach them basic social skills they do not give them at home — that is, to raise the children for them. The unfortunate result of government's willingness not only to do exactly that, but also to indoctrinate them thoroughly in obedience to the nationalist myth, is that the parent who objects to the system's judgments quickly finds he has no authority to place his own chosen values before those of the school in the upbringing of his child, from the most deeply committed Pentecostal puritan to the most libertine Libertarian.

The first fundamental change which would be necessary to "fix" the school system is that public school must not be mandatory, but an opportunity available to all, to take or leave, without regard to age or station. There should be no compulsion to attend public school, or any other school in order to gain mandatory state-approved credentials of education. The notion that every child must be industrially skilled and drilled in the history and doctrine of the state, even if by criminalizing the parent, is not a policy befitting any nation associating itself with the word freedom. If attendance in some government-regulated school is mandatory upon punishment by incarceration, and imposing that "benefit" is enforced by the techniques of high security and correctional behavorism, then by any name, the school is a prison.

The next most important change is to eliminate the concept of age-determined or time-determined progress. The public education system should be open from its most elementary classes to anyone of any age or background for whom the level of the subject matter is relevant. An illiterate adult of thirty, or an immigrant seeking citizenship, should be able to take second-grade reading in the public school if that is his level of need. A twelve-year-old able to meaningfully address hieroglyphic should be admitted to any class of her intellectual peers. The key to progress must be mastery of the subject, at any level. That means not only do we dispense with forced age-grouping, we make progression totally dependent on ability to demonstrate 100% fluency with 100% of the syllabus. No sliding by with your age group with C's indicating you learned half of the subject. When you have all the answers, you pass, whether it takes you six weeks or six years. Nobody says you have to pass to get another birthday or a job, but until you get it all, you can't take the next course in the program. Though classes might have members of many ages and social backgrounds, with very different intellectual abilities, they would have in common that they were all at the same level with respect to the subject.

Students should view their schools as sanctuaries where their personal differences and habits are not held against them, and not as forced stage sets where they must rigidly perform the actions of the characters assigned to them, under punitive stress. In the history of America, nothing has been more destructive to the nation than our own War On Drugs, which has caused to citizens, to our legal rights, our business practices, our communities, our foreign policy, and to the trust between citizens and the state, many times more damage than the effects of all the drugs this persecution is intended to prohibit. Even so, perhaps the most destructive effects are yet to be seen, the long-term results of anti-drug measures in the public school. Nothing more quickly arouses the willingness of the fearful sheep to surrender power and their rights to the sheepdogs than the cry to "protect the innocent children." More and more, our public schools are finding it "necessary" to conduct the activities associated with zero-tolerance enforcement of morality, security, and safety programs using the science and the modalities of penal institutions. School safety program designers are trained in police science. High schools are fenced camps, subject to restrictions enforced by uniformed police. Though use of "obscene language" to an officer is a statutory crime, armed campus safety officers may seize, arrest, and intimately search any dirty-mouth perp who speaks ill to authority. Though the school's demand for parent conference is mandatory as a legal summons, the system of campus discipline does not include an office called "student defense counsel" and the Dean's decision is not negotiable, but is a summary prosecution to which the parent has no appeal.

Whether this policy is "right" or not, there are inescapable consequences of raising our children in a prison-like environment. If they are treated like prisoners, even for their own good, they will learn to think like prisoners, and to see themselves as prisoners. It apparently eludes the entire power structure of our national school system that if you operate schools like prisons, it does not matter what is taught in the classroom. The lessons learned will be the lessons of life in the joint. Those are clearly observable. If one is to have any privacy, it must be sneaked. To survive the coercion of the inmates, one must learn to say nothing, or lie. To survive the coercion of the administration, one must learn to snitch, that is, to tell on other inmates (which betrayal is a major motive for mayhem). To survive at all, one must belong to an "organized mutually-protective group" which are almost always racial. Whether dealing with other cons or the keepers, the bottom line is violence, the fist, boot, club, knife, and gun, or ultimately the electric chair. You sneak, snitch, lie, join a gang, hate authority, and submit or dominate through force. No one raised in such an environment can be expected to become a successful part of a functioning democracy governing responsible free citizens.

It is not possible to teach a bird to fly with safety guaranteed. If it were so, then God would give birds parachutes. I wrote that like a joke, but I fear some bird-loving do-goodie will be moved to petition his senator to retrofit every American eaglet with a parachute before it attempts the potentially-fatal act of flying. Since it will take several fiscal years to implement the fail-safe Federal feather-chutes, someone will surely point out that the technology to protect the fledglings is already available. We have only to send out Federal Forest Rangers to put safety cages around all the nests. There was a time when School Safety Programs were conducted by the School Nurse, not by the police. It is not possible to teach a bird to fly in a cage. Those who will not be broken will destroy the cage if they must to get out, or they will destroy themselves against its bars. Those who accept their cages at best can only walk, and must be fed by agents of other government programs. Students "educated" in such an environment must ultimately make a choice between the only options offered by the architects of the penal state. Each must become one of the guards, one of the cons, or one of the outlaws.

The Drug War use of penal security in schools is only one of its fatal flaws. Another is federal requirements based on demographic academic statistics. Funding statistics have become the primary concern of administrators, which has led to breakdown of standards of academic excellence. Affirmative-action labor policies have further made the academic part of the education experience meaningless to the working-class student, at least with respect to his future employment. In areas like the Southwest, many students come from uneducated Spanish-speaking homes, and their resulting poor English skills place them far behind their non-Hispanic age peers. Opting as usual for the PC-posturing solution, the system has accommodated them by reducing standards for all, and by providing stereotypic special classes to those isolated as "culturally disadvantaged." Unfortunately, neither tactic enables the Spanish-home student to succeed in classes (or jobs) conducted in English. Since little Spanish is taught in our schools, most who come from uneducated Spanish speaking families learn only conversational vernacular. These people are not bilingual. They are illiterate in two languages. Since many jobs correctly require employees to speak the local Spanish, and in keeping with the policy of affirmative action, many such people become employed, but are technically unable to read and conform to the complicated government documents which define their job duties. When the Motor Vehicle Department, Social Services, and lower-level school administration, all data-and-communication intensive jobs, are staffed by bi-illiterate people, who is served by this refusal to confront the politically unspeakable truth?

Conservatives are right: Liberal forced-equality ideology has gutted education by eliminating direct competition in academics and reducing standards to avoid creation of politically sensitive demographically identifiable low-performance statistical groups. Liberals are right: Conservatives' reactionary return to spankings-and-sermons drill training will produce graduates who are expert only in the arts of living in a penal system, either as dour pious guards or repressed rebels. That is, both are wrong.

It appears to me several factors contribute significantly to the current deplorable state. Unfortunately, these are not matters which can be solved by funding another special-group program, nor by purchasing airport-security equipment for schools. They are consequences of very fundamental traditional assumptions, and of unassailable political postures. These include:

-- age-bloc-based, rather than performance-based progress through the system.

– denial of the system to persons not the "correct age" for classes.

-- grade-based, rather than completion-based passage through the syllabus.

-- failure to establish uniform evaluation standards of students.

– failure to determine promotion of teachers by genuine competition for excellence.

-- system evaluation by demographic bloc statistics, not performance of individuals.

-- mandating bloc-equal outcome, rather than offering equal individual opportunity.

-- lowering standards to accommodate age-progression of low-performance groups.

-- failure to utilize senior students as tutors of juniors.

-- negative peer-stature for academic excellence (vs. idolizing of athletes).

-- money, demographics and sports, not academic prowess, being keys to college.

-- failure of Constitutional protection against sectarian religious control of syllabus.

-- failure to defend historical truth from censorship for "political correctness".

-- emphasis on school as employer of labor, with lip-service to student product.

-- lack of "stick", an effective stress factor for non-destructive control.

-- lack of "carrot", a meaningful reward for personal academic excellence.

-- penal techniques to impose conformity, in absence of "stick" or "carrot" motivation.

When the use of our vast wealth and power produces social disorder in our schools and inferior graduates, it seems clear we are deceiving ourselves as to our priorities. I am reminded of a cathedral wherein the priests bicker over which icons are to be polished best, while the congregation fight and fornicate in spiritual poverty. Liberals and Conservatives each think schools should be legislatively tailored to their own politic. Lawyers litigating school issues think the system should be designed in the courts. Christians want power to conform the syllabus to Scripture, or payoff vouchers to make their catechisms into government funded schools. Unions want power to make schools a controlled marketplace for labor. Parents want schools to instill values and discipline they themselves have not. Society wants uncontrolled children off the streets, if not in school, in jail. I presume corrective measures lie far outside what is politically possible. However, I believe if the following five factors were made *sine qua non*, the quality of our graduates in all subjects would rise in a spectacular manner:

++ the ability to speak, read, and write the English language fluently.

++ the ability to apply and skillfully perform Arithmetic without mechanical aid.

++ the ability to conduct research, that is, to organize and perform self-teaching.

++ the discipline to concentrate on an assigned task, and to punctually follow a schedule.

++ the desire to excel in fair competition for meaningful reward.

When what is needed is a fleet of speedboats, there lies no solution in re-designing the battleship. Sooner or later the super-structure will become larger than the hull can support, and it will turn belly up. In these times of man's greatest affluence, and greatest intellectual accomplishment, we should sink the ponderous galley of state we call public education, and give to each student his own sail, and access to the wind.

"Di-di-dit dah-dah-dah di-dah-dit di-dah-dit dah-di-dah-dah dah-dah dah-di-dah-dah dah-di-dah dit dah-di-dah-dah di-dit di-di-dit dah-di-dah-dit di-dah-dit dah-dah-dah dah-di-dah dit dah-dit di-dah-di-dah-di-dah."

The Bi-Illiterate

I believe the American school system should unflinchingly demand fluent English proficiency of all for advancement, regardless of their ethnic background or home environment. Though Spanish speaking children who make up the predominant minority in the Southwest I know are certainly not inferior to Anglo children (nor to Germanic, Slavic, Asian, etc), neither they nor anyone else can succeed in education or in society without competent English language skills, no matter many artificial affirmative action sanctions or patronizing cultural programs the government dreams up to dump tax money into. It is obvious, however, that simply withholding promotion from non-literate students would quickly create racial age disparity in our classrooms. The minority kids would be older, larger, stronger, and sexier, and would likely exercise these advantages out of resentment toward their allegedly privileged younger non-minority classmates, who could be expected therefore to rigorously eschew visible academic excellence so as to gain schoolyard stature. The alternative taken has been to pass minority-language students without English skills by excusing their illiteracy as a disadvantage not to be held against them, and magnanimously providing token classes in Spanish as compensation. The resulting apparent racial disparity does not help the Spanish child to learn nor to gain self-esteem. Thus set up for failure, it is not surprising many Spanish students react with surliness and violence, or by dropping out. Race gangs offer peer-approved opportunity for both. Opting as usual for the PC-posturing solution, the school system has accommodated them by reducing standards for all, providing stereotypic special classes to those isolated as disadvantaged, and imposing order in the classrooms and the yard with school safety programs created by specialists in penal security, empowered to self-righteous intolerance by the presumptions of the drugwar. Unfortunately, none of these tactics enables the Spanish-only student to succeed in classes or jobs conducted in English. It creates a very real and very low "adobe ceiling".

Since little Spanish is taught in public schools, most who come from homes where only Spanish is spoken learn only the conversational vernacular of the uneducated classes. Able to converse with local people who speak only Spanish and also with those who speak only English, they are called bilingual. Unfortunately, they are not. It is more accurate to say they are illiterate in two languages. Since jobs such as social services and county offices correctly require employees to speak the local Spanish, many such bi-illiterate people become employed there. The liberal may consider that to be social justice, but unfortunately it means in practice such agencies are staffed by people who are technically unable even to read the government documents and complicated procedural manuals which define their job duties. Who is served by this refusal to confront the politically unspeakable truth? Nobody.

My suggestion would take a generation, but could offer a lasting contribution to the long-term progress of Anglo/Hispanic relations in The Americas. We in New Mexico hold a unique opportunity along the cultural interface from LA to Miami. Ours is the most Hispanic state, and we should not only mandate that every student be fully literate in English, but also mandate that every student, regardless of home demographics, be fully literate in Spanish also. Today's public school World History is still mostly about Anglo rule, and Anglo victories in war and industry. If classes in global Latin culture, conducted only in Spanish, were mandatory for all New Mexico students in order to pass to the next grade, the unequal pressure placed upon Spanish-home children would be balanced. Only then would the students have a racially-level playing ground on which to compete for excellence in education. Equally challenged to perform in an alien culture and language, the resulting generation of graduates would be the critical bridge we Americans need so desperately to bring our cousin cultures into the 21st Century side by side, instead of head to head.

This approach might well be taken in other areas with a large population who share a common foreign language, though such regions do not readily come to mind. Certainly many would clamor to have their language included in the local public schools, from Braille to Ebonics. Unfortunately, such clamor would quickly be exploited by lawyers and politicians to the absurd and unworkable. We're probably the only state with a chance of making it work.

This also presumes we should have a system of mandatory government schools at all. Who says I'm responsible to pay the state to "guarantee" everybody else's kids a diploma and a state job? Private schools, of course, should be free to offer or mandate any assortment of languages their owners and clients might mutually desire. If their graduates cannot write well enough to fill in a job application… hey, that's their problem. If anybody wants to, they can learn any language they want to without the help of any school at all.

You're Not In Control.

To save our children from drugs and sex, we are instructed in community service programs how to repeat seriously to them those things we are told are the correct lessons they should hear and believe, their own experience or ours notwithstanding. Like the surreally idiotic "fried on drugs" ads, the thrust of such counseling is to tell them horror stories using fearful images without substantiation or understanding, and to exhort them to obedience without further question.

My kids grew up in a dope-smoking environment, tried it, and decided it was not for them. Thus enabled to make their own choices, and aware of it, they quickly rejected most drugs in disgust for the garbage they are. You could bring a trainload around, and neither they nor I would consume one toot or pill, with or without prescription. There is no temptation from which we need state gunmen to protect us. Kids who grew up around people who have smoked dope since they were kids in the '60's quickly see that the horror stories are revival-tent drama intended to keep the sheep scared so they will permit protection by government power. They also see the children of the "protected" are most likely to have problems with control of vices. People who know they can take drugs or leave them can make their choices based not upon compulsion or fear, but upon their own evaluation of the risks and gains, as free people should. Those taught to believe vices will force themselves upon them are not in control of themselves. They do not know the truth about what they fear, so they submit to control, or fall victim to the real dangers out of ignorance. "Tell kids the truth," the drug warrior says. I agree, but the state has made it crime to possess the experience to tell all of the truth. What truth? Stories of the millions of us who live with drugs without horror are forbidden, and so is the truth that we are so enabled because we know the reality about which they are lying to the obediently ignorant, and we do exercise self control. Government welcomes neither such knowledge nor such self-rule. Prohibitionism does not exist because government wants to protect us, but rather to control us, and to protect certain interests in the marketplace. Enforcement causes much more damage to the lives of Americans than all of the prohibited drugs combined.

Same for that sinister threat to the moral fabric of our community, that old Demon Porn, from sepia postcards of fat girls in foundation underwear to interactive streaming video with playful nymphets willing to display their body parts to the camera on command. When it comes to sex, the puritans' cry is, "Keep the truth secret from kids." For myself, I find most porno stuff bland and unimaginative. Without the hostile feelings, treachery, crime, jealousy, psychosis, or horrid special effects common in the prime-time dramas of G-rated TV to create conflict, excitement, and tension between the sexes, the plots are usually flaccid. Best that can be said is the characters all seem to be having a mindless good time copulating away to bad elevator muzak, and nobody gets killed, hospitalized, sued, robbed, or arrested and hit with a stick. The First Amendment still protects what the puritans can't get the judges to define as obscene, but only as long as it isn't being sold within 1000 feet of a bar. I betcha there's a limit on how close a porno bookstore can be to a church or a school, too. I agree bookstores should be obligated to obey the law just like everybody else, but I wonder just who else does have to be 1000 feet from a bar, church, school, etc? People sometimes go to nearby motels to consummate whatever was stimulated by their prurient perusing. Shouldn't that be stopped somehow? Maybe if there was a limit on how close to a motel they could be? Say, can't you just visualize some kids thinking they were walking into a convenience store to get one of those magazines with the weightlifters in G-strings, or the interviews about TV-teens' sex lives, and find themselves exposed to...well, what is exposed! Maybe just expanding the code a little to include all those places where children go to buy non-X-rated magazines would prevent them from accidentally seeing... well, you know, people's... well, you know whats. Kids walk home from school on the sidewalks, don't they? Maybe if the smut-mongers had to be 1000 feet from any sidewalk, we could all begin to feel a little safer. How about 1000 feet from the surface of the earth...in the direction out of sight? Now there's a hell of an idea!

Contrary to both liberal and conservative government thought, we can cope with the reality, and we should. We can be in control of ourselves, and responsible for our actions, and we should be. There is nothing any government can give us that is a substitute for the truth, all of the truth, and the freedom to act upon it as the heart and mind direct. Tell the kids that truth.

Dressed-Up and Dressed-Down

School Board behaviorist wonks still believe forcing students to put on an outward show of uniform conformity is a good substitute for actually instilling those qualities the forced show mimics.

Anti-sex dress codes: At Las Vegas "prestigious" magnet high school for art recently, that year's student art show was attended only by the artists and their parents. Most of the other students did not know it was happening. Somebody noticed at the last minute that the advertising material the students had created included a picture (one of a dozen inch-wide thumbnails) of one artist wearing a garment which revealed her navel. Since that is a violation of the student dress code, the ad was banned from campus. Our city's big student art show might as well have been a Brownie party. At our magnet high school for international studies, classes in history have been forbidden to show the film Schindler's List in class, because it shows lines of naked people waiting to be gassed. Since display of the body is deemed prurient, no matter what the context, the film is classed with the obscene. Presumably if all those Jews had been well dressed, it would have been all right to show the obscenity of them being killed by their neighbors and state for congenital political incorrectness. Do the illusion-mongers of the Boards not know the kids have seen the film, and all the other realities they are forced to posture to conceal at school? Do they think the kids do not see them posturing in frock coats like the Wizard of Oz, operating the giant Happy Face while the big dog in the trench coat frisks them and locks them down for class?

Anti-gang dress codes: The lessons School Boards everywhere are teaching demonstrates they have not learned theirs. Unable to prevent students from making voluntary associations for peer stature and mutual protection, the Boards pursue line-item prohibition of expressions of such association. They would seem to hope that by enforcing prohibition of "gang symbols" they could eliminate the undesired behavior. Curiously, they also seem to believe if they could stop the behavior, that would somehow eliminate the attitudes which make gang membership so attractive to many youth in our society. The opposite is true. Formation of gangs as hostile underground groups is fostered by what is perceived to be oppressive policy enforced by a patrician bureaucracy. If that policy can also be made to appear absurd, the effect is greatly multiplied. The growing list of absurd prohibitions makes Boards look like frantic monkey mimics, banning first a hat, then a shirt, then pants, hairstyles, neckties, aromas, hand signals — whatever the underground displays. Who is then perceived to be in control, and who the knee-jerking fools? Trying to control behavior by prohibiting specific things creates the horrors which the prohibiters then attribute to the things they prohibited, so as to justify their prohibition. In their benighted attempt to control the few, they violate the rights of all, thus making tyrants of themselves. The music industry uses Gothic imagery for enhancing the dark emotional tones of the angry underground's music. When youth who feel those emotions in their lives show their appreciation by wearing the logos of the bands, the Boards attempt to suppress their self-expression of those emotions by prohibiting "Old English lettering" as Satanic. Such lettering is explicitly an indicator of one ethnic group: English, which happens to be my heritage. The gangs seem mostly an expression of Black or Hispanic angst, so that prohibition might be taken by some as an unjust defamation of Anglo culture. When a student draws an inverted star on his shirt and he is told by a teacher wearing a crucifix that he may not wear it because it is Satanist, he likely knows enough about the Constitution to recognize he is being had, which does nothing to improve his respect for either the state or the church. Crucifix tattoos and the Virgin of Guadalupe have been Hispanic counter-culture identifiers since the Pachuco days I remember in the 1950's, but I hear no one suggesting Catholic symbols be banned. Some people might take serious offense at racial defamation by the School Board, and artistic suppression by a politically powerful establishment of religion.

The de facto lesson taught by enforced prohibition of specific attire will not escape today's students. The solution to the gang problem does not begin with suppression of the expression, but by learning to understand what our children are seeking in their own peer groups that they are unable to find in their families or their society, and by giving them options which are better in their view. I am reminded of a hard-learned lesson of my military training: "You can compel obedience, but you must earn respect." In that distinction lies the difference between tyranny and democracy, between dogma and faith, and between indoctrination and teaching. Go to the back of the class, School Boards.

Nicotine Dogs In School?

If tobacco, number one killer of Americans, were illegal tomorrow, and the price went as high as the same amount of marijuana today, a suitcase of Camels would be worth $20,000.00. Might folks steal or kill or cheat on their badge for that amount of loot? Though it is still heresy to say so, and the issue is buried beneath the rubble of the Twin Towers, it is still clear the so-called drug crimes are not caused by the drugs, but by their prohibition. The oppressive, unjust, and anti- Constitutional sixty year drugwar has created in at least two generations a rightful resentment and mistrust of not only the government, but all institutions of authority. Nothing caused by the use of any drug known can compare with that in destructiveness to our society. Let us therefore be very wary of any rhetoric which would lead us to once again attempt to use the power of law enforcement to protect us from our own destructive desires.

Do those who call for Constitutional restraint on government power obstruct law enforcement, as Darth Ashcroft's minions proclaim? Drugwar proponents express surprise that any educator would oppose dope-dogs in public schools. They point out that dogs are the most effective weapon against student dopers, since it is impossible to resist being searched by them. They can even tell where dope has been, but is no more. Because they are effective, the minions of the Czar imply, whatever citizens' rights might interfere with their use should be abridged. If they are correct, and effectiveness is the gauge of moral validity, then why stop with halfway measures? After drug testing all teachers, deputize the clean ones and fire the others. Fence the schools, eliminate student lockers, and conduct pat-downs at the doors. Keep dogs on patrol, and demand body search and urine test of any student upon the dog's dope-alert. To be most efficient, demand dog scan, urine test, and "interrogative counseling" of all students wearing pro-drug symbols (slashed clothing, dope pictures, radical hair, body jewelry, rock band logos, or anything Satanic). Since it could be assumed many dope-smoking students come from dope-smoking homes, clearly the effective thing to do is to cut directly to the morally-destitute root of the student's problem, that is, the home where family values have so tragically failed. Place a judge on the school board with power to issue John-Doe-Jr. warrants for phone tap, DEA surveillance, and dog search of the homes of all students who alert the dope-dogs, whether or not they are in possession of forbidden fruit. Those in responsible positions who disagree with such penal techniques in school administration should have their credentials re-examined, after drug testing. Since the schools are used as voting places, how about deploying these wonder dogs to investigate all who come to vote? If law enforcement were given full use of all effective means of surveillance and management now possible, we would not have to obtain conviction to place all potential offenders under penal control. The land of the free imprisons more of its people than any other nation now, but then we would all be effectively imprisoned already.

I am pleased my children grew up preferring not to abuse themselves with the drugs so available, but I would rather they drank booze or smoked dope in a free country, than to see them forced to suffer hollow forms of righteousness under the moralist totalitarianism of such well-wishing duty-motivated classroom monitors as our Drug Czar, Attorney General, and the President's religious advisors. Their emotionally sincere but self-righteous tough-love "cut down the trees to save the forest" attitude would have been highly praised in the public security machines of Stalin and Mao. Won't someone propose a really effective final solution? If abortion is murder, should not a woman who aborts be executed? How about an undercover Life Enforcement Agency sting-clinic to attract her and bring her to the chair? If secondary smoke is potentially lethal, should not public smokers be shot down on sight like murderous abortion doctors? If that's too radical, how about a law which permits the diseased to file damage suit against any business or home they frequent which has not chosen to ban smoking? How about the LEA confiscating your car or your home if you smoke with the window open, then selling them to buy better smoke detectors, and anti-smoking TV ad time? What if that Beagle sitting on your foot is telling his handler about the Tiparillo in your sock, and you're about to spend the summer in a military prison camp to get your sense of social responsibility corrected? Tobacco addiction is a deadly serious problem, and we must address it, but prohibition by law and enforcement of obedience by police-state tactics is not the answer. Making war on drugs like tobacco is like using a power sander to treat acne. Zero-tolerance hell on zits, all right, but....

Hell Yes, I'm Anti-Terrorist

If an American blew up a Mosque full of Taliban in order to strike fear into the heart of all Islam, would that be an act of terrorism? What if he blew up a country full of Taliban? What if that American was the President? Would it be any more or less terrorism? It is becoming hard to tell what is part of the War On Osama, the War On Terrorism, and the War On Whatever We Imagine A Terrorist Might Do, and what is actually meant by the more and more often used word terrorist. The word is gaining increased ambiguity in its uses, but we all can likely agree a terrorist is one who perpetrates an act of extreme violence against a few persons in a social body, where no war against that body has been declared by his own state, for the purpose of arousing fear in its population, to some political end.

Acting by Executive authority, that is, as an empowered individual, President Bush has conducted an act of extreme violence against a small faction of a large group (Afghan Taliban, out of world Muslims, Arabs, and other Middle East oil producers), for the declared purpose of arousing fear in the entire large group. Whatever may be said about his justification, his objectives, or his state of Grace, one man, without his Congress' declaration of war, issued an order to conduct a demonstration of extreme power, to create terror in a world population. Creating fear of himself throughout the Muslim world by bombing a country, killing thousands, and replacing its government so as to strike at a few who were harbored there against US seems not in any significant way different from blowing up a church, a bank, or a supermarket to strike at a few in order to frighten the many of US. If the USAF is bombing Afghanistan specifically to scare Iraq, Arabia, Egypt, et al, then might it be correctly said that in responding to Osama's terrorism by bombing a country, Bush is just giving the terrorists a taste of their own medicine, using terrorism against terrorists? It might be fair play, but does it not mean President Bush and his team could justly be called terrorists too? Are we speaking of different ideology, or only of different scale? When we backed the Taliban in Afghanistan and paid them to conduct jihad against the Soviets in the form of acts of sabotage and killing, were they acting as terrorists then? Or were they not then evil terrorists, but courageous guerrilla irregulars serving the cause of freedom in their God's name?

Is a terrorist anyone who does something that frightens the

American people? anyone who says something that frightens the American people? anyone about whom the US newspeakers say something that frightens the American people? anyone US calls a terrorist? Or just anyone who frightens the US government? If those who believe in the creation of terror as a means to accomplish a political end are terrorists, then what of those for whom fear among their own citizens is welcome justification for taking power otherwise denied to them? Is the US agent who lets an act of terror happen attributable to an enemy so as to enable the seizure of power a terrorist?

What if you happen to believe such actions are wrong for America to do, no matter what you call it? What if you believe our government should not behave in ways that would be called immoral if practiced by a person, and we should not engage in acts of terrorism ourselves, no matter how we are provoked, or how many TV celebrity pastors say it is justified in their God's name? Does your moral belief mean nothing, if it does not support the President's decisions? If you someday attempt to take some action to attract attention to your voice of dissent, and to bring the President to account, and you are declared to be a terrorist, a promoter of anti-American thought, what then? As the definition of terrorism expands, so will the group of yesterday's patriots who find themselves tomorrow's terrorist suspects. If you are one who would sincerely desire to be a true and honest patriot, just what do you do as the words terrorism and dissent come to mean the same thing?

Instead of attempting to answer these questions, perhaps we should just agree that no act of The President of the United States Of America, his administration, US armed forces, or any of America's agents uniformed or covert, could ever be, or should ever be accused of, or even suggested as being... well, you know, the T-word. Let us agree then, though they may appear to do things which are technically similar, we are speaking of different moral genre when we talk about US and those individuals or groups who believe in using violence to create terror among the citizens of US and its allies. They are clearly and unquestionably terrorists, and since we oppose them for terrorizing us, we are anti-terrorists. And by God, we all should be against terrorism, starting at home. It's scumbag politics, strictly for bottom feeders.

We Are The Borg.

Like Christian fundamentalists, Libertarians are a minority of extremists who take as fundamental the literal meanings of the words of the Constitution of The United States of America. They have for three decades as a political party protested that American government has granted itself the legal paperwork to permit gross exceptions to each provision and guarantee in that document, however sacred it might be. Those exceptions to the rights and protections of the people from government have all been well established in the highest courts, and are fully enforced in the streets and the market. Libertarians have long cried, "Protect your rights, or we all lose them." They can now save their breath, for we have lost them, past tense, over and out, to keep us secure from communism, from racketeering, from dirty movies, from drug fiends, deadbeat dads and pederasts, and from unpatriotic liberal suspected terrorist supporters. We lost them when jurors were told they must vote to convict if the evidence shows the forbidden act, no matter how they feel about the justness of the law. We lost them when the makers of petro-chemical paint and fibers, the makers of pine tree paper, and the makers of synthetic drugs criminalized marijuana (and so hemp, their market competitor) as a felony to possess, thereby denying the convicted pothead dissident his right to defend himself and to vote for change. So it has gone. As the Libertarian Party grows, it will become an accepted perennial outspoken minority, permitted to whistle like a safety valve, like the Court Fool permitted to make jokes which gainsay the King. Whatever good elected Libertarians might do, however, the great beast of government will never voluntarily reduce its size, nor reduce its power to control its host population. We have gone from "protect our rights" to "get our rights back" and since we didn't then, we can't likely now. Bada bing.

Government might at best be a symbiotic parasite, but it is a parasite. Government produces no product or service to its host population not first taken from the worker and entrepreneur in tax upon productive enterprise. From the budget allotted to benefits government credits itself with providing, government deducts its own operating expenses. The more it can convince its host the benefits are worth the tax, government will increase its expenses to the greatest extent it can. It is unfortunately obvious if unchecked, the body of government will ultimately consume its private sector host. The host citizens will first be imprisoned by manipulated debt in their taxpaying roles and when the structure of workers paying off the parasite's IOU's ultimately collapses, both private and government workers will succumb, and the puppet masters will depart with the crown jewels to seek out new hosts.

We are already the Borg, each wired into the beast machine-plus-flesh. Of course we desire a secure home, a secure country. In the name of ensuring that, we have become the world's most advanced techno-socialist security state, even if still in the larval guise of a democratic republic. As the systems of surveillance, accountability, and enforcement mature, the group of powerful influences whose focus avatar is the man in The White House will know the location of each of us, who we are, what we do, with whom we trade, what we watch on TV (and therefore what we think), and they can examine at will our premises, our property, records, phone and internet communications, and the fluids of our bodies. Though they cannot yet watch all of us all the time, the power of government to do those things above to any individual it chooses is already a fact. The State of Maximum Security, as a way of government, is indistinguishable from prison. As in prison, the fully monitored behavior of the inmate citizen (that is, his willingness to accept the system, its control wires and body support tubes) is what determines his access to recreational areas, and the decoration of his assigned cell. Trustees can live in mansions with acres of yard, and administrators have private jets and make decisions announced to the inmates by a team of puppets with somebody's hands up their behinds. One popular TV show is a vote for which of the puppets should play the Leader in the War On Baddies this year. He lives in a movie set called The White House, and he and his family are a kind of reality-TV cast. It won't be long until they are all computer-generated synthetic characters operated by a team of writers and technicians. With the 3-D virtual and A-I tech just blooming, the effect will be to become the welcomed friend of The Leader himself, with whom you might daily visit and interact on-line in the intimate privacy of his own home. You just can't help trusting a guy you know that well, who is just that swell, face to face, shoulder to shoulder, upward and onward for the Red, White, and Blue. "Pray with me, Jim, who do you most want God to help Your President protect you from?"

Do You Really Pledge Allegiance?

I recently received an email post titled "The Oath of the Right-Wing Extremist" proclaiming to stand for allegiance to The Flag.

I pledge allegiance to the Flag of the United States of America,
and to the Republic for which it stands:
one Nation under God, indivisible, with Liberty and Justice for all.

Aw, horse chester. What high-horse blowhardism. The right-wing extreme certainly does not support these premises, for all their applauding the iconifying of them, or their characterizing themselves as loyal patriots, honorable mutineers taking back The Ship Of State from a rogue Admiralty. In fact, their behavior is quite the opposite. What do those words we children were taught to chant actually say?

A pledge is more than just a promise, it is an irreversable act of submission, as in formal marriage or joining a brotherhood of bikers. To "pledge allegiance" means to take one as your liege, that is your King, and so to faithfully serve - not to judge, not to obstruct or bring down, but to give fealty, obedience. "The Flag" is obviously not literal, but what it stands for does not mean a body of particular ideas you choose to agree with or not like an armchair barrister, it means the seat of authority. Especially in a Republic, that means the ones elected call the shots, and you obey whether you voted for him or not, whether he orders you to fight or to farm, and whether he wears your color hat or not. You do not follow command on ship, or refuse to, because of how you feel about the Admiral, or where he orders the ship to sail, but because his authority is what is represented by his Flag, and that you have pledged to serve. Personally, having been both a hippie and a Marine, I prefer a more libertine than authoritarian status quo, but that is what the words mean.

Next it says, "The United States Of America." That means the "one nation indivisible" and not allegiance to one particular State, or one particular Party. That national organization, that body of definitions, agreements, offices, and powers IS the Federal Republic for which the Flag stands, the legal corporate national entity which exists as defined by the Constitution and the Laws. It is that which we loosely refer to as "the government" or

"Washington" including the Congress, the Supreme Court, the Treasury, all the other agencies and bureaus, the lands and properties it owns, its accounts and assets, its population of citizens, and the Presidency, which is the seat of the Flag. You pledge allegiance to that Flag of that Republic as an existing thing if you pledge in reality, and not to some 1770's fantasy ideal you would imagine to be better, or to some faction within it you presume to define it apart from all the rest of us.

"Under God" would seem universally redundant, if we presume all of the created universe is under whatever we mean by God. The obvious error of the Christian right or any religious group lies in presuming that means God as defined by their establishment of religion, and the government should therefore in some way be subject to the dogma, doctrine, scripture, or influence of persons of power in that religion, that is, "loyalty to the higher authority" of their own interpretation and enforcement of God's Law. It is what the First Amendment was written to prevent, and what the Dominionists of the evangelical Christian faction of the hard right are deliberately and quite openly doing.

As for "liberty" it is abundantly clear the Social Conservatives of the right wing would define that to be liberty for all to walk freely within the lines they draw, and liberty for them to draw those lines where they will, in accordance with morality as they define it. Those who object they declare to be seeking not liberty to choose, but license to sin. For its connotations of promiscuity, the word liberal itself has become an unexamined label of wrongness among the rightniks, with a terrible dark stereotype presumed to all upon whom they stick it, like nigger or commie. What's wrong with liberals? Duuuh, Pelosi!

Across the political spectrum from right to left, and from authoritarian to libertarian, good people all sincerely wish for "justice for all" but every one of us can easily point to injustice somewhere in that system to which we pledge our allegiance, and within which we all no doubt sincerely hope to accomplish some good. To suggest that right wing extremists somehow have the edge on any of these things is benighted. As easily as they say others are not "real Christians" the right-wing extremists are able to say others are not "real Americans" - and somehow they believe only themselves are either of those, and therefore only themselves qualified to make the decisions and laws of a Christian America, and by God, they will defend that with their 2nd Amendment rights.

I am not saying I support fundamentalist obedience to elected leaders, or there should not be an active confrontational dialectic in the democratic process, but only pointing out that supporting the decisions of the elected officials of our government, whether that's how you'd have it done or not, is what Allegiance to the Flag literally means. It is what those words mean that the right-wing extremists are most objecting to under this administration, and most openly refusing to actually do, for all their touted oaths of allegiance, patriotism, and duty.

Americans who do not knowingly and wholeheartedly support the agenda of their blatantly sectarian coup de etad are advised to be prudently wary before voting for one of them, no matter whom they oppose, or how they wave Old Glory.

"The best aim of government is to protect the citizens' freedom; the best aim of free citizens is to look after the common good."

Why Not Vote Social Conservative?

"Social Conservatives" are good and sincere people, but they are the puritan crusaders, prohibitionists, finger-waggers, torch and pitchfork witch-hunters, censors of obscenity and of heresy, intolerant of perverts and false doctrines, each a self-justified moralist judge and ready executioner of the deserving sinner, likely motivated by a narrow but extreme religious viewpoint. Whatever you think personal liberty means, these are people who likely will religiously strive to prevent you from exercising yours, likely as not in the name of protecting your morality from self-abuse by license to sin, and protecting your children from the trauma of seeing you do it.

A century and a half ago, Lysander Spooner wrote eloquently about the folly of dealing with vice through enforced prohibition. In the 1930's we recognized the folly of creating a huge and profitable criminal class by the prohibition of alcohol, and that was repealed. Later the pragmatic on both sides of the law recognized the profitability of maintaining prohibition of many other such highly desired substances and elements of various vices. The consumer suffers from the actions of both sides in the wars on sin, but the street money for it and the budget money against it both flow.

Therein lies the unforseen horror. The fact prohibition is profitable for both the suppliers of the desired commodity and those who enforce the laws against them does not change the folly of what is being done, but multiplies it. Both sides soon create in the other the thing they fear, and everyone suffers the terrible destructive effects of each trying to resist and destroy the other. The damage done far outweighs whatever could have been caused by the prohibited substance or practice.

If dancing is outlawed as sinful because it leads to fucking, soon only outlaws will be dancing, and the self-denying who succumb to their nature will kill to fuck. Even one such killing will be taken as proof the sins of dancing and fucking should be more rigorously outlawed. The dance halls move underground and become more expensive, and more terpsichorian fornicators are hunted down, tried and appealed, imprisoned in huge new facilities, and hanged. The monster feeds upon itself, and grows.

Whatever you think of Barack Obama, the political ideology of the Republican Party, or the petty arguments of Congress over which of them gets all the money, it would be damaging to all of our personal and civil liberties to vote for any candidate who advertises himself or herself as a "Social Conservative."

Is Granting Freedom a Disservice?

I recently received this in correspondence on the subject with a friend, and I appreciate the chance to address it:

".....a woman's right to abortion is legal. That is not my problem with it. My first problem is that taxpayers should not have to pay for abortions. My second problem is that I believe the law does a disservice to women. If women have a right to choose, what are they choosing?"

If it is a disservice to give someone a choice to do something you think they should not, then you do them best service by taking such choices away from them, and ensuring they only choose right, right? If she has a right to a root canal, why should any health care program refuse to cover it? What makes the abortion procedure different, if not the moral judgment prohibitionists would presume the power to enforce? I think government should not pay for cosmetic procedures, nor for the pharmacopoeia of Dr.Feelgood drugs, but if abortion is called a medical right (and it is hundreds of times less expensive than the alternative, providing pre-natal and birth services), then who should say it should be excluded from the services covered, particularly on moralist grounds?

Your question demonstrates the apriori presumption of authority to define what is so immoral as to warrant prohibition. What are they choosing? The answer implied is "something too bad to permit." Whose business is it to judge her choices so as to take them from her by law? In a sense, she is choosing to call abortion a justifiable homicide, as homicide it unquestionably is. Those who admit an "incest rape" exclusion to permit the victim mother a merciful abortion are doing exactly that, claiming the right to declare that particular homicide to be justifiable, the right they will not give to her. Their issue is not the life of the unborn, but the moral circumstances of its conception, and their power to declare one homicide mercy, and another murder in accordance with their standards, and to employ the might of law enforcement to obtain conformance to their judgment.

However you define its physical, spiritual, or legal personhood, until you could take it from her and sustain its life yourself as in parturition, you have no rightful claim upon it at all, neither to protect, speak for, nor to vaccinate, assign an identity number, nor place into an institution of protective maternal custody for the unborn. Whoever you are, no matter how much you believe in your righteousness, no matter how devoted to God by any name, no matter how many of you vote, or if you use the guns and judges, that fetus is not yours to protect. It does not belong to you. It does not belong to the state, and even its soul does not belong to the church.

Whatever I might personally feel about any woman's choice to submit herself to carrying a pregnancy or not, or whatever I think God thinks about it, I would consider it a self-righteous usurpation of her God-given right to the ownership of her own body for me to subject her to my decision and bend her to my control by using the power of law enforcement in God's name. As for morally judging her choice, that part is between her and God, and none of us has a right to intervene, least of all by force of arms in God's name. Though it break our hearts, we ought bide.

"Your body is not property of the state to protect from your abuse. Your unborn is not the property of the state to protect from you. Your soul is not the property of the church, to protect by law from your sin."

Afghanistan Update

"Insurgent" used to mean somebody who comes in to organize against the legitimate government. "Partisan" used to mean civilians who organize against an occupying foreign regime. "Red State" used to mean Communist, where all get a job, a government check, and health care. Today, insurgent means anyone willing to stand against America's guns, God, and credit cards. Partisan is a dirty word liberals call Republicans, and folks in Red states vote to kick the sick old beggars and demand their papers. Ever read Orwell? "He who writes the dictionary defines the truth."

The people of Afghanistan are in the same position as political Independents in America who say voting for a GOP or DEM candidate is picking "the lesser of two evils" - or the new inmate deciding whom to let fuck him to protect him from the other (even knowing he's going to get fucked by both). The Afghan must choose between the mad executioners of the puritan authoritarian Islamic Taliban or the ultimate-armed robots and evangelists of the Christian American equivalent of Taliban. Both are clearly evil by any reasonable estimate. Allah beheads those who try to do something to help themselves — and Jesus bombs them from heaven.

Unfortunately, the war is not about them. Without the war, our economy would collapse. Troops are cheap, and sending even a few thousand, withdrawing them, honoring them, and burying them are politically visible actions, but if we quit sending the bombers burning 40,000 gallons of fuel every mission, and the USAF quit buying all that gas, EXXON would go broke! Likewise, if we quit bombing the opium fields to protect US big pharmo corporations from the third-world agricultural competition, our so-called health care industry would go broke! If we quit sending in our civilian armed security troops, and quit paying the Afghan s to hire them, we would have 30,000 unemployed religious-fanatic perp-shooting killer-cops-for-hire looking for work back in the inner city hoods of home. If we quit making war on the reed fields of Araby (as did Caligula)... our economy would go down like a pom-pom boy in the shower.

The President cannot get us out of that war. You know the scene: the men in the black suits take new President into the secret projection room, and show him The Movie. He turns white (gulp!), and quickly comes to a specuguine conclusion. "I spec you gwine do what you has to, Mr. President," he is told. "Y'shoulda seen the last boy we showed that to. Young Dubya like to pooped his pants."

The 1st Amendment Means Jesus Too.

From Day 1, 1776, we have violated the 1st Amendment prohibition of laws respecting an establishment of religion in several ways. One of them is freedom from the taxation other establishments must pay, even if doing the same thing, like publishing and broadcasting to generate revenue. A mistake then, worse now, as one extremist religious sect's marketers have created an industry rich enough to play the game of Senators and Presidents, in the hope of waging world war on the unsaved.

Another is the power to issue sex licenses... that is, legal marriage as defined by that establishment of religion's dogma, where all sex without that license is not just sin, but statutory crime.

Also the "blue laws" which regulate business and property use to conform to religious practice, when and what you can buy and sell vs Holy Day schedule, when you can drink, where you can put your business with respect to that church's premises, what books are not in your public libraries, what you can't teach in your schools, etcetc...

The Neo-Conservative Christian American Taliban (NEOCATs) believe their monopoly on the blessing of The One And Only Real God whose image is graven in occult symbols in their ancient scrolls like a mummified idol wrapped in papyrus entitles them to exemption from that Constitutional restriction, as they believe they serve "A Higher Authority" than the mere secular Constitution they would be sworn to defend.

Christians like these in America used to cover their heads with bed sheets to conceal their respectable faces while they took people they thought God loves less than themselves out and hanged them from the jigaboo tree. These days they wear respectable faces on TV to conceal the white hoods.

What is wrong with the Muslims is exactly the same as what is wrong with the Christians, the bigotry of believing the idol they worship gives them a monopoly on the blessing of God, the privileges and taboos of which blessing they should enforce with an army. Christians murder doctors, drown their children, and bomb thousands of innocent people in Jesus' name, not just back in Salem, but today. Brainwashed since childhood, fanatics of that ancient cult of guilt, fear, and spiritual blackmail are self-righteously eager to start a global nuclear holocaust and create Hell here in the Eden God gave us, to "bring Jesus back" — they having been raptured away to their mansions on Aruba while we fight it out for them. Last time this world had to face militant puritan Christians out to save the world from "liberal sin" we called it The Dark Ages for hundreds of years... and rightly so. Our Constitution has it right: you may believe in any mythical super-spook in the sky or boogieman down the volcano you want to, but you may not use the power of the law to force its "divine orders" on the rest of us, whether you get those from the Quran, Dianetics, the Book Of Urantia, or the Bible.

If you are interested in this subject, the impact of religious belief taken as equivalent to empirical reality, and the reasonable consequences of acting upon many of the precepts and prophecies of the Bible as being true, I'd like to recommend my book "Thank You Jesus, But NO Thank You." It is available in paperback on Amazon and is also available on Kindle.

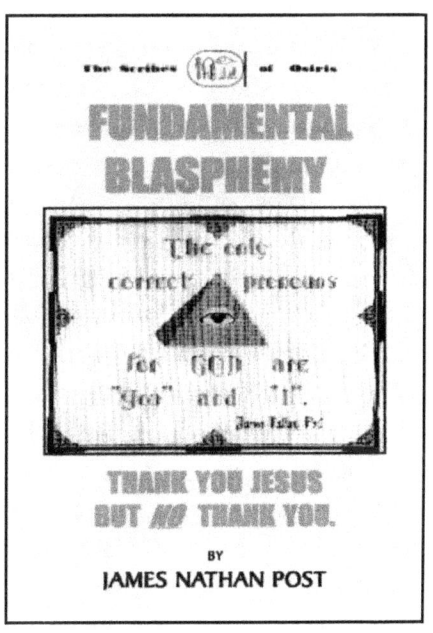

Is Real Money Possible?

If we ever again issued money with real Constitutional value, what would we do about the fact we are $11 Trillion in FRN debt to a private bank with global power? We smartly say, "Tell them to write it off," but can we actually do that? Can any debtor "repeal" the bank to which he is indebted? What would we tell the world when they come to cash in the trillions of FRNs they are holding as oil reserve accounts, bonds, and investments in US corporations?

What about all us non-corporate non-capitalized just regular ol' peckerwoods? Apart from a few coin-collection curiosities worth many times more FRNs than their face value, who among us has any real Constitutional dollars? Nobody. Mostly, we don't even have FRNs, we only have numbers in some bank's account somewhere, and most of us are upside-down mortgaged, credit-card maxed, and have no real property of any value whatsoever. If we take our digital FRNs to the new treasury, how many will we need to buy one real gold dollar? 2000/1? How many Euros will it take to buy one gold dollar, when a million old FRNs won't buy one Euro?

Just who actually owns America's gold now, the Treasury?... or the Fed which issued trillions more in FRNs than the Constitutional value of the gold "reserves" on which our certificated money was first printed, and replaced by fiat trade paper? Can the Fed "repossess" that gold collateral for non-payment of FRN debt... or has it done that already?

Would we use our new real money to buy the rare-earth metals and other non-US natural resources we need to defend ourselves if we shook our pretty high-tech sabers and told the rest of the world to eat their losses?

Do you suppose at some point the world-ignorant, provincial-minded, isolationist, bigoted, obese, addicted, mortgaged, and nationally indebted American people will have to be taught that our country, like all the rest, is simply a big self-defined club with rules and dues, just a corporation with a bank account and an (overdue) credit line, and not the unique, exceptional, and immeasurably superior ordained and entitled creation of The One And Only God Himself we have let the teachers, preachers, politicians, and pundits tell us it is?

I am no economist, and have always lived out of my hip pocket. But re this issue, and the balanced budget issue, the positions seem strangely detached from the simple reality I have known. You cannot pay down a credit card just by slowing the rate at which you borrow more. Even if you stop spending entirely, that does not pay the keystone, nor the interest, or the vig. Sooner or later, somebody must actually come up with the dough, or they'll break your legs and take the car. And if you have been borrowing to pay other bills, like food and rent, then you still must pay those bills. Passing a law that stops borrowing, and a law that says you may not spend more than you take in, does nothing about the fact that the bills to be paid are not about what we do or do not spend next year, they are about what we already spent... in trillions.

The question is not as the GOTP would have you think, about what President Obama will or will not spend next year, but what Bush already spent... and we still owe and must pay for, diminished returns or not. GOP's plan: don't tax the rich, who will then (we promise) employ the poor, who will then have jobs earning wages to be taxed to grudgingly pay for Obama's bailouts. In the meanwhile, we don't feed the poor, we tell the unemployed to blame the Mexicans for their poverty, and vigorously enforce puritan law to keep them in line... or in jail.

I am for stopping the bleeding, but let's hope not by cutting off the circulation to the extremities. Also good to try to see just exactly into whose gullet we are bleeding. Reds (funny, that used to mean socialist) would have us believe it is all going to the mexquitos, the hordes of poorer-than-us-taxpayers — when it seems pretty clear to a lot of us we are being bled mostly by the great glutted parasites who wear the robes of State, Church, and Mother Bank. But then, it seems most of us live on the tits of one or more of those, and most of us very well, even one as poor in money as I have been. Without them to feed us and to feed upon us, have we anything to eat but each other?

Freedom Is Only For A Few.

The rich and powerful of every political and religious stripe hate and fear nothing more than an informed and empowered populace. When reality is defined by what TV news-mongers and evangelists say, and your idea of "freedom" is a mortgage serviced by a rigorously demanding job, and the right to vote every four years for which of Massa Washington's boys gets to wear the Big Hat next, then the number of informed and empowered people is pretty small.

Most working-class Americans look to me like livestock on a treadmill with a feedbag and a virtual-reality hat over their eyes. Should we freedomists then strive to awaken and so liberate the sheep (like in the Matrix)? If you free sheep, they wander until led. They are still sheep, free or not. Most Americans have no idea what day-to-day freedom from their social and professional roles and responsibilities might really be like, and there is little they would do differently if offered unlimited freedom. We who exercise what we think should be freedom, outlawed or not, just learn to do it, living as outlaws among the lawfully ordered. It seems clear to me for that few who desire to exercise maximum freedom to still live in an affluent society, most of the people must prefer the ordered life, and must have that life. Whatever we revolutionaries do, it must not upset or disrupt the lives of the fat, dumb, and happy working middle class.

When a group of people are called "alternative" or "radical" or "fringe" that means most people are not that way, given freedom of choice or not. Obtaining a law by the vote of the majority which includes all of the fringe element is always going to be unlikely. It seems clear therefore that some of us are always going to be an "outlaw class" for exercising one freedom or other, and it is also clear that the form of order which best enables us outlaws to live among them as we wish is not the intolerant witch-hunting hangin'-judge Conservative, but the more diverse and inclusive Liberal.

If what you want is to live a very free personal life, perhaps doing things others might not do, with a minimum of government intervention in your life, then it is clear to me you should vote for the most progressive Liberals, and then responsibly live your life, rather than submitting yourself to loyally following and enforcing a severe code of honor, duty, and accountability, and living the life of a slave at arms, as good soldiers do. If you want that kind of life, don't vote Republican and start shooting at Senators, just go join the Marines. Really, I mean that. It is there such a self-sacrificing life of service is most valuable to our society, and most honorable, precisely because it enables the rest of us to live relatively libertarian and even libertine lives. To attempt to impose such a dutiful and puritan lifestyle on everyone, and to declare the freedoms being fought for should not be exercised, is a betrayal of those rights themselves.

A Marine says, "I give up my freedoms in order to give you freedom to do what I do not. I get up before the light so you can sleep till noon. I take orders and obey without question, so you can do nothing and serve no one. I am sober and straight, but I will kill for your right to suck a joint, whether that is somebody's reefer or somebody's cock. I will give my life to pay for the Food Stamps that keep your babies alive, even if they are all illegitimate. Though I may weep when my Flag touches the ground, I will stand for your right to..... aw, horsechester, I just can't do it! There is a line I can't cross, and that is it, bud. I won't have no pinko, faggo, dope-smoking, butt-poking, baby pumping, border-jumping, freeloading Food Stamp fatsos and Medicaid junkies making a pack of glutted-out Wall Street billionaires even fatter on my ticket, and then burning my Flag bitching about it! Goddammit, there's a point I just got to shoot somebody!"

Having been a Marine (and yes, you never recover), and also a libertine libertarian, I understand how being a Christian social conservative defending the Constitutional freedoms of a libertarian society is a bit like a monk who guards a whorehouse, and I also understand how unpleasant and unfree life can be when the Marine decides to impose his martial lifestyle and morality upon the house he guards. Be a Marine if you love that lifestyle, but vote Progressive for those whose freedom you defend.

Prophet or Psychotic?

On July 2, 1881, a failed radical political candidate named Charles Guiteau, convinced that President James Garfield would be the ruin of the Republican Party and so bring an end to freedom and prosperity in America ...shot him in the back. As a result of the "health care" available to Americans then, Garfield died a few weeks later of infection he contracted in hospital. Guiteau said God told him removing the traitor from the White House was a "political necessity" — and then he pled insanity. He was hanged on June 30, 1882, after having made several trial lawyers wealthy arguing on the public dime about the difference between prophecy and psychosis.

The issue is still not resolvable in the American court, every session of which begins with giving respect to The Bible, 1st Amendment or no. If a man crucified his son (or someone else's) because he believes God said he must do so as propitiatory sacrifice, could he be exempted from prosecution because of his faith? Could he instead be declared insane? Is not agreeing to participate (even after the fact) in exactly that sacrifice the most fundamental precept and requirement of being Christian? Without the blood of that crucifixion on your hands, you're still a G-d damned Jew on your way to serve Adam's sentence in hell. Right?

Did God really tell Billy Graham to tell George Bush it was His Holy Will to bomb Iraq? Or was it Osama Bin Ladin who received the Divine fatwa he faithfully obeyed on 9/11, thereby revealing the infidel Bush to be the idol-deluded mass-murdering psychopath? Or was Bush proved to be the saint and not the psycho after all because we were blessed by God with more bombs than Allah?

This is not just theological seminary chit-chat. It matters. A President who believes in these religious fantasies and holy wars has the atom bombs, real secular scientific and empirical bombs, and the power to use them. If she were willing to kill us all because she and her ordained Jedi cabinet all believed in the literal truth of Star Wars, wouldn't you say it matters that their belief be exposed as epic fiction, and their faith however sincere has been usurped by a nuclear-armed chimera, a demon out to lead us to bring about our own real Hell on Earth? Hear, oh Israel. Burn the Books, and repent of the Sacrifice.

Clean The Parasites Out Of Medicare!

Some things, like national defense, are best done by a disciplined and highly motivated agency of state, that is, by socialism. The correct way to solve Medicare is simple: socialize it, and remove the parasites. I do not mean those who need medical care, I mean the INSURANCE INDUSTRY which profits on every stitch and pill by what is in fact a rigged form of gambling, and for whom actually providing medical care is not the objective. No, providing medical care is on the expense side of their ledger, something they want to minimize. (This is basic MBA duuh stuff, like creating jobs. Companies do not want to create jobs, which are labor costs they don't want if they don't have to. Given money to expand, they prefer to cut labor and invest in more profitable alternatives, not hire a bunch of pedal-pumpers as some sort of political gesture. "Tax breaks create jobs," is a pathetic lie to get workers to vote conservative in fear of losing their jobs, and the unemployed to vote red in the hope of being hired.)

As with the care provided to wounded soldiers by the Army Medical Corps, government could pay directly for the actual care, at the lowest possible wholesale cost. ZERO to insurance premiums, and no fat commissions for commissioners and contractors. Should this be the only way then, and replace what we have now? NO. Keep the private sector business exactly as it is, and if you want to buy their insurance and receive their services, you go right ahead. The Federal Medical Corps would operate in coincidental competition with the private sector hospital system, but not as a controlling entity or sub-contracting agency. It would not impose standards on the AMA hospitals and staff, and it would not take its standards from those, but could operate as its Flag Officers and Cabinet Secretary determined best for its mission.

If you were willing to go into the FEDMED hospital, or a VA hospital, or an Army field hospital and take what you get there.... would that be bad? NO. Our military Medical Corps are the excellent example: they work for the same salaries as other officers and troops, with the same gung-ho attitude that means giving the most medical care (not making the most money) to those they serve (the sick and wounded, not boards of employers), from a sense of pride and true service to America, exactly like the grunts on the line and jet jocks and rotorheads feel. Ask the troops how they feel about trusting their medics to save their lives. What soldiers do every day is heroic, and what their medics do every day is miraculous. I believe such a uniformed domestic US Medical Corps, just like the Coast Guard or the Air Force, would have the same esprit de corps, professionalism and top-only standards as the Marines, and would eagerly strive to best serve every human being who came into the place with the best they have, regardless of that patient's gender, race, rank, religion, registration, or insurance coverage.

This would provide real medical care (not bullslick insurance coupons) to the deep class of Americans who are below even the working poor stratum, many of whom have never had insurance in their lives, though seniors now. It would really create good living wage jobs for thousands of people with medical skills, and for construction and maintenance jobs too. It would cost bupkis compared to collecting profitable insurance premiums with the IRS and the courts, and paying the profitable medical industry the gluttonously inflated costs of providing that same medical care. The socialist FEDMED system would be much less expensive than what we are paying now, and would provide better day-to-day "old country doctor" type common health care to all of us except the rich, who presumably will still choose to patronize the insurance companies and hospitals they have now, and good for them, as those hospitals are truly awesome and a blessing for those who can afford them. It is a win/win situation for both the best of a socialist system and the best of the free market too. Well, it will be a little rough on big capitalist medbiz and the insurance guys, but hey, a big racket is still a racket, right? If real care and real economy are the objectives, then you either take the rackets down, or you end-run them as I have suggested here.

End The War On Wetbacks NOW!

I have not read Arizona's "border security" law, but I have every confidence that it does not specifically admit the "profiling" of Mexicans. It only calls for all who are there without The Papers to be recognized as criminals and treated appropriately. Even given such a semantic technicality as a passcard, it is abundantly clear what it means in practice. The probability of anyone being stopped, subdued, interrogated, and searched in Tucson because they have a suspicious epicanthic fold or might be an illegal Norwegian is simply ZIP. We all know what the "War On Wetbacks" law is intended to do.

Here are two proposals which I believe could offer New Mexico the opportunity to be a positive force for solving the growing discord across our nation's southern border. These are (1) Marijuana, and (2) the Mexicorps.

(1) Let us make an end run around California (as Albuquerque does with respect to Hollywood) and make Las Cruces our state's competitive entry in the exploding new market in legal marijuana which is saving the economy of California. I have read that the famous Hatch valley chile production has seriously dropped off for various reasons. There is hardly a better place in this country for the production of high-grade marijuana. Instead of allowing Monsanto to create patented GM industrial pot seed to exclude the small farmer, we should ban such seizure of the market by growing only with clone cuttings as those underground agriculturalists do who have created the fine hybrids the medical industry would like to take credit for. There is no such thing as "medical marijuana." Those beautiful and profitable seedless hybrids were created by outlaws hiding from the DEA's gun-packing goons in cellars, caves, and canyons to serve the millions of Americans who recognize from personal experience the benefit in our lives of this natural relaxant, a true "anti-depressant" with no harmful side-effects whatsoever.

Let us therefore be the state that welcomes, certifies, and harbors those Mexicans who will come here, move into such new labor-residence communities as my friend Tres Stahmann's family used to maintain on the great pecan plantations of Dona Ana County, and work to produce this beneficial and profitable crop. They will not be a burden to our state, but instead a true asset who not only carry their own weight, but will make us the most agriculturally affluent border state in our free land. If we go one "Liberal" step further, and offer such laborers classes in the English language and the history of our country, we could produce a new generation of bi-lingual citizens with a well-deserved sense of gratitude and patriotism.

(2) Within the structure of our very fine even if poorly funded New Mexico National Guard, let us create a Mexicorps, a corps which welcomes the immigrant (however he got here) willing to sign up for a four-year tour of duty in which he or she will receive basic military training, classes to become fully bilingual and biliterate, and a program of education leading to full naturalized citizenship, medical care for themselves and their resident families, and a GED or college entry as appropriate. There are today millions of men and women in Mexico and here among us who would eagerly leap at such an opportunity to be of true service to America, and who would re-energize our military forces which are struggling to find new recruits to relieve those now forced to serve three or four tours in our efforts to help the people of so many countries around the world. Again, this would make of these people not a burden on our social services, but instead a true asset to our nation, like the Irish, Polish, Chinese, Italian, and so many other immigrant groups who have contributed to the growth and success of this nation which once welcomed the "poor and hungry" of the world not as handout seekers or second-class outsiders, but as the very lifeblood of a growing land of the truly free.

Let Arizona and Texas make themselves into prison states and wargrounds, places where Mexicans are hunted with guns and driven into lives of crime and violence. Let them have the gangs and terrorists their cruel, unjust, and foolish "non-racist" pogroms make of people who only want a better life. Let them suffer the hell on earth their prideful heartless folly produces. We can be the place which recognizes that Mexicans make good Americans, and our Rio Grande valley from Mesilla to Bernalillo will blossom with righteous progress.

Are Mexicans Paying their Dues?

"Mexicans who come here contribute nothing," I hear the Rightniks crying. That is not true, especially not true just because they aren't paying income taxes. I believe the working-man's term for it is "sweat equity" which they pay into our economy by working very hard for less than a citizen must be paid, which enables the employer to sell his produce at a profit without making it too expensive for the working American to buy. Those are some very hard dues those people are paying, harder than most Americans would rather have to pay than to cough up their taxes.

We should open the border fully and marry Mexico, not keep her on her knees at gunpoint at the fence. You think that is naïve? You are so right, of course. The real American way would be to clear away a DMZ (De-Mexicanized-Zone), build a Tortilla Curtain, guard it with State and Federal guns and robot military camera airplanes, and start shooting those invading criminal drug terrorists. As we did with suspicious-looking Japanese in WWII, we would then round up anyone suspected of being allied with or likely loyal to the Mexican insurgents, and put them in a chain of residence and evaluation camps. Call it "Sheriff Joe's Gulag," in honor of that law enforcement hero whose head was found on a bullfighter's pike (or would be if caught). Halliburton and Blackwater could be paid on a DOD contract to operate it all, which would provide jobsjobsjobs for thousands of good Christian boys in uniform, khaki, green, black, and blue.

To affectionately refer to Arizona's Mr. Arpaio as "Sheriff Joe" for ruthlessly interpreting and enforcing the law is hardly different from calling Mr. Himmler "Marshal Hank." I am reminded that no Jew was killed in Nazi Germany except in accordance with the published Law of the Land, and with paperwork signed by a duly appointed officer of the court. I am always surprised so many Americans believe if something has been made into Law, it is therefore just. Personally, I find it hard to trust those who believe if the paperwork is done right, then whatever they do is right. Having once immersed myself in a number of religious studies, including the bloodthirsty ancient occult mythology of the cult of Abraham, I am likewise wary of those who publish Bible quotations in our courtrooms and claim therefore that whatever they do there is sanctioned by God.

Most Mexican immigrants, legal or not, work harder for what little they get in a week than the megabux desk-jockey CEO works in six months. The Rightniks make it illegal for them to work, then call them lowlife when they go into crime. They risk their lives to work as dirt-grubbers to feed the children they sneer when they call "them" and then cram them ten deep into prison cells where they are forged into cadres of extreme anti-American homicidal fanatics. As a movement of charitable Christians in the Land Of The Free, today's religious right are hypocrites, assholes, and fools.

Mexicans Make Good Americans.
We should have married Mexico
Not kept her on her knees at the border.
Instead be build The Tortilla Curtain
Armed with burrhead white boys
Eager to have a new enemy.
I think it unwise to arouse the Jaguar.

Bubba Goes To The Doctor

Like the classic joke of the two Jewish ladies at the restaurant who agreed the food was inedible, but the portions too small, it is sometimes difficult these days to tell if we are getting too little medical care, or too much.

Bubba was delivering a truckload of shingles to the doctor to fix his roof. He walked into the doctor's office and the receptionist asked him what he had. Bubba said, "I got the shingles." She wrote down his name, and medical insurance number and told him to have a seat.

Fifteen minutes later a nurse's aide came out and asked Bubba what he had. Bubba said, "I got the shingles." So she handed him a twelve-page form starting with his height, weight, and a complete medical and credit history and told Bubba to fill out all the pages, and then to go wait in the examining room.

Half an hour later a nurse came in and asked Bubba what he had. Bubba said, "I got the shingles." So the nurse gave Bubba a blood test, a blood pressure test, an allergy screen, and an electrocardiogram, and told Bubba to take off all his clothes and wait for the doctor.

An hour later the doctor came in and found Bubba sitting patiently in the nude and asked Bubba what he had. Bubba said, "I got the shingles."

The doctor asked, "How long have you had these shingles?"

Bubba said, "I got into this shingle thing back when I was nineteen."

Doc said, "OK, here's a prescription for some stuff you can put on your shingles. If you've still got shingles in two weeks, come back again."

"OK," said Bubba. "Do you want to look at these shingles now?"

Doc said, "Naw, I know what shingles look like. You say you got shingles, I believe you."

"Can I get the shingles off my truck now?" Bubba asked.

"I never heard of anybody getting shingles off a truck," the Doc said with a laugh, "but when you do, you let me know."

Bubba got his clothes back on, and he went and got the shingles off the truck, and he took them up and laid them on the roof.

Two weeks later, Bubba got a bill for $640 for the entry processing, the tests, and the examination. His insurance denied the claim because he had admitted that he already had the shingles since he was nineteen. He objected that he had only gone there to give the shingles to the doctor, and he didn't understand why he had to take off his clothes. Bubba couldn't figure why they seemed to be so confused and offended by that.

"How did you plan to give the shingles to the doctor?" the insurance guys asked.

"I'm supposed to see they get laid up on the roof," Bubba replied.

They were shocked. "You say you got naked and gave the doctor shingles getting laid up on the roof? That could be a considered a sex crime, attempted blackmail, or biological assault, all of which would abrogate your policy." Bubba had to pay.

Bubba found out soon that he had picked up a virus sitting in the lobby with all those wheezing sick people and their snot-gurgling kids, and he picked up a super-staph infection sitting naked on the doctor's bench. Soon he had a wretching cough, and boils on his asshole nothing would cure. He was prescribed antihistamines, antibiotics, antitussants, antidepressants to keep from feeling low, and antipsychotics to deal with the side-effects of the other "medicines".

Because of the boils, he lost his job driving the delivery truck for the roofing company. Without the job, he lost his insurance. He would take a second mortgage on his house to pay for the addictive prescription medicines he must now take, but he lost all his equity in the collapse of 2008 (oops, sorry, I mean the Obamalapse of 2009).

To keep from losing the house over his medical bills, he divorced his wife and let her have it in the settlement. Bubba now lives on a homeless care program, where he gets free medications, pain-killers, tranquilizers, and a winter coat. He survives by visiting his ex's kitchen door every evening after she gets home from work. She feeds him, but won't let him in because of the smell, and the restraining order her mortgage assistance program demands. If he got a job, he would lose his meds, and he can't get through a day without them.

The doctor is suing Bubba's old boss because the roof still leaks.

In Texas Good Dogs Heel.

I just read that Rick Perry, Texas' latest Bible-dazzled village-idiot oil-patch corporate-muppet Governor has proposed a system of toll highways, freeing the taxpayer from spending to repair the old ones. One contractor will be given an exclusive concession to borrow money (interest to the bank), receive subsidy from the Fed ("I voted against it, but I'll take it,"), create jobs which will pay wages which can be taxed to pay for it all, and operate the highways at a profit instead of a tax burden (rah rah!). Those who can afford to pay the tolls can drive to their jobs so as to pay the taxes like good supportive citizens. The freeloading malingerers who are too lazy or shiftless to work can use the old failed socialist Franklin Delanobama roads to get to California to apply for Stampos De Foodo. The corporation will get a Teabag tax break and pay none, the Executives will move their profits offshore, and the CEO will fund a PAC to pay Rupert Murdoch for the air time to re-elect Rick Perry. Convinced by John Hagee that God is blessing him for his Party affiliation, Rick will buy a new car, and some Tiffany for his wife ("Mine's bigger than Newt's").

I'll say it again, whether meant as praise or an insult, Rick Perry is authentic Texas. I read about Rick strutting his stuff and puffing his pistol about how a coyote looked wrong at his dog, so he shot it, and left its rotting carcass for the birds. This is the same guy who gets weepy at the full-military funeral service given for a K-9 Police Dog. I respect the good dog, whose name means "Faithful" and who will die to protect you if you are his Master, or die to kill you if he thinks you're the one he's protecting him from. I likewise respect men who feel and serve that way. However, as Masters mostly dislike those who will not faithfully call them Master, it is pretty rough to be identified as one of the coyotes for failing to be tagged, refusing to heel, or to roll over and permit yourself to be sniffed, defanged, and fixed. I've been to Dog School, won ribbons fighting in the cockpit, and I've even worn the wool pretending to be a sheep, but the way Perry and his party's evangelical puppet masters advertise themselves as looking at things, I think I'm one of the coyotes... well, one of the goats, anyway.

Here's a winky note on the mental evolution of Texism. Never much into the limp-wristed fuss of interpretive dance, the last generation all danced together in the complex cooperative geometry of the Square Dance, with sideshow solos by a few acknowledged to be fancy hoofers. Good folks, good neighbors with good fences. Still good folks, today's Texians line-dance. One dimensional, arm-in-arm, lock-step, tap-toe, two to the right, tip your hat, and drill baby drill. What hasn't changed is, "Don't know the step? Not from around here, are you? ... stranger."

"Good morning. Do you have any fresh fruit, marijuana, assault rifles, illegal aliens, Madonna videos, or nicotine-enhanced cigarettes with you today?"

Texas Wants To Secede?

Secessionists: a pack of blowhard clowns... but killer clowns, the modern American horror movie. I find it ironic the same GOPers cheering how Abraham Lincoln was their great president are yowling to secede from The Union now that the Socialists have thrown their party's war-profiteering oil-patch Jesus-freaks out of DC. Wasn't Lincoln the one who suspended the Constitution and waged a war that killed half a million Americans to ensure that no state could secede? Are we one nation indivisible, except for Texas, 'cause they're more American than the rest of us peckerwoods?

Texas? Without the USA's domestic market for car and airplane fuel, and its jet-powered military buying the gas they make from Arab oil, the Texas oil industry would go belly up in days in the face of free competition from Venezuela, Mexico, or the new Republic Of Alaska. Pull out NASA, the US Air Force and Navy, cancel all contracts related to any of those with Texas corporations, including the beef, and put a trade barrier along the north border. Having no love for Texas since the place got ripped off from them two hundred years ago, the Mexicans would likely put up a wall on their side of the border. New Mexico would dam up the Rio Grande and fill the reservoir lakes, and Texas would be back to dry-dirt clod-kicking and taco stands.

Are you Texans first, and Americans second? How American is that? Are you Conservatives first, and Americans second? How Conservative is that? Are you Christians first, above all political loyalty? To paraphrase a familiar quote, "Our President's house hath many mansions." Whether you like us all or not, we are a diverse people, and our interwoven differences in social values, rights, and responsibilities create an evolving tapestry, not a defined pattern to be enforced. Just what part of America do you not acknowledge as part your own house, such that you should bring strife that troubleth the nation?

Motanomics: Marijuana Money

When I got back to New Mexico in 1969, having started smoking pot in Nam to relax after a good hot LRRP extraction, I could go to friends in the valley and buy a pound of basic rough Mexican mota for $60. It was not harvested like modern pot, full of sticks and seeds. Usually only about half of it was smoking stuff, but it was pleasant, cheap, and harmless, altogether superior to getting drunk, which often as not is none of those things.

About five years ago here in Albuquerque, I could buy two kinds of smoke. One was Grade, the beautiful domestic sinsemilla hybridized by outlaw free American farmers hiding from the DEA's goons with their guns and dogs in basements, attics, and caves. These were running about $200 an ounce. The other was the Mexican import, called schwag. It was good basic weed, all tops, but pressed into blocks like chewntbacca because of the needs of smuggling. I could buy a quarter pound for $180, sell three ounces for $60 each, and smoke the other one. Everybody was happy.

Two things happened. #One, in 2007 Pres. Cheney instead of shooting wetback pot mules in the Rio Grande, gave the Mexican DEA some money and a bunch of guns and told them to do it for him, and to start a real war on the smugglers. They did, disrupting the established old family system, and initiating gang wars that have killed about 30,000 people and have switched the market from mellow marijuana, which is agriculturally dependent and hard to smuggle, to methedrine, which is the favorite drug of zombie warriors and brewers of evil potions. As a result, Mexican schwag is now hard to find, and much lower quality. QED, George Bush can claim his Halliburton-built "Tortilla Curtain" has worked to interdict the dope traffic. #Two, the medical industry got its permission to be the exclusive legal sellers of pot... by calling those beautiful outlaw hybrids "medical marijuana" as if they were miracles created in their laboratories, and not the evil dangerous Devil Weed they have been persecuting, prosecuting, imprisoning, and shooting us over these last fifty years.

As a result of these things, I can now get a prescription for medical marijuana, presumably by whining to Doctor about PTSD. That would probably cost me a couple hundred bucks, after office visit, entry filing, tests, consultation, etc. Then I could go to a pot store and buy some prescription health care benefit cannibis iatricus. I admit it is beautiful weed, a true credit to the American grower... but the cost usually runs about $60, not for a pound like back in '69, or an ounce like back in '06, but for one eighth of an ounce, which will make five or six nice slender joints. Do the arithmetic: at that rate, a pound will cost you $7680.00. That is what marijuana costs now that it has become part of the American health care system.

The legal status of marijuana and the War On Drugs have always been about the market, not the morality, alleged mortality, social consequence, industrial use, or medical value of that most beneficial weed. The powerful will imprison you, kill you, or wage war upon nations to control that market. Free it may grow in God's Heaven, but not in America.

Death Of A Salesgirl

A One-Act Play

She: Would you like to do a couple of lines? *(A delicate trace of blood begins to trickle from her nose.)*

He: That's just for beginners, Baby. Let me show you how we do it up-town, and your dreams will all come true.

CURTAINS

Would I Serve Charlie Manson?

There is a passage in my novel SACRIFICES where my character makes a connection with himself and Tex Watson, leader of the Bel Air massacre team. "We both took our orders in moral trust from our leader, who wished us to use homicidal violence to make a political point, to object to someone's life and customs. Both of us were praised by our families. Assured we were doing what God wanted us to do, we each led a team of motivated killers into the neighborhood of strangers where we interrupted their dinner and killed them all. We did the same things, for the same reasons. The difference? Tex had the blessing and order of Charlie Manson. I had Lyndon Johnson's. Another difference? Tex did it once. I did it every few days for a year. Tex is imprisoned for life as a criminal and a psychopath. I am a decorated veteran, proclaimed a hero. Yet does not some part of me rightly sit there in that cage with him?"

How about Bill Calley? I was a gunship pilot. I rode a flying dragon, and I had a pair of six-guns that shot 40 rounds per second each, and a fistful of rockets that would each level a house. When we took fire from a village, we did not stop to interrogate the residents, to inspect their ID papers nor to see if they were grandmothers to separate the combatants from the indigenous. We rolled in hot and shot the place up. Yes, it was war, and yes, we got clearance first, and yes, they were insurgents even if in their own country, and their families only unavoidable collateral damage. All that is true, so I've got my excuse, and the medals to prove it. Yet even with the horror of that morning in My Lai, however, I'd not expect Lt. Calley has a bigger box of bones to carry than I do.

I'm Ok with all that, as I take my personal service in uniform and in combat to be honorable and in good faith. I am eager to recommend today that young Americans should certainly volunteer for a tour of military training and service, and to consider a military career. Even so, I am all too acutely aware that such viewpoints as those above may sometimes trouble the veteran in ways that might produce the symptoms of PTSD, yet are unspeakable, the ultimate heresy and horror of thinking that the terrible things we did in the name of God and Country might have been wrong.

Defend the Constitution? Against Christians?

About that Constitution some claim to love so fundamentally, and call on our leaders to respect and obey. America is NOT a Christian nation. It was very deliberately and wisely created as a secular nation, Newt notwithstanding. My copy of the First Amendment says, "...shall make no law respecting an establishment of religion...." That is, the law may not be used to promote or enforce the dogma or doctrine of any establishment of religion, including any and all sects of Christianity. It also says, "....nor prohibiting the free practice thereof..." That is, even religions which Christians hate cannot be prohibited or persecuted by law, even if some individuals among them perform anti-American acts. There is no question about the Constitutionality of this, whether we like it or not.

If 9/11 had been perpetrated by a small group of fanatical renegade Zionist Jews, would it then be all right for the USA to carpet bomb Israel, or to deny the right to build synagogues in America, or to start identifying all the Jews and refusing them airline tickets?

The few Muslim Americans I know are exceptionally patriotic, though struggling today with being demonized and their children abused in public and in school. If the Bible-whacking Jingoists treat them badly enough to turn them against us, whose fault is that? After turning the 40 million Mexicans and Mexican-Americans who are already in this country into our nation's angry enemies, do we really need another internal enemy who used to be our friend?

The basic error in the Holy Wars lies in the most fundamental principles which are at the root of all of the factions of the religions based on the occult idol known as The God Of Abraham. The three major factions, Judaism, Christianity, and Islam, are each now nuclear armed and prepared to destroy the world to prove their version of the absurd soap-opera of Eden is more true than the others, and God will give what is left of the world to them alone. If you really care about God, the Earth, the United States Of America, or the human race, you might take a second look at that story.

Claiming Medals Falsely

For a shape-shifting con-man, or a VFW bar hustler, lying about being a veteran, or having rank, or receiving decorations just seems all in a day's work, like lying about your education. The guy who gets caught reveals what kind of character he is. My pet hate regarding how people treat veterans is the use of one's veteran status for or against him depending on whether he is or is not a Republican, or a Jingoist, or a Christian. A swift boat is the same kind of weapon as my gunship, light and heavily armed, zero armor, designed to get in close and trade fire. The job is to go looking for trouble, and getting seriously in harm's way. Somebody was willing to go through the laborious procedure of getting him highly decorated, yet Lt. Kerry's honorable service is attacked by the rightniks, not on the basis of being untrue, but because like Jane Fonda, he stood up and declared that as a nation and sometimes as individuals, we were abusing the Vietnamese. I bear witness to having seen some of what he was talking about, and to have been party to it.

Though Lt. Bush wore the wings of the Eagle, he was a duck. Having spent a million of the taxpayer's bucks learning to fly a jet fighter, when other men were dying using that rare and critical skill, he used it only to fly from one Officers Club to the next to get his flight pay, like a personal sports car. Yet the same folks praise him as an Era-Vet Hero, no doubt for defending the border from the Mexicans. Cpt. Ronald Reagan spent his war years starring in propaganda films in Burbank, and as a hard working actor, he spent the rest of his life playing the same role in one political reality show after another, as pitchman for his Party's product. John Murtha did not take a shortcut to become a Marine General. There is no shortcut. Yet the same folks who cheer Reagan as their icon swear Murtha must have been a closet homo or something all along, because no real Marine Corps patriot with half his right mind left would say his President (even if the most rear-echelon REMF) was wrong about his Cheneyed-up Book-Of-Revelation war for all the oil and all the souls of Araby. For these folks, so quick to claim every coin they see tossed has two right sides, it isn't about whether or not you served The United States Of America in combat back then, but whether or not you serve the Party now.

My last three months in Vietnam I was Awards And Decorations Officer for a helicopter company. Almost daily I saw good men, our

Kingsmen flight crews and support people, making heroic decisions and choices, and performing self-sacrificing acts of extreme risk to accomplish the mission or to protect the lives of others. These men all fulfilled the stated requirements for receiving many of the awards and medals, in Spades, like the Aces on the front of our ships. They did their part toward earning those decorations, not just on one rare heroic day in their tour, but every few days or so. It of course goes without saying that very few of them actually got the medals they deserved.

The admin process was the obstacle. First, somebody had to go through the steps of formally putting somebody in for something. Somebody then had to go find and interview others involved in the action, when they weren't out getting shot at, and to get their statements. Next, there had to be a good writer in the loop, as the recommendations had to be very rigorously formatted, to include certain very specific language describing the action prescribed in the regs. To be accepted by other admin people higher up the pile, people up at Division who read a stack of them every day, the description of the action had to read like a good adventure novel. Then each page of each recommendation had to be duplicated in seven copies. Seven. The paper those who "support the troops" sold to the US Army those days was the crudest heavy acid-woodpulp stock made, not even newsprint grade, simply the worst paper in the world's history. While paper made of hemp (yes, that hemp) or papyrus lasts thousands of years, the records of the Vietnam years are blackened and crumbling today. Our typewriters were huge ancient newsroom Royals, on which things were literally pounded out. Using carbon paper, it was possible to make one clear copy, and one barely legible fuzzy one. To make seven copies, every page had to be typed without error three times, or four if that last fuzzy one wasn't legible.

I kept two clerks working full time just typing up recommendations for awards, and I wrote a lot of hyperbolic descriptions of the truly very heroic things we Kingsmen were doing out there every day. I wish I'd had half of the super document processing tech we have today, and a lot more of that elite club of gray old vets now could say, "Yeah, I've got the bones, with a V."

I believe we who wear such things, and hold them in high esteem as I do, are most likely to agree that having them is no big thing among ourselves, and they do not set those who have them apart from those who do not. Even so, the recognition by a grateful nation that you can show to your grandkids when it's all just history to them is a meaningful thing, something to be held in honor for. When so many who deserve that honor were not recognized, it is truly an indication of a very weak and not-so-clever character for a person to claim that honor to himself, when it is not deserved. Pretending to be a veteran to pick up girls at the country club bar is one thing. Whether by innuendo or outright lie, saying it for the purpose of obtaining political power is a BIG RED FLAG. Next he'll be claiming the ghost of Ronald Reagan told him God wants him elected.

Fighter Pilot
A Short-Short Story

Lt. "Snort" Norton relaxed in his chair and guided his robot jet to a target six thousand miles away, using his heads-up virtual screen to see through the plane's eyes. It was just like being there. His enemy were ragged men guarding opium crops they sold to evil druglords to buy ammunition and food, so he was morally justified and highly motivated.

There they were. He zoomed in until he could see their faces. "Gotcha," he said as he finished off his coffee. He put the target bogey right on them and hit the button on his joystick, releasing the bombs to kill the drug terrorists, and seed their fields with mines, so nothing could be grown there again.

Suddenly the building suffered a terrible shaking and collapsed from an earthquake which crushed him instantly. Lt. Norton was declared to have been killed in action, and was awarded the Distinguished Flying Cross.

Do Violent Games Damage Minds?

Do football, boxing, and computer killer games damage our children's minds, or prepare them to be good soldiers in the reality of a world always at war?

We hear a lot about the damage being done to the minds of children by their super-violent computer games and TV cartoon shows. If such damage is actually possible, then what should be done about a TV channel for adults that glorifies killing alien people with strange cult beliefs, promotes hatred and fear of things they invent to frighten the viewers, considers people who make terms for peace to be weak, and leads viewers to believe that their actions are led by powerful ancient supernatural beings who can take over your mind and make you do bad things, decide who wins the ball game, and make hurricanes happen. Doesn't that sound like FOX NEWS? THE 700 CLUB?

It is not new. It is the same old game, training our children to become soldiers. Today's cutting-edge soldier is a fat kid who grew up on X-Box games, sitting in a bunker in Nevada with a soda and a bag of chips, using his computerized robo-bomber to locate and zap the drug-terrorist devil-worshipping bug-heads in the caves of Saddam Engamorra. It starts with ball games at recess in kindergarten to football, in which boys are taught to sublimate their dawning sexuality to the violence of the game (by showing them their sexiest classmates' panties with the unspoken promise that she goes to the winner). They learn to become organized, submit their will to the group, and to regard all who are not members of the group to be thereby a little less than themselves, and to put all of their physical and emotional resources into proving Bulldogs can kick the Wildcats' asses. It is only a short step to taking up the sword, or the ICBM, and sparing no life to prove the Yanks can beat the Gooks any day of the week.

This is not done secretly, but proudly, calling it "discipline" and "esprit de corps." It does not surprise me to see American men in uniform swaggering the streets of foreign places talking down their enemies as "gomers, faggots, and pussies," like they did their high school ballgame rivals. The program works very well, and I am first to agree that the best of my contemporaries driving the 101st's gunships, my section leader Cpt Charlie Rake and Lancer 6 Maj Ken Fitch, were both Oklahoma football players of distinction. I'm not saying it is a bad idea, just that is what violent games are for, and if we intend to keep producing generations of warriors, then we should keep celebrating the games. Likewise, we must recognize that as long as we keep using the games to teach our culture to our children, and to select its heroes, then we make warriors of them, and we will endlessly make wars for them to fight, for our team's colors.

If you are interested in this subject, the effect of our children's lives being more in the virtual worlds of their games, and in the way we train our soldiers, you might enjoy this collection of science fiction stories about that which I wrote in the early 1970's, and which are still very prophetic today as so much of what I described then has come true already. King's Knight, A Science Fiction Anthology is available on Amazon, and also on Kindle.

A Higher Law Of Physics?

Does nobody get it? The First Amendment clearly, wisely, and generously states that anybody can practice any kind of religion they want, but NO law can be made just because it says so in any establishment of religion's book of dogma or doctrine, including the Bible, and therefore no religion can be respected in public school as being even hypothetically equal to empirical science or evidentiary history as representing the truth. Santorum, Perry, Bachmann, Gingrich, Romney and the other TV political evangelists blatantly promise to disregard and disobey that First Amendment because they believe they are obeying "A Higher Law" than the mere secular Constitution they would swear to uphold.

How bizarre it is to see supposedly intelligent educated people fumbling to sidestep the law by declaring the leftists worship a religion of Secularism, and Creationism is a science.

In making their case that science is only theories, and trying to semantically end-run around the Constitution, Creationists have a strange view of "proof." Science does not begin with the "faith" that you have the answer, then you look for evidence that supports it (and reject that which does not), but the other way round. They are as quick as the OJ jury were to declare that the mathematical possibility somebody else would have the same DNA signature was one in one-hundred-seventy-nine-million was good enough for "reasonable doubt" to declare that because the archaeologists found a place called Jericho and the walls have fallen down that means science has thus proved every word in the Bible is true.

Creationism does not agree with science, it is the antithesis of science, the denial of evidence, and the abandonment of reason. There ain't nothing much stupider than "faith-based science"... or more dangerous and less democratic than Faith-Based Government.

For Stupid Voters, Keep It Simple.

Orwell had it right. Police are not the pigs, they are the dogs. The pigs are the patricians, the politicians and CEOs, intelligent but amoral, and they live only to fatten themselves. Remember the little pig Snowball, who tried to create public works to benefit all the animals? The pigs who traded the working horse Boxer to the knacker for a box of jam had Snowball assassinated, called him a Jonesist, and then took credit for his ideas. They recognized most of the animals were not so smart, sheep, geese, and cattle, for whom the fine points of rhetoric went right over their heads, so they reduced every issue to a slogan. Today's Neopublicans have done just that, and now have given us six such slogans which will answer most any question that can be put to them. Here they are:

- 1. Don't Tax the Boss.
- 2. Drill, Baby, Drill.
- 3. Red, White, and Blue.
- 4. Back To Jesus.
- 5. Remember Clinton's Penis.
- 6. Duuh, Pelosi.
  Go ahead, try it.
  "What morally justifies us?" Red, White, and Blue, Back To Jesus.
  "Save the economy?" Drill Baby Drill, and Don't Tax the Boss.
  "How to save the education system?" Back to Jesus, and the RWB.
  "What about corrupt Republicans?" Remember Clinton's penis.
  "What is wrong with Democrats' policy?" Duuh, Pelosi.
  "Why make war against Islam?" JC, RWB, & DBD, a trifecta.
  "How to make the Congress honest?" Back to JC.

What about vice, crime in the streets, and in the science labs and hospitals? That's JC too, an unending zero-tolerance War On Sin. What about when they sin? One screws his secretary, gets Mama to pay her off and hires her husband on the public nickel. So? Obviously, Remember Clinton's Penis, but what about someone who cooks the CIA and lies to the public to start a war for corporate profits? What about that? Hey, he didn't get a blowjob and lie about it, did he? Clinton's Penis trumps any Bush card. Go ahead, try some, but be careful. They are just so sensible, and so believable, and so easy to remember, you might find yourself believing them.

Who Do We Shoot First, Bubba?

Have you ever been grilled by a goon squad? I mean, "Have you ever been lawfully detained and professionally questioned by a tactical unit of properly-uniformed and well-groomed God-fearing peace officers acting in accordance with acknowledged public-safety modalities to obtain voluntary compliance while ensuring the safety of the officers?" No? Nor have I, but I suspect being treated as a suspect these days might undermine my sense of patriotism and social cooperativeness in this land of freedom and human rights. If you happened to be shot in the process, do you suppose your survivors would be comforted to know it was done only with the greatest reluctance as a last resort in accordance with Ordnance 264-A, in response to the shooter's partner's declaration that it appeared you were about to pull an AK-47 from your undershorts, and his dog alerted that he smelled Mexican funkle-spinach on your breath?

I made the point to some of my 2nd Amendment friends that as a deterrent to Federal tyranny, a group of local boys with assault rifles would be no use at all against the invincible technical superiority of American military and law enforcement power. A reader replied, "If that were true, there would be no need for infantry soldiers in the modern army."

Perhaps he is correct. Saddam's modern army infantry — about 100,000 of them — lasted about eight days, and as Mr. Bush said, the military mission was accomplished. Eight years and $800B later, however, we have not defeated the local malcontents armed with hidden illegal rifles and homemade booby traps (when we made them, they were booby traps; now we are the boobs, they are IEDs). Clearly, only what we call terrorism could possibly be effective against the US government's boots, badges, and UAVs. The result of taking such action is not newfound Libertarian freedom, however, but a brutal police state in which the job of our country's heroes in uniform is kicking down the doors of civilians and sustaining collateral damage... that would be your family, right? Do you really think turning Burque into Basra is better than having a niberaligger for President, and public health care for the minimum wage class as good as Cuba's?

I've asked before, and of course neither the militia guys nor the hermits with the flintlocks can say. Ok, you have your rifle. Just whom do you expect to have to shoot first? A Senator? A cop, Iraq vet, mother of three, come to take possession of your Pappy's old M-1? (Easy to boast you would, but really?) National Guard troop? IRS employee's lounge? Do you start shooting first, or just wave your piece and yell rebellion until somebody shoots at you first? Are you going to make a grand show of suicidal standoff and go down for the cause a martyr, or become a guerrilla insurgent, call yourself Al Kading and join the snipers shooting US Marines?

Lets say there are a pretty good sized group of you, and you are well enough organized to actually take over the government and security of the State of New Mexico with your rifles. What are you going to do? First you stop all those socialist welfare parasite entitlement programs, cut off the benefit checks and fatcat pensions, and shut down the propaganda day camps called public schools, right? You'll establish a flat tax, that is, whatever you flat demand, just like the IRS, because you know without the power to tax there is no state. You established de facto martial law to get in control with your infantry, so you start rounding up the Mexicans and checking their papers, and fully arming for the War On Gangism, which is gonna be no quinceanaria, ese, aie la puta madre. As most of you are vets to begin with, and the revolution was not without bloodshed, the hospitals' first mission will be to support the troops, and then they can conduct free trade with the liberated citizens of your New Old America for access to their surplus medical services. You'll show us the Spirit of '76 for sure, right? We'll all be glad you restored our freedom and ready to vote for you in the next election you hold, right?

All that said, I personally believe we should be able to take the Constitutional word "arms" in its most complete and effective sense, that is, as any kind of equipment specifically intended for lethal combat with other human beings. To limit that definition to what arms meant in 1776 is ludicrous. To further limit that to "sports" rifles is a humiliating show of obeisance. The citizen should be able to possess the actual modern means to oppose potential tyranny, at least including any personal weapon being utilized in the armed services, and to pack them on their person anywhere in the land. Armed. Really armed. For misusing that power the price should be very high, but the right to possess it in a land of the free should be absolute. Good luck with that, nu?

Afghanistan 2008: Osama Thanks Allah

I was asked by a dear friend, a patriotic American Muslim and lifetime activist for just causes, to write about how we might actually do some good in Afghanistan and Iraq. I find myself only able to express the horror of what we face, and how it is that is what we have caused. This is the America I stand against, not the socialists trying to rein in the robber barons and give beans and bandaids to the working poor. Though we have been there almost a decade, and will likely be there for many years to come, this is why we have lost the wars in Afghanistan and Iraq. Yes, past tense, lost. If we had actually left Iraq when President Bush said the mission was accomplished, we might have won what we said we were there to do. Instead we occupied the country and attempted to set up (once again) one of them who would utter our orders in their language, a cacique. As in Vietnam, even having the most powerful military might on the planet, sooner or later we can only make some show of "victorious withdrawal" and slink out.

Osama Bin Laden, if he is still alive, is on his face five times every day thanking Allah for making his September 11 mission more successful than he could possibly have dreamed. His tiny mission team consisted of fewer men than a platoon of Marines. They were educated and traveled young men, most of them middle class or wealthy like Osama himself, and almost all were Saudi. None was Iraqi, and none was Afghani. Using only borrowed equipment without armament, they conducted a single mission against a country which is defended by the world's most powerful Air Force and a warning system manned by thousands of Americans spending billions of dollars. The result of that successful mission was to motivate the hubris-driven leader of America, the provincial and ignorant privileged Sunday-school simpleton George Bush, to initiate a war against two countries his advisors had dreamed of for years, hoping to make great profits for themselves "supporting the troops."

Acting upon that single mission, George Bush made aggressive ruthless unprovoked war on the innocent people of two nations which had nothing to do with that mission, other than sharing its planners' religion, and harboring them where they had a right to be at the time. Osama's tiny organization of a few fellow Saudis protesting America's use of his country as a staging ground for aggression against their neighbors has now grown from twenty courageous, pious, and self-sacrificing heroes to a global network of tens of thousands, all committed to finding a way to bring us down. Nothing Bush could have done would have been better for Osama's objective. America has bankrupted itself, squandered our military might, and smeared our reputation over the entire globe, confirming the resolve of our enemies, and making enemies of millions of people who were once our friends. That September attack may have been the single greatest tactical mission since that bold squad of footsoldiers smuggled themselves into the city of Troy in a wooden horse.

Though the capitalist warmongers of the Christian Right who made of that September mission their Reichstag Fire to motivate seizing power in America claim to be led by their ideology, it is not the ideology of statesmanship, but of wealthmanship they follow. Nor is this the first time we have done this. In Iran a few decades ago, an elected democratic government was covertly undermined by the CIA and replaced by a puppet monarch dictator who enriched himself at our trough by dealing with our corporations for his country's oil reserves. Since the otherwise peaceful clergy of that country removed that cacique and took over the government, America's right wing oil barons have struggled for decades to find a way to justify destroying Iran. To that objective, we elevated Saddam Hussein to dictatorial power, and financed his war against them. Likewise in Iraq and Afghanistan, the oil reserves have been the big chip which moves the capitalists of America. Though it has enriched a few corporations, that war has bankrupted America, reduced our personal freedoms enormously, created a vast Gestapo-like police state structure, and turned most of the world's nations and people against us, or at least to distrust us, and rightly so. We American patriots have been reduced on one hand to a disappointed and mistrustful group who have seen the righteous principles we believe in violated at every turn, and on the other hand a horde of flag-waving jingoists, prideful bigoted fanatics and racists, who are ready to send all but their own image of "real Americans" to the worst hells they can conceive.

In the 1950's, we sent our CIA into the newly-created nation of Laos, formerly five French colonies which had been forged together under Japanese occupation in the 1940's. They had just created a modern democracy in their country, and had a working government consisting of many political parties and ethnic groups. That government was called Pathet

Lao, which means Free Laos. It would seem to be exactly what we claimed we were trying to create all over the world. That was, unfortunately, a lie. We declared since they admitted a Communist Party to that broad coalition, they were a Communist country. We used our covert forces to install a former monarch from one of those colonies as the "rightful" leader of the entire new country. We armed his palace guard, called them the country's defense force, and permitted them to drive the Pathet Lao into the jungles. Unable to legally finance that new dictatorship through our Congress, we let them take over the lucrative opium market which China had conducted peacefully there for hundreds of years. That opium trade was conducted through the "French connection" we had built dealing with the Sicilian syndicate we call the Mafia in order to control the commies in the longshoremen unions of Marseilles during World War II. The money came from the streets of our cities, where prohibition of the drug keeps the prices up, and was used to buy black-market Russian weapons...so it wouldn't look like we were behind them. When we lost the war in Vietnam, we bombed the fields of Laos with land mines to prevent them from growing the opium...or anything else. That in practice comprised an act of genocide against the Hmong people. The Pathet Lao deposed the cacique we had installed, and they control the country today.

In Afghanistan today, we send airplanes costing fifty million dollars each, which burn enough gas on each mission to supply an automobile for fifty years, to drop million-dollar bombs more powerful than Tim McVeigh's truck on a handful of ragged illiterate mountain men with rifles who are guarding fields of opium. We do this in the name of protecting Americans from that natural pain reliever, while the corporations that fund our warmongering leaders' campaigns have addicted millions of us to patented synthetic versions of that same drug. We are killing the Afghanis to protect their market from the superior natural product. This hypocrisy has killed thousands of them, and also has killed thousands of us, truly making ghouls of those corporations' executives, men who have grown obscenely rich gorging themselves on the death and suffering of others.

Those who take their religion seriously are also aware that the arrogant goons of our mercenary security forces, and the bigoted fanatic religious cult within our government are attempting to create Christian cabals within the new states, and are spreading their heretical form of god-man idolatry among their children with smuggled-in Bibles, and obsequious evangels promising them heaven if they will just kneel and swear to obey

Jesus Christ and Pat Robertson now. Not satisfied to destroy their homes, their cities' infrastructure, their economy, their culture, and their government, we are determined to kill their God as well. In return, we offer them women's suffrage, and the BigMac.

Whatever comes of our attempt at occupation and economic exploitation of Iraq or Afghanistan, or how many of them are able to enrich themselves taking advantage of the money we pump into their countries, no Iraqi alive will ever forget that in the name of freeing them from a single despot, we have reduced their ancient and beautiful land to a rubble pile in the desert laced with deadly depleted uranium, and we have killed a million of them in the process, and we kill more of them every day. Like the children of our SWAT-patrolled inner cities, every little kid growing up in either of those countries dreams of the day he might someday be able to kill just one of those grinning armored goofs who are passing out candy one minute, and kicking down their doors and killing their fathers the next.

Today in Iraq, and in Afghanistan, after a trillion dollars and almost a decade of futile mayhem, there is not a single square meter of land where a common American citizen could safely stand, without being protected by a guard of armed men. Unless we are able to somehow suddenly change ourselves from the ravenous worm to the butterfly, I think it is not unfair to say as long as there is one man left in either of those countries who still has a free mind, a heart, a soul, and a pair of balls, there will be no such place, and no peace.

About This $2Billion Cut?

It is the policy of our government to pay every person who holds or has ever held the office of President or Congress for any length of time at all, their full salary for life. To my knowledge, there is no other company or institution which offers such a pension to every former employee. For the vast majority of Americans, if you no longer work for a company or agency, you are no longer paid at all.

The current salary paid to incumbent and retired Presidents and members of Congress averages out to about $180,000 each, forever and ever after. If the number of them is 535 plus the two in the White House makes 537 in office at any given time, and the number on the list of retired former members of the Congress or White House still alive and receiving that pension was found on a wikipedia entry to be just over ten thousand of them, then the total which would be paid to them annually is just over $1,896,660,000.00. The round-off figure is $2Billion. Dollars. Billion. That is being paid, presumably from now on, earmarked as a lifetime entitlement benefit, to everybody who has ever been in Congress.

Many these days are calling for budget cuts, for trimming off the suet, the wasteful, and the undeserving. How about they start this "mutual sacrifice" business by putting that on the table? After all, you have to be a millionaire to begin with just to get that job, don't you? Many of those in and out of office now receiving that aforementioned $2Billion bucks are people who would let the air out of their own Granny's wheelchair tires to score a cut that big in the other guy's budget, or who already have. No? Well, they would sure as hell let the air out of YOUR Granny's tires, wouldn't they?

Now to be fair, I know they're only talking about that fat half-black border-jumping bean-bandit Granny in her electric wheelchair going to the Food Stamp office with her nine grubby little anchor-baby half-brother bastards to get her monthly lobster-fest and to whine up some good Obama-Meds to give her worthless dog-pack of deadbeat dads to knock her up again. They're only out to get her, not YOUR Granny. And they're doing it to save you taxes, don't you get it?

We Need Arms For What?

For the problem of deciding just what "arms" we ought to take steps to obtain for ourselves, whether covered by the 2nd Amendment or not, I'd say the answer depends on first getting a clear picture of just whom you expect to have to shoot.

#1: Government troops. Fuggittaboutit! When we talk about our legal right to "arms" we are at the level of a semi-automatic rifle and a sidearm. You want to start domestic violence against Federal and local law enforcement? As a gunship jock in the days before the stand-off satellite-aimed stuff, I have some sense of how small groups of men armed with rifles stand up against US military tech, even if they are well organized, and indomitably motivated to resist the power of Washington. As we proved in a few days in Iraq, even 100,000 men marching with rifles or dug in with 1000 tanks are only an inconvenience to modern US warfare and law enforcement. Resisting a Federal badge with your AR-15 is at best a suicidal gesture in which you might kill a few good American heroes in uniform, and do some collateral damage too. You'll make the News, and Tommy Lee Jones will play you in the movie.

Anyone who thinks good Christian Republican kids in blue uniforms will not turn their guns on other Americans has not spent 40 years in the deep sub-stratum of poverty+ level outlaw country in America, as I have. I hear the refuseniks swear they won't shoot the white-hooded bubbas with the deer rifles out to kill the Black Stalin in the White House, but if the revolutionary folks even look to them like liberals, hippies, faggot sheep-lovers, anti-war cowards, pro-Moozlum sleeper cell raghead jihados, or jewelry-nosed, dope smoking, probly-gangsta, baby-raping Mexican sex-slave traders, socialist eco-nazis, femi-nazis, aborto-nazis, and all the rest of them ACORNAZI Satan-tolerant anti-Christ Obamzies.... God help them! I expect if you could hear the thoughts of those heroic veterans in blue, they likely wouldn't be about doubt and forgiveness, but more like, "WhooEEE Dawg! Take out the garbage! Call in the gunships! My team is keeping a body count down at the Sheriff Joe Memorial Chapel. God Bless America!" You sure you want to be on the receiving side of that equation?

As for discussing arms technology that might effectively resist US SEALs or SWATs (which discussion could arguably be considered an act of terrorist conspiracy), you should ask an Afghan vet... I mean, you know, one of them. Given a credit card at Home Depot and the weekend to do it, could you build an IED that will stop a tank... or even a Subaru?

2. Gangs. This one is tough too. When bourgeois order breaks down, especially under a militant security regime, the structure which survives best is gangism. Mexico is a perfect example. The pot-smuggling industry on which northern Mexico's sub-middle-class economy depended was well ordered, large old families with acreage, connections, a living for the peasant farmer, etc. We armed the Mexican DEA and turned them against that structure. Now the only structure ruthless enough to deal with the armed DEA and still serve the market is the gangs. They dropped most of the pot, abandoned the farmers, and switched to meth and guns. We pack them into prison and turn them into tightly organized utterly ruthless cadres of homicidal raiders... who hate you a lot more than you think you hate Borax Obonga or the Bible Nazis. Belonging to a tougher gang is your only hope, and you'd better have access to black market arms a LOT more powerful than the sports plinkers Massa Washington will give you permission to own, whether you vote Red Hat or Blue Hat.

3. Your neighbors. This is the most likely, and the easiest to take care of. You start now with a purse pistol, and classes to know how to use it. Learn. You recognize that it doesn't matter what armament the law says you may own, it only matters what you do own. You tell no one what you own. You keep it clean and out of sight. If you live in a place where you truly expect you are going to need it for self defense, you might consider the wisdom of a pre-emptive cleansing of your neighborhood before waiting to be placed in an untenable defensive position... and get away with it.

My advice about firearms in general is something like the First Rule Of Fight Club, that is DADT.

Christians Hate Your Freedom

We are told by the Republican Christian apologists for Holy War that the Muslims are killing us because they hate us for our freedoms. That is true. Their version of the Abraham myth (just like ours) tells them to convert the unsaved and exterminate the disobedient. In the same way, and for the same reasons, Bible authoritarians hate many of us for our freedoms and are willing to use the power of law enforcement and even vigilante murder to prevent us from exercising what they call "license to sin"... (rewriting the Constitution if they have to).

The only difference between the Taliban and the Dominionists is their hats (anyone who thinks public beheadings beneath the honor or sanity of American Christians has forgotten the ducking stool and the jigaboo tree). They are both fighting over absurd differences in the same psychotic fantasy ancient occult mythology of guilt, fear, and spiritual blackmail. The Republican Pharisees want to put that mentality in command of the greatest nuclear army on Earth. If Satan were more than a scarecrow created to frighten gullible children to cringe and kneel, he would be laughing his big red hairy ass off.

So what? So what if the reality is clearly that the whole Abraham story, from "let there be light" to the little soap opera in Eden, to the half-god water-walker from Galilee strung up like the carcass of a goat set out to appease the fearsome dragon in the cave so he won't come into town... is all simply a story that has been taken as real for the last few thousand years. Does it matter? We are like the 100th generation of Star Wars fans, and for 1000 years, it has been a capital crime to declare Luke Skywalker never existed, that George Lucas lied, and to refuse to submit to the Divine Rule of the Jedi. We now have the power to destroy the Earth, and ourselves on it, like lemmings in uniform, reciting our rules, sacrificing our scapegoats and daughters, led by lunatics in chasuble.

So what? Particularly those of you who are not so dazzled by your sincere faith as to recognize the story is a valuable moral epic fable, and those of you who truly respect the fine political principles of the Grand Old Party, think very seriously about voting for a witch-hunting puritan holy-warrior with a revival tent view of the world and a hunger to reap the golden harvest of politically invested seed money just because he happens to be the Republican.

As for the horror of re-electing (gulp!) a socialist, lets face it, Obama is not the flaming liberal left-wing blablabla the righties conjure up to scare you, or the people's champion the lefties thought they were getting. If you cannot bring yourself to vote for Obama, then vote for one of the many independents who still represent those good old Republican values, and spare us all from whatever Texan Cotton Mather or Dixie Jane Of Arc the Republicans run against him. It is not about Democrat vs. Republican any more. It is Democrat vs. NEOCAT, the Neo-Conservative Christian American Taliban, who now control the GOP.

Is It Divine Vision?

"The computer is a mirror
in which I can see through the eyes of Thoth."
Alex St. Luc, Enosar Emeritus, The Scribes Of Osiris

We take it for granted already. To know everything, anything, anywhere, now. In all of history, and even in our own lives, that was only for God. There was a time only a few years ago when most of the information in the world was printed on paper and available in catalogued libraries. That might sound like a terrible restriction today, but in its time it was a revolution. Before Gutenberg, there were few books, and only a few had access to read them. Most of what everyone knew of the world, they had only heard. After Gutenberg, all of the established institutions began to change as larger numbers of people knew more and more about the world. The changes were not something that was predictable at the time. It was only after a generation or two had grown up with access to that information that they developed not just new ways of doing things, but new ways of organizing themselves and relating to each other.

If the invention of writing is the First Literary Revolution, and the Printing Press the Second, then the Third Literary Revolution is the Internet, the great commonly-shared data cloud of access to all of the information in the world, instantly. I can call up, that is "invoke" the content of every book in thousands of libraries, in every language, and thousands of films, and newspapers across the world, daily. I have access to cameras, even pictures from outer space, anywhere on earth, right now. All of the information anyone knows, or has ever known, is now available instantly, to everyone, anywhere. Only a few years ago, such access to knowledge could only belong to God. Only Thoth, the Ibis-headed scribe who represents the "intellect of God" could know all things at all times. Now we all have that. We are become as Gods. Though some of our science fiction writers have been exploring the idea for a century or so, this is going to change the nature of being human in ways we cannot yet predict.

The generations of people raised with that Internet and its Siamese-cousin the TV, living in that omnipresent data cloud (which knows who they are and where), and all connected to each other by social networks of varying exclusivity, will not think and feel much like the more individualized and isolated lives we live today. The Latterday 19th Century Teaparty type still trying to remember the Alamo for Jesus on election day will appear to those people like a blind old fool who wandered in from the desert, and has never even experienced a vivi-pansensory encephalo-hologram projection. "He wants to disband the Sodality Of Terra and the National Consensus and let everybody vote for two guys who will make all the rules… and they get to decide how much we pay them! Haw haw haw! When did you find your way out of the cave, Gramps?"

"You can't teach an eagle to fly in a cage, especially if you are training him to be a sheep. If you run your schools like jails, even for safety's sake, your kids all learn to be jailers, jailbirds, or outlaws."

Obama Kicks The Can

Obama Kicks The Can, the headline reads. "I don't personally agree with gay (or any other alternative) marriage," he says, "but I wouldn't veto it. QUACK QUACK QUACK!" So he behaves like a DC Duck and kicks the can down the road another block. What a disappointment.

He kicked the can on Afghanistan... the progressives who elected him wanted the US out of that sordid money-pit, not just a few "troops" but also the jets and bombers (and their DEA target-identifiers) and the thousands of our Blackwater-type mercenary "security officers" (and evangelical missionaries) employed by the cacique Afghan regime using money we give them. He sent in 30,000 grunts, and now says he'll pull them back out during the rest of his term... which means he will not bring out any of what we had in there when he began. Kick....

He kicked the can on Marijuana decriminalization... it's moving along only because the government is giving the medical industry the exclusive right to sell it. It is only about selling permission to sell it, not about the value of the substance itself, nor about our right to decide for ourselves. With Dr. Doctor's magnanimous letter of blessing, "medical marijuana" is now the new miracle drug. Without those papers to get you past the piss test and the prosecution, you are still a degenerate criminal addicted to the Devil's weed. Obama says law enforcement should look the other way on the personal use of marijuana, but keep it illegal except under circumstances of tax and license controlled by the individual states. Kick....

Same with the sex... given the right papers from Church and State, sex is a heavenly sacrament, family values, bride price and dowry in itself, blabla... Without that permission, sex is a lurid demonic sin that will get you jailed, sued, stoned to death, and damned to Hell. The Church is demanding the State issue sex permits only in accordance with its own standards, and Obama is kicking that one down the road too. Kick...

Too bad, we had hoped for (or feared) so much more from him. So, what could be WORSE? What is unfortunately much worse is that the other party is running only the Bible-driven jingoists of the oil-patch Right, self-deceived to believe Jesus wants them to reap the benefits of sowing campaign seed money by joining the class of powerful billionaires they serve in the legislatures, and to take Dominion of the world in His name. Fifty million good Americans, sincere and hard-working people, patriotic with Purple Hearts to prove it, pious and hopeful believers in Christian utopia are cheering them on. Beware my friends, you Good Sheep of His flock, for these are wolves in chasuble, and they would lead you not because they love sheep, but because they know the price of wool, and the taste of mutton. Think the War On Drugs has been bad, and the War On Terror is worse? You just vote to give those people the power to wage War On Sin.

Can We Afford To End War?

Pull out the troops from Iraq and Afghanistan? Absolutely, they should never have been sent there. But can we do that, without imploding our country's oil-based economy? We have reduced each of those to a cacique police state on behalf of our own petro, pharmo, and military industries. The USAF is the world's largest single client of petro-fuels. Every B-52 mission burns a lifetime of gasoline for one of us (40,000 gal, at 2000 mi/mo in your 25 mpg car, is 42 years worth). If we not only withdrew our troops, we also withdrew our bombers, could our petroleum industry survive the loss of income? Would the petro CEOs pay for propaganda "news" time to place their agents in high office to keep the war going just to keep selling that fuel to the Pentagon? If the CIC and the CEO are wearing the same pair of pants, isn't he just writing his own check with every mission he authorizes, and putting it on your tab?

Even if we withdrew our uniformed troops, would that mean we were no longer sending people there, and spending our money to do it? No, we have an un-substantiated number of civilian armed security personnel, estimated at least at 100,000, each paid much more than a soldier for doing a similar job. If we shut down our covert and civilian activities too, how would our economy deal with 100,000 unemployed extreme security enforcement specialists returning to America looking for work?

Read the news. US helicopters going down for "mechanical problems" report 3 or 4 troops lost, and a couple of DEA agents. Afghanistan is not about terrorism. It is a real shooting theater in the War On Drugs. Yes, opium smoking has its downside, but nothing compared to the personal and social downside of criminalized heroin addiction, or of prescribed addiction to oxycontin, a synthetic opium manufactured by US pharmos. The war in Afgh is waged now to suppress the opium which competes in a free market with the synthopes our corporate drug kingpins sell through our "health care" racket industry. Lets not even start on the pharmacopia of addictive mind-altering psych-meds prescribed by the billions to our veterans for PTSD, their problem of feeling less comfortable now about what they did than when they marched away to drive the Devil out of the holy lands. Would the pharmo CEOs pay for propaganda time to get people elected who will keep the US military machine fighting the War

On Drugs all over the world, so as to keep selling all those deadly "medicines" to the scrip-addicts of America?

Between those who want to sell the USAF the products of Obombiran and those who want to sell the VA the products of Obamacare, we are stuffing the right and left pockets of the same small group of very fancy pants. If we stopped doing both of those things, and taxed their war profiteers to pay our war debts, would we all lose our jobs?

"The average B-52 mission burns 40,000 gallons of jet fuel gas. That would operate your SUV for over 40 years. Who pays for every gallon? You do."

Self-Evident Tax Facts?

I am no economist. I have always been a low-income person, unsuccessfully self-employed, and have never had savings or owned a share of stock. I did have credit cards once, and I learned some things that seem obvious, but which appear to elude the economists and most Americans.

#1. It is not possible to reduce debt merely by reducing the rate at which one goes deeper into debt. That is what "reducing the deficit" means. To reduce the debt, at some point someone must actually pay it.

#2. Unlike business, government sells neither product nor service, and earns no profits. Government has only two sources of revenue: borrow from the bank on the people's credit card, or collect taxes. Borrowing does not reduce the debt, it increases it. Only by taxing somebody can government pay down the debt.

#3. Those who have nothing cannot be taxed. There are only two groups of Americans who can be taxed: the capitalists who own the money, and the workers they pay for their labor. If the voters can be persuaded to free the capitalists from taxes, then clearly the only way to pay the debt is to tax the workers.

To propagate the illusion that neither the capitalist nor the worker gets taxed, the Repubs claim to ease the debt by taking away the little bit the government gives to those who already have the least, and the Demos "reluctantly" let them. Then the government borrows more money from the banks, gives it to the capitalists who (we hope) employ more workers, who can then be taxed to pay the debt. The capitalist gets the money, and charges interest you must pay, and gets the hours of your life and the fruits of your labor... and you pay for it with tax on your income. Why?

The answer is tragic. The Repubs cater openly to the capitalists, in ideology and action; the Demos to the "middle class" — that is, the well-employed and well-mortgaged workers. Neither will mention, or even give a name to that huge stratum of us below the middle class. There are two groups of these: the working poor, less-than-$10/hr folks, and those who have no working income at all, and live on government support or petty crime. The Repos get the workers to vote against their own interest by inciting fear that the Demos will tax away their jobs and give the money to that lowest stratum, often as not by pointing out they no speakee English, are not real Christians, and have more children than white people do. It is a shame they do it, and it is a shame that it so often works.

Is it true that if government provides a service to all of its people, that is "socialism" and should be avoided? If democratic government does not actually provide some real and tangible service to the people, all the people, then of what good is it? Do we really believe the best government should be a propaganda machine of power and law enforcement by which the capitalists are enabled to control, indebt, and exploit the people as a worker- soldier- consumer- taxpayer mass? If enough of the anthro-livestock are living fat, dumb, and happy lives, and the rest of us varmints are kept under tight enough control, is that really the American dream come true?

"If the true intelligence data is top secret, and speaking it is treason, doesn't that mean everything they tell us must be something other than the truth?"

Americans Too Smart For Them?

I keep hearing about how The People in America today are too smart to be flim-flammed by exploitive rabble-rousing politicians with materialist ambitions and ravenous egos driven by psychotic religious obsession.

I wish I could agree, but I'm afraid it looks like the politicians and those who market them have it right. Political strategists like Karl Rove may seem cynical but pragmatic when they prove that the American people are not comfortable with intellectual explanations of complex issues, and do not trust educated candidates who attempt to rationally promote what they are for. They are more easily swayed by campaigning that gives them a reason NOT to vote for the opponent. Generally, these reasons are simplistic and pander to people's baser prejudice, superstition, pride, and fear. No matter what the candidate's many assets may be, it takes only ONE such reason to refuse to vote for her, and the other is elected by default, no matter how little he might actually have to bring to the office.

Our political landscape is being razed by exploitation of the simple-minded mass psychosis of literal belief in the absurd myths, fables, and fantasy of the Bible. At issue is whether the Constitution or the Scripture shall be used to determine what shall be free, and what shall be prohibited by law enforcement. In objecting to Muslim sharia, they would establish by law a Christian equivalent, judging all on the basis of the moralist posture they proclaim entitles them to power. Because of religious influence on syllabus (among other things), the quality of our national education is a boil on our face among civilized nations... and "the people" are crying the solution is to end public schools and pay the preachers to do the teaching.

The working masses (the only group besides the "rich" who have anything to tax) are whipped to such a fearful frenzy they'll lose their jobs and mortgaged homes that they march in the streets declaring their answer is, "Don't tax the boss. Don't feed the poor," and bleating the alternative is socialism, and refusing to vote for anyone their bleat-leaders inform them is a socialist, never mind what he says, or what they think socialism means beyond being taxed to feed the Mexicans.

The same troop-supporting law-enforcing Bible-banging burrhead moralists who fill up the prisons and wage wars to oppose popular addictive herbs grown in the Third World are themselves addicted by the millions to synthetic versions of the same chemicals made by the corporations that fund the elections of those who perpetuate the prohibitions, and the wars, both of which are very profitable.

Our most acclaimed and highly rewarded national heroes are neither statesmen nor scientists, but athletes and entertainers, who are expected to behave like shills at a carnival, their conspicuous consumption being the measure of our esteem, and to emulate their gluttony our greatest desire. Our interest in their lives consists of imagining with whom they have sex. Likewise we are most concerned for the sex lives of our political leaders. Who cares what one's background or accomplishments are, when the legacy of a world-class statesman in the American popular mind is reduced to getting his stogie smoked in the Big O?

The rich and powerful are who they are because they are aware, even if cynically, that the masses of the people really are sheep, or other such barnyard livestock, and they really are motivated and controlled by things you'd think even stupid people would recognize and reject. I have been blessed to know a lot of really aware and intelligent individuals, but it is all too clear to me that The People who have prayed to God to make them His Good Sheep have had their prayers answered long ago. Isn't it self-evident that even the very good shepherd does not keep flocks because he loves sheep, but because he knows the price of wool… and the taste of mutton?

As for my yelling some kind of warning that things are going to go wrong if we don't pull our heads out... well, I have been the last thirty years or so saying IF we don't do this or that, then certain bad shit is going to happen. The People did not do those things back then, and a lot of the shit I said has done shat. Past tense. Things we did not protect back then, we have lost, and likely cannot get back, no matter whom we elect or assassinate. Yes, the American people have proved we are at least as stupid and tractable as "they" think we are. So don't worry about it. The smart guys are in control. Take your Soma, and go buy a car. Go see Vagilina's new movie. You'll feel swell!

Am I an allrightnik, just have to be right? No, there is nothing in the world I would like better than to be proved wrong about this. Please, tell me something you see being done that is smart.

Church And State: An Illicit Union.

We hear a lot of fire from the Religious Right about the "radicalization of Muslims" being a danger to America. True, but the greater danger is within... the radicalization of Christians. The overt movement to bring the power of radical Christianity to control our federal laws is in fact a sectarian coup de etat intended to subject the Constitution to conform to the Bible, and to take up the sword of law enforcement to impose its values and taboos, as they see them. That is exactly what would be meant by "Christian sharia", and which is prohibited by the First Amendment, and they all know it... but they sincerely believe their religious restrictions are more highly moral than your constitutional freedoms, their faith more true than your science, and they are therefore justified in bringing their idol into the legislatures and giving it the last word.

What is wrong with that? The basic premises of all versions of Abrahamic religion, which includes both Islam and Christianity, contain prejudice, discrimination, justification for genocide, bigoted exclusionism, racism, sexism, and some terrible self-fulfilling prophecy for which they are willing to bring about nuclear war in God's name. It matters that these radical ideas be dispelled as the mythology and sorcery they are, even though they are the fundamental principles of the world's largest religions.

My particular pet target the last thirty years or so has been the so-called "religious right" whose rise I warned about in the prophetic declaration Fundamental Blasphemy. Though the spirit of God is very dear to me, and I hold many Conservative views, I agree with both the Bible and the Constitution that for a religious body to get into bed with secular power and embrace the deadly sword of civil law enforcement is "fornicating with the kings of the earth" and should be avoided. To use the power of law enforcement to punish some act just because a reference can be found in some religion's scripture forbidding it is "respect for an establishment of religion," whether you are quoting Moses, Mohammed, L.Ron Hubbard, or The Book Of Urantia. This is exactly what the 1st Amendment is written to prevent, and what the Neo-Christian cabal in today's government is deliberately attempting to do, and quite openly.

Insofar as the Biblical paradigm for political rule is not democracy at all, but a Kingdom, run by a self-anointed bureaucracy which imposes the absolute authority of a totalitarian Monarch in absentia, then making and enforcing laws by quoting Leviticus, Matthew, or Revelation is exactly what would be meant by the term "Christian sharia." Much as I admire and support both Church and State, I am acutely aware that their union is and historically always has been not just illicit, but destructive to both. There is no faster way to corrupt your church than to start whoring her out for votes and dollars in the wicked game of politics.

Let us not forget the last time that particular establishment of religion gained absolute political power, took up the sword against infidels, put heretics and scientists to the torch, and made gilded palaces for its princes. We called it The Dark Ages for a thousand years.

"When a religious body gets into bed with secular power, the Bible calls it 'fornicating with the kings of the earth' and calls that church a whore. There is no faster way to corrupt your church than to whore her out for dollars and votes in the dirty game of politics."

Who Wants A Job?

Like to play around with numbers? Let's say you are single, and have no dependents. You get a minimum wage job. If the MW is about $6 (to keep the arithmetic easy), and you work 40 hours, your gross earnings are $240. Your SS and IRS deductions will each be about $10. If you drive about 25 miles going to work and back, and you get 25mpg, you'll spend about $15 a week on gasoline getting there. Liability (only) on a cheap old car will run you about $72 a month, or $18 of that weekly check. Lunch is probably a burger combo on the run, at $5 a day, or $25 the week. After those deductions and daily expenses, your weekly take-home is about $157.

Not included in those figures is a payment on the car you need to have the job ($120/month?), uniforms or other special clothes, using a coin-op laundry for cleaning ($7/week?), makeup and grooming ($5?), and parking costs ($5?). If these are included, your net discretionary income is $110 a week.

That is to say, you must spend almost 50% of a minimum wage income for taxes, transportation, lunch and the like, just to service the job. Counting the two hours you must commit to rise, dress, and drive, the lunch hour you aren't paid for, and eight hours of sacktime, you have five hours a day left in which to live the life you are working for, and $22 each working day to spend. If you are very careful, and save $5 of that each day, you will be able to buy a pizza and a 12-pack of beer for the weekend.

Not included in these figures are your rent, utilities, other food, and whatever you do besides eat, sleep, and work.... oh, yes, and your health care.

Get a better job, you say? How about a good job, breaking that $10 per hour barrier? OK, start with $400 a week gross, and deduct IRS and SS at about $30. You'll be able to afford a newer car, raising your payment to $60 a week, and adding comprehensive doubles your insurance to $30. You'll be able to eat at a restaurant for lunch at $10. You will likely need to improve your wardrobe, and add dry cleaning costs, as well as professional grooming. Even only doubling those from the very frugal costs above, that will consume $40. This goes way up if you are a woman. You drive to work in a nicer car, wear a nicer outfit, and you get to sit down to eat. Now you are left with $190 you can call your own (before your rent and living costs, and your health care), which is $38 per working day. If you are very careful, and save that extra $8, you will be able to take your sweetie to a movie on Saturday, and buy a bag of popcorn to go with that pizza and the 12-pack.

It surprises me to hear people whine they just don't understand why our youth, when told they need education to get a job, decide they don't want one of those, and they drop out of school to hang out with their friends selling weed to the working man to buy the beer.

"I was Mr. Nice-guy until I discovered you can draw more flies with bullshit than you can with honey."

On Veterans Day: Winning Vietnam, and Iraq.

We of the military did our part in Vietnam very well, well enough that many soldiers still say today, "We could have won that war, had we let the military loose to do it." Sadly, that is not true. Yes, we could easily have destroyed them completely, but we could never defeat them, for the same reasons we hold most precious when they are expressed by General Washington at Valley Forge. Had we chosen shock and awe and crushed them, installed an "elected" cacique to give our orders in their tongue, and enforced his authority by patrolling the streets with our invincible army, we would still be there today, as we will forever be in Iraq and Afghanistan, maintaining the same kind of security as guards in a big prison, or SWAT teams in a bad neighbrohood. If it happened to you, you would call it slavery by military occupation, even if you were assigned a nice hooch, and privileged to register, surrender your terrorist firearms, and vote for which of them you would obey. They will never forget the cruel irony that they are imprisoned in their own land by armed alien invaders in the name of protecting their freedom.

Winning a war is much more subtle than the ball-team mentality which is best for conducting conventional military operations. Military power is one piece in the game called war; it is a very big piece, but it is not the game. Who won in Vietnam? Ho Chi Minh (a Commie for better or worse, sorry about that), who in a single lifetime of struggle, unified his country, and freed it from the colonialism of France, the USSR, China, and the USA. Yes, I know, he was on the other side, but like Rommel and Saladin, that fact makes him no less a hero.

I hope it's working out for the Vietnamese people I once fought for, and against. However they decide who wears the hats, does the paperwork, and runs up the flag, they seem to be good at capitalism, and pleased to practice it honorably with the rest of the world. I hope they can keep that up, and don't end up getting bought out by China, indentured to the owners of the great factories who will employ them, and then indebted to credit cards at Wal-Mart, the American company store.

Taking Away Your Rights? Awwww…

TAKING AWAY YOUR RIGHTS? AWWW… HOW COULD THEY DO THAT TO YOU?

Regarding things being made illegal these days which have long been taken as our rights, some of us have been fifty years enduring the distress and disadvantage of living among people we knew would have us arrested if they knew we were doing things we thought we had a right to do, even knowing they had been made illegal by some powerful board of men in suits somewhere.

The 18th Century America that gave us The Bill Of Rights, the 19th Century America that gave us "one nation indivisible" and the 20th Century America that made us the most powerful nation on Earth, are gone. The 21st Century American is looking like an obese old ex-fighter and too-successful businessman living in a big house with a guard, wearing his gold watch and Veterans hat and running old war movies, surrounded by a horde of his own predatory super-consuming progeny and increasing numbers of folks from other places who bring nothing here but their hunger. Our military is becoming a privatized mega-policeforce of computer kids who drive robot bombers, and armored robo-troopers kicking down doors in the hostile neighborhoods of the world.

I try to deal with what is obviously the reality, like it or not, and I endeavor to be tolerant. You know for sure that ain't always so effing easy to do. Even so, I am what I am, and damn thankful I still can do what I want to… even if sometimes I may not do it without breaking the law.

I do know where Billy The Kid's secret hideout was, and I've been an outlaw in my own country for a long time, technically speaking, even if always a patriot. If you want certain rights or freedoms, there is a point when you have to take those rights and do those things you want to even though they are against the law. Technically, that makes you an outlaw. That doesn't necessarily make you a criminal, a real bad guy, though the law will treat you the same, and often as not so will your neighbors. You can become an activist, and march with signs in the streets, or blow up buildings demanding your rights be legalized, or you can more sensibly learn to live among the lawful, whatever the law is, as the potheads, chile-pickers, homos, gun-nuts, tax-refusers, assorted religious groups, and the like have these many years learned to live among the rest of us. The Real America these days is largely underground. "Welcome to Outlaw Country, pilgrim. You remember what they used to say — when gums are outlawed, only outlaws will be packing Double Bubble. You're a Black Jack man? I'll see what I can do."

The Blind Clown
A Short Short Story

There was once a blind clown who made his way at the carnival pretending to be a mystic, telling people what he thought their world looks like, painting them a beautiful picture, flattering and delighting them. Of course nobody ever disagreed with what he said, everybody loved him, and he became wealthy and famous, for a carnival clown. In spite of his good fortune, however, he wanted so badly to see the beautiful dancing girl that he let an old wizard sell him some magic tea, and he got his sight restored. He looked around at the world, and laughing, hanged himself.
THE END

Rights Are Illusion. You Have None.

Since the Federal Government won the war against the states 1865, we've known all the last century that a world community with power greater than any state's is not only necessary, it is inevitable, that is, if we are to survive without destroying us all. Hopefully, that will be a democratic community, in which all the states agree to accept and obey the collective decision. The alternative is a world techno-dictatorship, a global penal state armed against itself, in which half of us will wear the uniforms, to keep the other half of us in order.

The United States Of America, one nation, is now globally in a position similar to that of Virginia and Pennsylvania back then. Whatever form the new structure takes in practice, or how it is disguised to be presented to a world of homicidal nationalists and religious fanatics, it appears it will not be based on granting to any of us the quaint and idealistic old US Constitution's Bill Of Rights. The USA, like Virginia, will continue to exist as an administrative jurisdiction, but the real power in the world will be directed to objectives broader than the limited interests of US capital owners and US military dominance of the world. Welcome to the 21st Century. Our grandfathers' idealistic image of America the land of the brave, tolerant, neighborly, honest, armed, and responsible red-white-and-blue free and sovereign citizen is no longer representative of what is actually happening, in spite of the millions declaring they are ready to fight at home or abroad to preserve the illusion.

As for our "rights" we so proudly proclaim, as a Libertarian, libertine, and outlaw free-trader in illicit commodities, I've been painfully aware for decades that we really don't have any of those that cannot be abridged, and all of our actions and decisions are predicated upon the permission of persons in whom power is vested, that is, in the legislators, lawyers, judges, and politicians, who are given command of the use of force, from the cop's nightstick and shotgun to the atom bomb. The Drug War has always been a good "thermometer" for evaluating how far it's gone. When the system of government is able to examine your life, your home, your possessions, your movements, relationships, business transactions, your records, online activities, phone calls, the contents of your pockets or body cavities, and the molecules in your blood or urine, either secretly or on demand, such that it becomes impossible for you to obtain and consume a joint of marijuana... and then to forcibly seize, arrest, declare you a felon, imprison, dispossess, disarm, and disenfranchise you for having done so... well, the use of such words as "privacy" and "freedom" and "justice" and "rights" are simply fantasy. If they will do that to you over marijuana, just what might they feel entitled to do over issues that justify extreme measures?

"He who hires himself as attorney has a fool for a client, especially if trying to prove the judge is a crook."

The Cost Of Real Medical Care.

When I was a boy living on the New Mexico border, my Gramps and I often took the pleasant walk across the Santa Fe bridge into Juarez, to shop, enjoy the street musicians and kiosks, have a Manhattan (yes, we could) and an enchilada, and return to be met by a big friendly guy in a bus-driver suit who asked our citizenship, and said, "Welcome home, Gents."

Until even very recently, if I needed a tooth pulled, I could call for an appointment, usually that day, cross into Juarez, fill out a one page form, get a shot of novocaine, and lose the tooth for about $30. I could go to any corner pharmacy and ask for any pain killer I knew the name of, and buy it for about 20 cents a pill. Getting back was not so easy, even ten years ago, with the long lines of cars, the grim-faced uniformed troops with the guns and the dogs, the long inspection sheds many are diverted to, the X-ray machines, the proctoscope checking for an uzi up your wazoo, all of them seriously reminding me I should not complain because all that is necessary to protect our free market economy from people trying to duck the tax collector, and to protect my children from the Mexican Devil Weed marijuana. Even with all the bullshit at the border, the actual medical care I received cost only about $50, including the pills.

A few years ago I had some dental work done in Las Vegas. I had no insurance, but I hit a nice little jackpot, and decided to put the money where my mouth is, literally. To have a tooth pulled there, I paid a $55 office visit, a $100 admittance fee to fill out six pages of my personal, financial, and medical information, $150 for xrays, $40 extra for the laughing gas, $400 to pull the tooth, and given a prescription to go to a pharmacist and pay $50 more for a handful of aspirins doped with a little artificial opiate and a few broad-range antibiotics. And considering that as a relatively poor guy, I'd lost a lot of teeth, it took my whole five-figure jackpot to fix it all.

The dentist (Asian, an expert in cosmetic work) commuted weekly from his home office in Sherman Oaks, in his private plane. I do not regret that all of my jackpot went into my nice Hollywood smile, and I treasure what's left of my teeth. Even so, I am today bothered by the knowledge that simple dental and other medical care procedures could obviously be provided very inexpensively, and someone paid a working wage to deliver them, but the actual bills charged are many times that, whether paid by you or charged to your insurance. The big difference, which looks like it could be so easily bypassed in fact, is the enforced monopoly established by, among others, the AMA and the FDA.

I recently read that the markup on the actual cost of the active ingredients in most prescription drugs is from 1000% to 10000%. The difference goes to pay off the $60,000,000.00 it costs a manufacturer to get each drug it sells through the FDA's approval program, and the manufacturing, the packaging, advertising, documenting and publishing, and the distribution, the wholesaler, and drug-store retailer... not to mention that each sale must be conducted through a Federally licensed Doctor whose exclusively-protected credentials cost him upwards of $500,000.00 to obtain, and which debt he is entitled to service in setting his fees... not to mention that every corporation in America that owns establishments of medicine has an investment division which borrows money on the establishment's worth, uses its cash flows selling medical care to service the loans, and then plays the money in the market. Like the car makers, the drug makers are really not in the car or drug business, but are in the investment business. To exist, they must have the cash flows, whether we need more cars or more drugs or not. Though I am reluctant to call the owners of the great drug companies pushers and ghouls (in spite of all they have done), it seems all to obvious that it is in their best bottom-line interest that each of us should be prescribed drugs we cannot stop taking. If the IRS collects what we pay for them, and we are told they are free, so much the better.

I have never owned a share of stock, nor even had a savings account, so what do I know? Yet it seems to me though the actual medical care most of us would like to have access to could be very simply and inexpensively provided, it is abundantly clear that to provide lifetime full-service care to even just our veterans and Senators by paying the charges of the medical industry, the drug industry, and the insurance industry as they now exist, there is not enough money in the entire world.

VA Hospitals For All Of Us?

Veterans have always been a discomfort to the Kings. Soldiers are, after all, expected to be motivated by a spirit of sacrifice... not simply looking for reward like mercenary contractors. Veterans need things, but unlike repairing a damaged truck, money spent maintaining them does not increase their useful value to the King, that is, beyond the propaganda value of "honoring" them with medals and speeches. Kings love the dead. Words can be put into their mouths to rally the living, and their portraits hanged like unpaid bills only the blood of the King's enemies can pay. Kings erect grand monuments (close to the Castle, under the Flag) which they tout as honor to the fallen soldiers, but which actually glorify that for which those patriots are declared to have sacrificed themselves... that is, the reign of Kings.

It seems clear to me that separate hospitals for the veteran operated by the government comprise a form of "socialized medicine." Curiously, many of those calling most loudly for the state to provide care for veterans are the same ones objecting most to the idea of socialized medicine for the rest of the population. The situation offers two options: one would be to close the VA hospitals and provide Federal payment of insurance to guarantee the veteran, and everyone else, access to the AMA's private-sector protected-monopoly corporate medicine system, and the other would be to expand the VA hospitals to include everyone.

Such an expanded Federal hospital system would not replace the existing medical industry, but would operate in direct competition with it. The medical and insurance industries both seek to obtain the highest profits the traffic will bear for what they provide. Given a gung ho attitude about genuine service like our present military medical corps, the FedMed Corps could strive to obtain the most actual medical care at the lowest cost to the taxpayer. To be competitive, however, it must be set free of AMA licensing or union requirements, must be permitted to provide any medical procedure or prescription at the lowest cost, in accordance with its own standards, and to pay wages equivalent to military salaries. It has no investment managers, no stockholders, and pays no dividends or bonuses. The AMA's private industry can continue exactly as they are, and people who can afford it may buy into the insurance industry to pay for their services. No government program, however, should pay a private hospital for services available at a FedMed hospital. That way it is not a matter of them choosing only one way or only the other, but instead, giving you the citizen your choice of the best service socialism can provide for you and the best service capitalism can offer you, if you can afford it.

The other alternative, the one that seems to be blown around The Castle these days, by the princes of both houses, is to socialize only the payment of insurance premiums, so as to give the less-affluent more affordable access to the AMA's hospitals at their own profitable rates. Nobody is talking about actually providing medical care to anyone. No, they are talking only about providing medical insurance, and getting the IRS to collect their profitable premiums from all of us. In the meanwhile, veterans, and many others, go without...

Why Do We Pay For The VA?

Veterans benefits are a form of socialism. No other employer besides the state is either obligated or able to pay lifetime pensions, subsistence, and health care benefits to all of its present and former employees, much less entitled to tax everyone to pay whatever it costs. A system of hospitals on the Federal budget which offer free medical care only to a group of present or former employees of the US Government in certain capacity is a form of socialism. I'm not saying that as an indictment, but just a fact. The active Socialists in America want exactly that... a system of hospitals exactly like the VA, but where any citizen can go. The loss of profit to our medical industry and insurance industry would destroy the free-market economy!

So why should paying Veterans benefits be tolerated? Why are Veterans selected for what are after all socialist entitlements? What is there about being a "Veteran" which should justify a person's being placed for life in a certain category of beneficiary of Federal funds? Whether drafted or volunteered, with some benefits dependent upon having been in combat, this is presumably a reward for placing life at risk for the State, whether willingly or not, notwithstanding the fact that many veterans' jobs did not place them at risk at all. Likewise not withstanding the fact that many in other State and private jobs must risk life every day, and are not being given those benefits. What makes being a Veteran so special? Is it merely a propaganda gesture, a show of "honor" so as to motivate the next generation of sacrifices?

Drafted or volunteered, it is presumed you are there to the death. You have agreed to offer your life in service to the Flag, and to the Republic for which it stands. It is not just a job, something you do for the benefits like a common profiteering corporation mercenary, it is a sacrifice, for God and Country. So if you were willing to die for your country then, shouldn't that same spirit of sacrifice rule your relationship to the Flag now? So you don't sleep well; take it to the Chaplain. So you lost a couple of parts; be a hero, and hand out Buddy Poppies to inspire your replacements. You were willing to die for freedom's sake then, so why are you complaining about a little suffering now? "Freedom Is Not Free" — you remember that? Somebody has to make the sacrifices. Veterans should not be the ones whining for benefits, but the first as always to step up to the plate... and pitch in a little silver or a little blood. Right?

You who would like to put an ***end to socialism*** in America, and an end to the practice of exclusive medical entitlements given only to certain government employees, should begin by demanding that the term "veteran" should be discontinued, and that no Federal funds or other benefits or advantages should be given to any person merely because of that qualification. Wearing any government uniform is a job, risky or not, and as in the private sector, no employer should be obligated (much less entitled) to pay anything to any of its ex-employees. You should insist that the VA hospitals in America are a form of socialized medicine, which give favor exclusively to certain employees and ex-employees of the government, at the expense of the private sector businessman and taxpaying employee, and the program should immediately be discontinued, and the assets sold to the private sector, for honest competition in the free market.

REALLY END SOCIALISM IN AMERICA?
END THE VA HOSPITAL SYSTEM!

On the other hand, maybe you ought to take second look at just what you think you mean when you speak of socialism as though it were some kind of fundamental sin.

"Beware of those who think if the paperwork is done right, whatever is done IS right."

Total Separation Of Medicine And State?

The Libertarians inform me that Obamacare is wrong, and the correct fix for our abysmal public health system is total separation of medicine and government. I believe they might be on the right track here, if by TOTAL separation they mean to end the laws which make it illegal for anyone to provide to anyone else any kind of ameliorative care without the certifications of the AMA. Open up medicine to true free competition, and the cost would plummet. End government enforcement of the medical industry's monopoly on the right to sell medical products and services, and more important, their right to define what is and what is not medicine such that they should have a market monopoly on it, and the price of common health care would go down like a pompom boy in the shower. You'd still pay a ton for a robot heart, or a transplant, but you could get a couple of stitches or a tooth pulled for the cost of an oil change in your car.

I'm all for private business, large and small. I know it's not what they teach you to get that MBA, which I don't have, but it seems to me there has to be a point at which something is more important to anyone selling a product or a service than the money he can make doing it. I could be wrong about that.

Don't whine to me about how we have to have the government in there with their law enforcement pistoleros to "protect us" from quacks, or from our own vices. A real free market would quickly weed out the medical quacks. Like being able to tell whether a line of cars is fine engineering, or painted up lemons, we are able to tell the good healers from the quacks without even a lot of education. The healers will clean you up, sew you up, get your body running correctly, and teach you how to take care of it. The quacks will sell you a lifetime prescription for symptom-treating pharma-ceuticals that are poisonous and addictive as junk, so you can't quit taking them.... QUACK QUACK QUACK!

What about the good doctors? There are certainly many of them. But… when it costs half a million bucks and more just to get that MD, and half of that every year to buy insurance to protect themselves from predatory suit, and they must charge the patient for superfluous tests made to protect the doctor from the potential plaintiff's lawyer, the system does not favor the individual who would like to be a genuine health care provider to the commonly-paid citizen.

The political solution to the health care problem? Fuggittaboutit! You could elect the ghost of Lincoln, or Roosevelt, either of them, hell, you could bring back Ronald Reagan, and as long as the discussion is not about providing actual health CARE to people, but only about using the IRS or the Courts and Police to provide mandatory health INSURANCE premiums, we aren't going to succeed, and we'll continue to drop dead addicted to phony opiates and tranquilizers, or go bankrupt for a week's stay in the Healin' Hilton. As long as so-called "free market conservatives" think if the CEOs and stockholders are making money our health care system is working, we people won't have real health care, employed or not. Don't forget that for the medical industry, providing health care benefits is not the profit part, it is the expense part, and they will do their best to minimize it. Ever scratch your car? You find your insurance company has a staff of "adjustors" whose job is to find a way to justify paying you less, while raising your premiums. What makes you think medical insurance is different? As with the salaried people who work for the corporations: paying "workers" is not the company's objective, it is just another of its expenses, which they want to minimize. The objective is Conservatively clear: enable the few who hold the papers of ownership of the corporations to make money, and the more the better, ad absurdum. It is basic trickle-down theory, whether under feudal lords, gangsters, CEOs, Popes, or kings, that as long as the rich are getting richer, the rest of us will grow fat on the crumbs falling from their table. Shepherds do not build folds because they love the sheep, but because they know the price of mutton and wool. Don't look now, Little Bo Peep, but what is on that table is lamb chops. Baaaaa! Baaaaa!

Not My Gun, Mr. President!

I hear a lot of yowling on the right about Obama taking away our guns, and how the new law mandating the use of only coded ammunition is evidence of that. As I've written before, gun possession for me personally is pragmatic, and has nothing to do with the law. If you need to be armed, and you are not armed because you are obeying prohibition, you are a suicidal chump, and might as well just get in line for the showers.

They're not taking away your ammo, only your privacy. That's been long gone anyway. It's not different from registering your guns. You may have them, but not secretly. What's wrong with that? It only makes it harder for people to do criminal things with their guns, and harder for people who might use them against the US government, that is, who become domestic insurgents... terrorists. Presumably these days, defending their True America from the socialist welfare-state regime of the crypto-Muslim President Afrobama, those would most likely come from militant non-minority extreme nationalists with a puritanical and evangelical religious agenda, the Christian Americanist equivalent of Taliban. (NEO-CATs?) Since those folks aren't going to be operating in secret, but in public and proud of it, it won't matter to them who knows who bought the bullets... which leaves only the muggers and the gangsters at a disadvantage. Right?

Bearing arms to protect ourselves from government gone wrong has been a joke for many years. Even if you've got a real AK (not a de-nutted M-14), or even if you've got a couple dozen other old VFW barflies in cammos with AKs, the best you can hope for is to kill a few hundred people - Americans — to make a "statement" of some kind with your last gesture of sacrifice.... you become suicide bombers, so to speak. You make the news, they outlaw civilian cammos, and Tommy Lee Jones plays you in the movie...

Next... the inevitable national identification card, with built-in RFID, and ultimately, the high-security sub-dermal chip.. which lots of people already have. Wave your hand at the icon, and the guard snaps to attention and says, "Sir!" ... or.. he zaps you with an immobilizer, and checks your body cavities and your DNA. Welcome to the Borg, Program. Take your Soma, go for a ride, and have a nice Soylent Burger for dinner. This is not a warning. I am not telling you we have to do something or this is how it will become. You were told that thirty years ago. This is how things are now.

Don't waste your time trying to outgun Agent Smith. Learn to dodge bullets, and slip through walls.

Whatever they do with the law, it is a good idea to be armed. It is not possible to be armed to defend ourselves from the US government, right or left. You can forget about that. It is increasingly important that we be armed to defend ourselves from each other, to defend our homes and our neighborhoods. It would help if the law permits us the right and the means to do that, but if the law forbids it, I don't recommend you let that stop you.

"No government which must arm itself against its own people, and which must conduct its activities in secret from its people, has any right to call itself a democracy."

Iran's Final Solution?

Is Iran seeking a nuclear "Final Solution" for Israel? If Iran's desire is to own a bomb, the easiest way to get one is certainly not to create a complete nuclear weapons construction facility, beginning with the enrichment of uranium ore. That is a huge undertaking, and to do it concealed from world intelligence is inconceivable. Furthermore, if their objective is to nuke Israel, they only need one, not an arsenal that could neutralize the objections of the already nuclear armed US, Russia, India, Pakistan, and China, all of whom are Iran's principal trade partners. The easy way would be to simply buy one. Even the oldest and crudest obsolete ex-Soviet nukes will still work just fine with a little tweaking, especially if you don't mind they are really "dirty" falloutwise. For a country who has friends that can spend $10B on a luxury hotel, the notion there is no black market which would serve them is also inconceivable.

Though the best delivery system for their purposes is likely not a rocket but a boat, or a camel, sub-orbital rockets capable of reaching Israel from Iran or from closer Muslim nations can be made by science fair kids these days... like Rutan and Branson, who are heroes of mine. Hell, they could start an astronaut program and buy a dozen of the old R-7's the Russians still use for orbital access; they're kind of like the AK-47 of rockets, and could conceivably bomb any place on earth

That would be bad enough, but these folks have also made it clear they are willing to kill any number of people and destroy nations in their process. We of the tabloid-propagandized wage-slave American population therefore have two serious problems: Islam, which is being whipped to a bloody froth in its desire to destroy the Great Satan by war with America, and also the Neo-Con "religious right" movement in America which is equally ready to plunge the entire world into war which will render vast areas of the earth uninhabitable as Chernobl for the next few thousand years... not to mention that the use of explosive devices to destroy armed satellites in orbit would render the LEO an uncrossable mine field that would end space exploration forever, making us, in the cosmic long-run, an egg with an uncrackable shell. All the sides in the virtual-world fantasy game they are playing out for-real on our planet think they are doing it to fulfill their own side's prophecies, and so to find favor with God, as defined by the idols they worship.

The only possible escape from the self-fulfilling prophecies of the Adam-Abraham story is a global epiphany, the recognition by the faithful of all versions that it is fundamentally a fiction, a story evolved to explain life and give people a sense of purpose and a moral compass. It is a good story, and well-intentioned, even if it is based on centuries of ignorance, poverty, war, and fear. BUT... that does not change the fact that is a fiction, and its characters, values, taboos, and demands are only ideas taken as reality, no more absolute than the definitions and roles agreed upon by Dungeons and Dragons players.

We are bound, not by the hard demands of life, nor by our guns and bombs, but by our ideas. If we accomplish sane and righteous freedom and peace, it will be through freeing our minds, not by killing each other.

US Constitution For The New World?

I consider the US Constitution to be the pinnacle of human accomplishment in such matters. Nonetheless, certain things seem clear to me. Our Constitution is in practice an historical curiosity. It has no God-given right to exist, nor any more absolute authority than Leviticus, Dianetics, or the Rules of Golf. In practice, its every limitation on government power, and every protection of the individual from government has long ago been abrogated, edited, and exegisized on the streets and in the courts, and covered with a ton of paper from the Supreme Court down. The Drug War folks turned it into a hemp-linen rag used to shine their badges and boots. It's like that ad on ebay: It has had two new heads, and three new handles, but it's still George Washington's axe.

Global politics is the simple, self-evident, and inescapable fact of the 21st Century, no matter how much we agree that the Founders were right back in 1776. Every inch of Terra has been mapped, and the Internet puts all of us in the world in instant communication. This fact makes One World Government INEVITABLE, because it is now possible. The only question is how much influence the US has, and how that world shall be run.

US Constitutional freedom granted to all would instantly produce bully rule most everywhere, as libertarian Bill Of Rights freedom depends on people voluntarily respecting each others' rights, which calls for a level of social sophistication shared by only a few these days, even in this country.

The democratic approach to world order recognizes that, which leaves two choices: one, Empire, rule by force, high-tech security, and wealth; two, some kind of voting cooperative (democracy) in which no single nation's DerLeader is King. And, yes, that is more "socialist" than pure authority wielding the sword of law in freedom's name.

This administration, starting with The President, is more educated, experienced, and knowledgable about international affairs and the ways of other peoples than any ever before it, particularly the last one. Texas notwithstanding, the 19th Century is over, and born-again oil-patch Christians are not the only people who love God... and vice versa.

It is time we dispensed with the benighted provincialism of believing when we say "we," we mean only Americans, or worse, only Republicans, or worse, only Christian Republicans. I know the Book says singleness of vision is a fine thing, but if folks would just open that other eye, they might discover a certain perspective about things...

Day Of The Jaguar?

The criminalization of being Mexican and making war against them is the second stupidest mistake we have made in the last decade, the stupidest being granting unaccountable power to the covert elements of our government by the deceitful initiation of the unjust wars of aggression against the people of Iraq and Afghanistan.

If that smirking Hermann-Goering-doppleganger Arizona Sheriff Joe Arpaio were ever to be caught alone in Mexico within 100 miles of that border he is so ready to start shooting people over without his gang of club-packing "corrective" goons it is a crime to refuse to grovel before, his head would be on a stick in ten minutes and his body bloating in the sun like a rotting beached whale. Anyone with the most simple sense of the difference between justice and kneejerk punitive law enforcement would have to agree that he deserved it.

The border to Mexico should be wide open, and Mexico a place as it once was, where any American could go with their families and be welcomed, and our country a place where any Mexican could come here and with no more fanfare than it takes to register to vote, sign up for the right to be here. Mexicans make good Americans, or at least they used to before the right-wing fascists of our Republican government made enemies of them by initiating the armed war on drugs in their country. They should be made welcome here, and given the opportunity to do honest work, admitted to our schools and armies, instead of being driven into the criminal underground in order to survive as they try to help their families.

At some point, when we have built the DMZ (De-Mexicanized Zone) on our border, and battalions of armed peacekeepers crouch on that line in the sand with rifles pointed south, we will be violently shown that the enemy is then behind them, already here across the border, about fifty million of them, some citizens, some with papers, some with power, and some with nothing but their hunger and their rage. That, sadly, is exactly what the "patriots" of the police state are waiting for, to deal with immigration reform the Arizona way, with guns and privatized prisons.

As everyone from Macchiavelli to Orwell has pointed out for centuries, the militant authoritarian security state needs two enemies to survive. One is an undefinable foreign enemy, preferably a strange race and religion, one not limited to a particular nation or even a particular activity or ideology. Those are the "terrorists" to be feared and so hated, and endless war made against. The other is internal, justifying the treatment of every person in the country as a potential enemy, a suspect, and therefore subject to the law enforcement modalities of the penal society. That internal enemy are now the Mexicans, whose crime is simply to be here. The third most powerful factor in such a system of control is a crime which almost everyone commits. Whether through use of prohibited natural herbs or misused prescription addictive pharmos, that crime is the drugs. When all of us are either suspects, defendants, convicts, or on probation, it no longer matters what rights the citizens have by law, because those categories of people no longer have the rights of citizens. Where those common and popular crimes are made felonies, for which you are disenfranchised, a point is reached where only those working for law enforcement still have the right to vote. Eventually, such as in the great tragedies of Russia, China, and North Korea, everyone is in prison, either in chains or in uniform.

Whether it is still possible to stop the tragic and increasingly violent hostility between America and Mexicans is hard to say. When even the Libertarians are howling that common human rights and simple dignity and compassion are only for "us" and not for "them," then it becomes difficult to say we still ought to have hope. Having been raised on the border at home among the Mexicans in Billy The Kid's Mesilla, I have great affection and respect for that culture. I am also all too well aware what a terrible mistake it is for foolish Americans to arouse the jaguar.

Mexican Drug War Progress?

It wasn't but just a few years ago that Mexicans coming up here were mostly two groups, the marijuanos and the braceros. The braceros were honest people who came to this country, the country of their dreams, to work hard for less money than the poorest American workers are paid. They appreciated the opportunity. They were not murderers, rapists, or thieves, but people with the family values to suffer risk and hardship. Because of them, the agriculture of California, Arizona, New Mexico, and Texas was made profitable, and our economy flourished. It was pretty hard on the Mexicans, but they could still earn enough to send home more money than they could make back in Mexico. Everybody was happy with the arrangement.

What the marijuanos brought into this country is a highly desired commodity, highly desired by tens of millions of Americans. Though it is not addictive, and nothing is stopping anyone from quitting it, those millions all agree that it is such a benefit in their lives that they say it is forbidden to them unrighteously, and they are willing to become outlaws to exercise what they believe should be their right to do, and they buy it and smoke it. It was about the only thing a Mexican could carry on his body and smuggle up here which he could be certain he could get a good price for. The Mexicans who grew the marijuana lived out in the country, and they had a good protective relationship going with their local authorities, and because they were growing the only possible money crop on the land, they could afford to send their children away to college, perhaps even to travel like American tourists do. Everybody was happy with the arrangement.

At some point somebody in American politics started getting up steam among working voters complaining about seeing Mexicans with jobs and food stamps, when they were paying the taxes, and how somebody should stop the Mexicans from coming across the border. The politicians didn't want to let on they knew the farms would fail if they had to pay legal wages, so they had two solutions to the problem. One was the California system. When you find Mexicans without papers, you put the women with American-born children into state housing, and you put the men in jail as dope smugglers and deadbeat dads. You've also got the Texas solution. You put up a keep-out sign and make the river run red with the ones that don't. That seems to be the Arizona solution too. They are down there making themselves a Taco Curtain, two fences with the ground cleared out in the middle, a DMZ. That's a De-Mexicanized Zone. I was in Vietnam, you know. I was on the DMZ, where we had the First Cav Division, my division the One-O-Worst, the US Marines, a fleet of Navy jets, and Air Force bombers that flew five hours to get there and dropped more bombs on each mission than a whole squadron of B-17s, and we still couldn't keep people from getting across that strip of enforced border.

A few years ago American drug companies who keep marijuana illegal because it can compete with their products put the pressure on the Congressmen they own to give money to the Mexican government to arm their DEA and send them out to make a real shooting War On Drugs against the people growing and smuggling marijuana. One way or another, that was pretty much everybody. To a good old Texas boy like George Bush, getting the Mexicans to solve his smuggling problem for him by shooting each other on the other side of the border was not just the most effective thing possible, it was funny as hell. Twenty thousand wetbacks and Mexican dope dealers have died down there, and we haven't fired a shot. Then they blame the murders on the marijuana. Them good old boys are laughing their asses off. If that ain't Drug War victory, I'll kiss a pig.

The entire local economy of the northern states of Mexico is built on the smuggling and labor markets, legal and illegal. From highly placed officials to local estate dons, to the soldiers and the campesinos, there was a structure which peacefully and successfully conducted trade in a market which everybody must pretend they know nothing about, but everybody is making money doing. Suddenly there's an invasion, with the trucks and the helicopters, and men with sharp new uniforms and machine guns, and people are shot, and arrested. People are betrayed, and imprisoned, and they become vengeful enemies of other people, and where before they were peaceful and loyal citizens, even if technically outlaws, they become truly the enemies of the state, filled with hatred for their own country's government, and especially for ours. There is chaos, and they are at war.

The structure of connections which grew, marketed, and distributed the marijuana was suddenly disrupted, but the most fundamental truth is still true. Marijuana is still the only crop the common people can grow there for which they can make more money than doing brute labor.

Suddenly the dons, the estate holders, are gone, and the commissioners and deputies who maintained the protected order are gone too, killed or arrested. Crops are destroyed, and the growers must go farther underground, farther out in the country. There is a market which still must be served, however, if the economy is to survive with or without the gringos' war. Suddenly there is hard competition for the seats of power, for the protection of product, and the protection of place in the market. The enemy of them all is the terrible killing machine the Americans sold their government, with its helicopters and black-armored robo-soldiers. They are also the enemies of each other. Each of them has been taken into the dark rooms and made to betray the other. Each of them has lost someone, betrayed by the other. Now they are truly at war, a war among themselves, and against an invincible high-tech overlord that comes in like from outer space and punishes them by killing the survivors, and destroying their fields and homes.

In such an environment, there is only one structure of organization that can survive such odds, and that is what is called Gangism. When I was a boy, the first thing we learned in the Cub Scouts was The Law Of The Pack. There were rules you did not break, nor fail to obey. You advanced by accomplishment in defined goals. As in a close family church, or a military unit with esprit de corps, the others are like brothers to you, but closer than brothers. Their fate is your fate, their fight your fight, and their respect your only desire. Akela is the leader, the top wolf in the pack, and when he speaks, all the other wolves stand up straight and listen. It is about loyalty and obedience, and being true to the values and goals of the order. The gangs are like that, but more so. They are truly wolves, and not packs of donkeys or babbling geese, or even good dogs. Wolves. The real wolf leader is not a discussion moderator. He could kick all the other wolves' asses, and if you don't want to take him on, you roll over and wag your tail. The price of disloyalty is to be torn apart by the other wolves, or at least, banished from the pack. When the pack hunts, you eat. When the pack fights, you kill or die.

Only the gangs are disciplined enough, and ruthlessly violent enough, to survive against the power of an armed DEA. Therefore, the new organizations that succeed the old ones will be gangs, instead of the post-feudal estates of yesterday. In America's jails, new gang members are recruited by pointing out that those without their protection are prey to the black gangs, and the skinheads with the swastikas on their faces. Their families are identified and placed under pressure by agents on the outside, and they are made to understand the law of the pack. They accept the demands of blood-in, blood-out loyalty. To be accepted, they must commit crimes that bind them for life, and they know if they try to leave, they will be hunted down and killed by their former brothers, and their families will be killed. This produces an organization of great and implacable power. There is nothing surprising about this idea. It is the foundation of the Catholic Church. You must agree to take part in the murder by ritual sacrifice of the innocent Jesus to get in, and if you commit heresy or disobedience, you are burned at the stake. Blood in; blood out.

Certain big changes were done to the market by making war in Mexico. Marijuana is not easy to smuggle. It requires lots of land to produce, it is large in volume, it smells strong, and for its weight, is very low profit. It is favored by a clientele that are generally peaceful and easygoing, and likewise is grown by people who just want to be peaceful farmers. Its use does not lend itself to the gang system of social structure or marketing. The Mexican marijuana market has dropped off to almost nothing, and the quality of what gets through is very low due to the processing needs for smuggling. That is not grounds for congratulation, however, as it has been replaced by something which is truly dangerous, terribly and unquestionably lethal. Even heroin is not a drug that lends itself as well to the gang system as this new horror. Most people who use heroin are not desperate criminals, and only the weakest few actually destroy themselves with it. When a heroin user has a good supply, and he is in control of his addiction, he is at peace, and able to conduct a regular life. He is a threat to nobody. It is only when his supply is cut off that he becomes desperate, and dangerous.

However, there is a drug which is perfect for the life of the gang, and that is methedrine. It does not require a large agricultural base, and so it does not profit the common growers in Mexico, nor suffer their vulnerability to interdiction by the DEA. Great amounts of it can be made quickly in small movable laboratories, from products that can be bought on the open market. It has almost no smell when finished, can be compacted into a very small space, and is easy to smuggle. Even a small amount is worth a lot of money. It is the most addictive substance ever created, and its users are most dangerous when they have it, as they are driven to action by a feeling more powerful than adrenaline. Like the extreme use of cocaine, it is an ego expander, and its users come to feel themselves invincible, and their thinking unchallengable as revelation. They feel no pain, suffer no fear, and they have great delusions which drive them to fight and to kill ruthlessly, for the thrill, and for the right to tattoo another merit badge on their chests. When they are suffering from withdrawal, they will do anything, literally anything, to get it. So, of course, will their clientele. An organized gang of angry Mexicans which traffic in methedrine to an American clientele they hate is a calculating predatory monster with which there is no reasoning, no compromise.

A few years ago we had a Mexican problem, we thought, because we had basically good people coming up here selling marijuana and working for the lowest wages in a country they hoped someday to live in. Now we have Americans dropping dead by the thousands from the cruel addiction to the methedrine, and we have prisons full of Mexicans who are being forged into cadres of highly organized extreme homicidal death squads who hate America and Americans, and from any reasonable point of view, justly. Instead of the open border and peaceful relationship with our nearest and should-be-best neighbor which I enjoyed growing up in New Mexico, we now are arming our border with robot airplanes and soldiers with guns, fanning the flames of racism on both sides, and making another nation of people our hated opponents.

We have made enemies not only of those Mexicans who are trying to get across the border, but of those who are already here. There are about fifty million of them, some born with citizenship, some with papers, some with millions of dollars and powerful positions, and some who have nothing but their hunger and their rage. I like to say Mexicans make good Americans. I know them to be good family-oriented hard-working people who make the best of friends. They are also a people with the cultural heritage of the Mayans, for whom the celebration of death was the very fabric of their society. The people of Aztlan accepted the idolatry of the Catholic Church precisely because it is a cult of human sacrifice. As the toreador in the arena demonstrates so gracefully and so cruelly, Mexicans are a people who dance with Death.

Like our Muslim problem, today's Mexican problem is our own Frankenstein. What the anti-Mexican right-wing Drug War proponents in and out of government have given us is already ten, a hundred times worse than the pot mules and chile pickers against whom we started this blood bath, and it is just beginning. Al Qaida was once just a small club of effete religious intellectuals who conceived and executed a single elegant tactical plan. As a result of the reaction of the same American leaders to that mission, there are now thousands of them, enemies we created who were once our friends. Take a lesson, for likewise, I warn you, to arouse the spirit of Mexico against us is to awaken the Jaguar.

Thanksgiving Day Grace

We Americans are the most affluent people who have ever lived. We have abundance of everything, and could care for everyone's needs. Yet everywhere I see us obsessed with obscene and insatiable greed, one of the deadly sins.

While half the world is starving, we say we are suffering an epidemic of obesity, which for all the apologies we make can only be the result of common gluttony, another of those sins.

We have the knowledge and the skill to treat and heal almost every disease or disorder we can identify, yet thousands of us die in our homes and in alleys for want of care, and millions are cruelly addicted to terrible deadly substances that were once called vices, and now are called medical benefits, miracles, for which we will sell our treasures, our skills, our bodies, and our souls.

Our religion, in all its contesting forms, call upon us to be tolerant, compassionate, and generous to all of our brothers and sisters, children of the one God in which we all say we believe. Yet today we stand on the brink of global destruction on the most unprecedented scale, not in trepidation, in reluctance to enter upon that hell only in the most desperate defense, but eagerly, in the bigoted pride of believing those who do not use our name of God, or wave our Flag, are somehow less than us, less than human, no better than cockroaches to be exterminated, exterminated with mocking laughter, and cheers of self-congratulation (woof! woof!) as though dropping a bomb on someone's home is the same as throwing a touchdown pass, an act for which we make men national heroes, and drape them with gold.

It was not many years before the lives of those still among us that the world lived in isolation from one another, and the fastest forms of communication were the rowboat and the horse. Today at the touch of a button, we can instantly talk to anyone, anywhere on the world. Yet our use for this unity seems to focus on the promotion of simple materialism, cheap thrills, and anonymous lust, another of those sins. Insofar as I have spent so much of my life in pursuit of those things, I am humbled.

Yet in the face of this avalanche of global evil I can look around this room, at this little group who have gathered here this way so long, and I know your hearts, that you have always wanted only to do good in the world, and you have sought to personally know The Holy Spirit of God, by whatever name or concept you imagine that to be, and you have always tried to pursue lives of wisdom, virtue, honor, truth, and love. Therefore I am deeply and humbly grateful for the blessing of being able to stand here, on this day of Thanksgiving, with you. Let us all be of good cheer then, and love one another, in the name of God. Amen?

CONTENTS AND INDEX

CONTENTS

CONTENTS

CONTENTS

CONTENTS

INDEX

ELECTIONS // Crackpot Patriots // Who Needs Freedom? // Affirmative Action White House? // Really Cut Government Spending? // Prison, Punishment, Public Good // Freedom Schmeedom. It's Over. // Talkin' 'Bout My Revolution // Revolution In What Direction? // Uncomfortable Truth // Why Not Vote Conservative? // Texas Wants To Secede? // For Stupid Voters, Keep It Simple. // Obama Kicks The Can // Americans Too Smart For Them? //

ENFORCEMENT // We'll Protect You, Body and Soul. // Prison, Punishment, Public Good // Who Protects Us From Protectors? // Who Is Using The Dark Side? // Lord Vader's Kids // Nicotine Dogs In School? // Hell Yes, I'm Anti-Terrorist // We Are The Borg. // Who Do We Shoot First, Bubba? // Taking Away Your Rights? Awwww… // Rights Are Illusion. You Have None.

FREEDOM // Who Needs Freedom? // Freedom Is Only For A Few. // Freedom Is Our Community Standard. // Freedom Schmeedom. It's Over. // Freedom From Power Groups // We Are The Borg. // We Need Arms For What? // Christians Hate Your Freedom // Church And State: An Illicit Union. // Taking Away Your Rights? Awwww… // Rights Are Illusion. You Have None. // Not My Gun, Mr. President! //

GUNS // "Annie, (we're here to) Get Your Gun!" // You Are A Terrorist. // We'll Defend You, Trust Us. // Who Is Using The Dark Side? // Lord Vader's Kids Who Do We Shoot First, Bubba? // We Need Arms For What? // Not My Gun, Mr. President! //

HEALTH CARE // Who Wants Cancer Cured? // An Open Letter To Pro-life // Do We Have Bodily Rights? // Is Granting Freedom a Disservice? // Clean The Parasites Out of Medicare. // Bubba Goes To The Doctor // The Cost Of Real Medical Care. // VA Hospitals For All Of Us? // Why Do We Pay For The VA? // Total Separation Of Medicine And State? //

MARIJUANA // Marijuana: Martyred In The Market // A Drug-War Questionnaire #1 // A Drug-War Questionnaire #2 // FAA: Just Another DEA Tool // Who Wants Cancer Cured? // The War On Drugs: We lost. // Motanomics: Marijuana Money // Rights Are Illusion. You Have None. // Mexican Drug War Progress? //

MEXICANS // End The War On Wetbacks NOW! // The Bi-Illiterate // Are Mexicans Paying their Dues? // Day Of The Jaguar? // Mexican Drug War Progress? //

PATRIOTISM // Do You Really Pledge Allegiance? // Crackpot Patriots // Memorial In Vain // Our Flags: Burn the Ban. // New Emperor; Same Old Clothes // Claiming Medals Falsely // Who Do We Shoot First, Bubba? // Why Do We Pay For The VA? // US Constitution For The New World? // Thanksgiving Day Grace //

POLITICS // Would I Serve Charlie Manson? // Defend the Constitution? Against Christians? // Claiming Medals Falsely // For Stupid Voters, Keep It Simple. // Afghanistan 2008: Osama Thanks Allah // About This $2Billion Cut? // Christians Hate Your Freedom // Obama Kicks The Can // Americans Too Smart For Them? // Church And State: An Illicit Union. // VA Hospitals For All Of Us? // Iran's Final Solution? // US Constitution For The New World? //

RACISM // Affirmative Action White House? // Is Pro-Muslim Anti-Israeli? // OK To Call Black Terrorists Niggers? // Don't Call Me Skinhead. // Racism, Favorite American Insanity // Yo, Bro, Do I O Yo? // No Slave Mentality, Please. // The Bi-Illiterate // The Bi-Illiterate // Day Of The Jaguar? //

RELIGION // Defend the Constitution? Against Christians? // No Christmas in Town Hall? // Is Halloween Satanic? // Our Unholy Holy War. // Don't Blame Me, It's In The Book // If Not Santa, Then Why Me? // Uncomfortable Truth // Choose Life, Or We'll Kill You. // Ready For The War On Sin? // Moses' Myth, or DNA? // Keep School Satan-Free. // The 1st Amendment Means Jesus Too. // Prophet or Psychotic? // A Higher Law Of Physics? // Christians Hate Your Freedom // Church And State: An Illicit Union. // Thanksgiving Day Grace //

SEX // Father Washington, Save Us From SEX! // Just say NO!... to Smut Busters. // Ready For The War On Sin? Is Granting Freedom a Disservice? //

TEXAS // In Texas Good Dogs Heel. // Texas Wants To Secede? //

VETERANS // Memorial In Vain // On Veterans Day: Winning Vietnam, and Iraq. // Would I Serve Charlie Manson? // Bubba Goes To The Doctor // Claiming Medals Falsely // Who Do We Shoot First, Bubba? // We Need Arms For What? // VA Hospitals For All Of Us? // Why Do We Pay For The VA? // Total Separation Of Medicine And State? //

WAR // Hell Yes, I'm Anti-Terrorist // Our Unholy Holy War. // The Big Bad Bush / Bin Laden Bash // Is Pro-Muslim Anti-Israeli? // Afghanistan Update // Claiming Medals Falsely // Do Violent Games Damage Minds? // Who Do We Shoot First, Bubba? // Afghanistan 2008: Osama Thanks Allah // Can We Afford To End War? // Iran's Final Solution? // US Constitution For The New World?

Raised at White Sands, the post-WWII rocket base in New Mexico, the son of a research engineer and an artist, James studied Physics at New Mexico Tech, then served as a Marine jet pilot, and as an Army combat helicopter gunship pilot in Vietnam. Though highly decorated in combat, he was drummed out of service as morally unfit for smoking marijuana. He then immersed himself in several religious forms including Tao, Wicca, Scientology, and Christian Fundamentalism, while taking flying jobs for the Forest Service, an international airline flight school, and some "commodities importers" of the Han Solo variety, editing a line of "new-age" books, working as a $1Million/month high-rolling bogus sportsbook player in Las Vegas, public-access TV producer and host, and other curious callings. First published at twelve, he has always been a writer, in his words, "A blowhard would-be-professional opinion monger, and weaver of fantasies and spells." He now lives in Albuquerque, and has over 20 books in print on a wide variety of subjects.

Other books by James Nathan Post:

SACRIFICES -- A Novel Of The Vietnam War

SEDUCTIONS -- A Novel Of The Seductive 1970's

MERLIN'S PAWN -- A Doubled-Down Runner In Vegas

KALISNACHT -- A Cult of Serial Killers, Out To Save The World

KING'S KNIGHT -- A Science Fiction Anthology

HIGH ARENA -- Post-Apocalyptic Flying Action Adventure

HEALING WATERS -- A New Mexico Romantic Adventure

MURDER BY STARLIGHT -- A New Mexico Mystery

SEDONA ESOTERICA -- A Trio of "New-Age" Studies

FUNDAMENTAL BLASPHEMY -- Debunking Bible Idolatry

With Shelly Waxman, J.D:
The Case Adventures Of Sam Cohen, J.D.

With Bajram Angelo Koljenovic:
 Blood Of Montenegro -- An Epic Family History

With George Mendoza:
 Spirit Man

www.postpubco.com